THE RIDDLE OF ALL CONSTITUTIONS

THE RIDDLE OF ALL CONSTITUTIONS

International Law, Democracy, and the Critique of Ideology

SUSAN MARKS

OXFORD

UNIVERSITY PRESS

*This book has been printed digitally and produced in a standard specification
in order to ensure its continuing availability*

OXFORD
UNIVERSITY PRESS

Great Clarendon Street, Oxford OX2 6DP

Oxford University Press is a department of the University of Oxford.
It furthers the University's objective of excellence in research, scholarship,
and education by publishing worldwide in

Oxford New York

Auckland   Cape Town   Dar es Salaam   Hong Kong   Karachi
Kuala Lumpur   Madrid   Melbourne   Mexico City   Nairobi
New Delhi   Shanghai   Taipei   Toronto
With offices in
Argentina   Austria   Brazil   Chile   Czech Republic   France   Greece
Guatemala   Hungary   Italy   Japan   South Korea   Poland   Portugal
Singapore   Switzerland   Thailand   Turkey   Ukraine   Vietnam

Oxford is a registered trade mark of Oxford University Press
in the UK and in certain other countries

Published in the United States
by Oxford University Press Inc., New York

ISBN 978-0-19-926413-1

for Colin and Sonia

Preface

This book draws on work presented in a Ph.D. dissertation at the University of Cambridge. I was fortunate in having as my supervisor James Crawford, and wish to record my deep gratitude for his encouragement and advice. I am also grateful to the University of Cambridge and Emmanuel College for giving me a year's leave in which to work on my dissertation, and to Harvard Law School's Human Rights Program for its hospitality during that year.

The names of four international legal scholars feature with particular prominence in this book, and I take this opportunity to emphasize my indebtedness to each. Thomas Franck and Anne-Marie Slaughter put the question of democracy onto the agenda of contemporary international legal scholarship. If on occasion I single out their work for critical comment, I hope it will be clear that I do so with the aim of strengthening the immensely progressive potentials which I believe their arguments to have opened up. David Kennedy and Martti Koskenniemi put the question of theory onto the agenda of contemporary international legal scholarship. It was their inspirational writings which, by a somewhat circuitous route, led me to the perspective I offer here. Both also provided specific guidance in relation to my evolving arguments at crucial points along the way.

In writing this book and the dissertation that went before it, I have benefited from the generosity of many people. For help of various kinds at various stages of this project, I want to give heartfelt thanks to Marie-Claire Belleau, Nathaniel Berman, Rosemary Bloom, Julie Brown, Deborah Cass, David Freedman, Dan Hunter, Neil Leach, Jayan Nayar, Stephanie Palmer and Nathalie Prouvez. I also want to thank Simon Olleson and Fiorentina Azizi for valuable research assistance.

I have long been aware that my greatest good fortune was the one that came to me earliest. This book is dedicated to Colin Marks and to the memory of Sonia Marks, my treasured parents, allies, and life-guides.

SUSAN MARKS

Cambridge, October 1999

Contents

Introduction

According to some international legal scholars, a 'norm of democratic governance' is 'emerging' in international law.[1] That is to say, democracy is acquiring the status of an 'international human right';[2] a legal standard of 'democratic legitimacy' is crystal-lizing;[3] 'democratic government' is becoming established as a criterion in the recognition of states;[4] and the groundwork is being laid for 'some form of collective democratic security'.[5] According to other scholars, such claims must be viewed with profound scepticism. To proclaim the emergence of a norm of democratic governance is to subscribe to an 'overstated universalism', which ignores the fact that outside Europe and Latin America there is little evidence of any 'trend toward democracy'.[6] More than that, it is to fuel the idea that 'democratic countries should do everything possible to promote democracy in the world', including military intervention.[7] In consequence, the 'risk of imperialism looms large',[8] as does the danger that international law would be deprived 'of its indispensable role as an overlapping consensus among societies that otherwise radically differ on fundamental matters'.[9]

This debate and some of the wider issues exemplified in it are the subject of this book. My concern is not to investigate the *basis* of the claim that an emerging norm of democratic governance should now be recognized, but rather to determine the claim's *implications*. I have not conducted an empirical analysis of the extent to which there exists a 'trend toward democracy' of global proportions. What I have sought to explore is the link in this context between empirical analyses and political outcomes, between factual assessments and evaluative considerations, and between academic commentary and social change. I thus sidestep the question of whether the democratic norm is well founded in international practice, and go straight to the issue of whether it represents a good idea. My argument can be stated very simply. I think the sceptics are right to warn that the risk of neo-imperialism looms large. Indeed, I believe that the problems with the postulated norm of democratic governance may go further than these scholars suggest. On the other hand, I do not accept the conclusion, seemingly drawn by some, that the attempt to secure explicit international legal support for democratic agendas should therefore be dropped. I think the proponents of the norm are right to bring democracy into the vocabulary of international law. Indeed, I believe that democracy might valuably be made more central to international law's vocabulary than, for their part, these scholars suggest. Instead of renouncing the project of promoting democracy through international law, I argue that international legal scholars should rethink that project. I offer a tentative proposal of my own in this regard.

In formulating my proposal, and in developing the argument from which it arises, I make use of a distinctive analytical tool: the concept of *ideology*. This is, quite

[1] Franck 1992 and 1995, ch. 4.   [2] Cerna 1995, 329.   [3] Fox 1992*b*, 253.
[4] Slaughter 1993, 236.   [5] Crawford 1994, 4.   [6] Carothers 1992, 262–3.
[7] Ibid. 266.   [8] Koskenniemi 1996, 231.   [9] Roth 1996, 236.

patently, a tool which can be—and has been—put to a large array of different uses, some of them deeply problematic. As John Thompson observes, 'there is much that is misleading and much that is erroneous' in the tradition of reflection upon ideology. Yet, as he also observes, there is much that is worthwhile as well. From this tradition we can 'distil . . . a residue of problems which retain their relevance and urgency today'.[10] These problems have to do with the way symbolic practices work to constitute and stabilize the position of dominant social groups, the way ideas support power. I indicated above that my concern is with the implications of the claim that an emerging norm of democratic governance should now be recognized. I can now be more specific: my concern is with the relation between that claim and prevailing power. I seek to consider the democratic norm in terms of its potentials both for sustaining relations of domination and for transforming them. I use the concept of ideology to help in this regard. Given that this concept has so often been deployed misleadingly and erroneously, I devote the book's initial chapter to a discussion of precisely what I intend by ideology and how I hold it analytically valuable.

Let me now indicate the plan of the rest of the book. In Chapter 2 I outline the thesis that a right to democratic governance and democratic standard of governmental legitimacy today belong in international law, and summarize the responses of those who take a more sceptical view. In doing so, I set the arguments in the context of wider debates about the occurrence at the twentieth century's end of a 'worldwide liberal revolution'. Chapters 3 and 4 are where I examine the 'democratic norm' thesis with the aid of the concept of ideology. Chapter 3 is concerned with the notion of democratic governance that underpins the postulated norm. Like ideology, democracy is, of course, a hugely contested concept, with many meanings competing for ascendancy. For the purpose of the new norm, 'democratic governance' is understood as government produced in a particular way. What makes governance democratic is that political authority is conferred through the mechanism of periodic competitive elections, backed up by civil rights (freedoms of expression, assembly and association, and so on) and a constitutional order dedicated to the rule of law. That is not an uncommon way of understanding democracy, but it has important limitations, which are analysed at length in the work of scholars from a wide diversity of traditions. The thread which runs through much of this work is that, important though the institutions and procedures of representative government clearly are, they cannot be allowed to exhaust the meaning of democracy. To permit that is to give up on the idea that democracy is about self-government, and not just about legitimating government by others. It is to cancel democracy's historic promise of popular self-rule on a footing of equality among citizens, or at any rate cease striving to enhance the extent to which that promise is fulfilled. Those who argue for the norm of democratic governance are quite aware of these points. However, they consider that, in the context of democratic reconstruction, it is necessary to begin with a more limited account of what democracy can mean. In this international legal scholars echo an assumption

---

[10] Thompson 1990, 2.

informing many international initiatives for the promotion of democracy—an assumption which some political analysts have criticized as ideology.

Chapter 4 is also concerned with the notion of democratic governance that underpins the postulated norm. Here the focus is on another aspect of democracy's significance. For the purpose of the new norm, democracy is understood as a form of national government. It is taken to have its site or frame within nation-states, just as ancient democracy had its site or frame within city-states. Clearly, the history of modern democratic politics is inextricably linked with the emergence and consolidation of the states system. In recent years, however, theorists have begun to question whether democracy can continue to be conceived exclusively in national terms. As a result of processes of globalization, the fate of national communities is increasingly shaped by decisions taken outside the framework of national political institutions—in other countries, but also in international organizations, informal meetings of national and international officials, and the 'private' domain of global markets. And if this is so, then the democratization of national institutions begins to appear a decidedly partial approach to the establishment of democratic political arrange-ments. Though no-one believes that the problems involved are likely to be easy or quick to resolve, many today contend that, if we want democracy in national settings, we must find ways of bringing democratic principles to bear in international and 'transnational' settings as well. Without doubt, those who argue for the norm of democratic governance are aware of this reasoning. For them, however, the central challenge is to secure the extension of democracy to more countries. Their assumption appears to be that global democracy requires to be built through the accumulation of national democracies. Can this assumption too be criticized as ideology?

The thrust of the argument up to this point is in part to vindicate the scepticism with which some international legal scholars have received claims regarding the emerging norm of democratic governance. If this argument is compelling, it is tempting to conclude that international law and democracy do not mix; that the move to turn international law into democracy's champion was a well-intentioned but misconceived project that should now be halted. I believe this temptation should be resisted, and in Chapter 5 I consider how current proposals for a norm of democratic governance might be rearticulated so as to meet the concerns to which they give rise. As this indicates, I do not share the view, sometimes expressed, that democracy is a Western form of government, with little pertinence in other parts of the world, and hence little place in international law. There are, of course, understandable reasons for that view, given the history of Western hegemony and international legal eurocentrism. But, in the words of David Held, '[u]nderstandable as they are, . . . these reasons are insufficient to provide a well-justified critique: it is a mistake to throw out the language of [democracy] because of its contingent association with historical configurations of Western power.'[11] There is considerable evidence that those struggling against oppression agree. As Claude Ake remarks, '[t]here is no part of the

[11] Held 1995*a*, 282.

world where democracy is not relevant, if only as an emancipatory project. There is no undemocratic country I know of where democratic struggles are not being waged.'[12] From this perspective, democracy is to be rated an 'ideal that belongs to all humanity',[13] a 'universal aspiration, rather than a merely localised form of government'.[14] The reference here, it should be noted, is not to any particular institutional structures or constitutional arrangements, nor even to any consensus with respect to a wide range of values and beliefs. Rather, it is to the basic democratic ideas of popular self-government and political equality—ideas which are universal, not in the sense that they will or should be uniformly interpreted and realized, but in the sense that they circulate globally and play a part in political life across the world.

In the last chapter of the book I leave behind the specific issue of the relation between international law and democracy, and turn to the more general question of the theoretical framework within which that issue is addressed. In international legal scholarship theory often appears as a kind of arcane diversion from the main business of working out what is actually going on at the coalface of state practice and *opinio juris*. The classic question of international legal theory is 'Is international law really law?' and, as one prominent international legal scholar observes, debate over that question has largely exhausted itself (for the moment, at least).[15] Does this mean that there is less occasion than ever to divert into theory? If so, then the liberal attempt to depict international legal knowledge as a matter of immediate observation has been fully successful. As liberalism's critics convincingly argue, however, knowledge about social practices like international law is not a matter of immediate observation, but is instead mediated by ideas which help the observer to determine what is worth noticing. In establishing the facts of customary international law, I necessarily draw on presuppositions about the world, among them presuppositions about the nature and purpose of the enterprise in which I am engaged. These presuppositions shape my decisions about what is most relevant, important and telling. And these decisions in turn shape my assessment of what is going on. As Terry Eagleton puts this point, '[t]here is no such thing as presuppositionless thought';[16] there are only more or less explicit presuppositions.

Theory, in the sense of the ideas that inform enquiry, is not only a problem for liberalism, however. Critical scholars too are apt to avoid explicit discussion of theory in this sense and limit themselves to allusive references, for fear of lapsing into 'totalizing' thought. Yet, as others point out, exposing normative assumptions is by no means incompatible with retaining a context-sensitive and open-minded stance with respect to those assumptions. Even so, why expose them? Why does theory in the sense indicated matter? Because international legal scholars are not just commentators upon international law; they are participants in its making. Some recognition of this can be found in article 38(1) of the Statute of the International Court of Justice, in which the writings of jurists are deemed a subsidiary source for the determination

---

[12] Ake 1993, 30.   [13] Boutros-Ghali 1995, 4.   [14] Beetham 1995, 2.
[15] Franck 1995, 6.   [16] Eagleton 1991, 3.

of international legal rules. Some recognition can also be found in the institution of the International Law Commission, through which scholars gain influence in relation to the 'codification' and 'progressive development' of international law. In neither of these two contexts, however, are the extent to which, and the ways in which, scholars help to shape international law fully registered. Using the language of social theorists, in neither of these contexts is the 'reflexivity' of international law fully captured. The consequence of this reflexivity is that, as earlier sections of the book will seek to demonstrate, analyses affect outcomes, knowledge is bound up with power. The issue then becomes: what outcomes will be pursued? what dispositions of power will be fostered? Viewed in this light, theory appears itself a prime target for ideology critique, insofar as it is made to appear extraneous and obscure, yet could scarcely be more material or more worldly.

With these points in mind, I try in Chapter 6 to render explicit the approach which has informed my own investigations in this book. I can convey the general drift of that approach here by referring to an observation made by Eagleton about Marxism. This is that, far from rejecting bourgeois ideals, Marxism 'takes with the utmost seriousness bourgeois society's talk of freedom, justice and equality, and enquires with *faux* naivety why it is that these grandiloquent ideals can somehow never actually enter upon material existence'.[17] Whatever might be said of the fate of this perspective within Marxism, my approach to international law is similar. I take with the utmost seriousness international law's claim to be part of the modern project, with its 'bourgeois' agenda, and enquire with *faux* naivety why it is that more is not being done to realize the ideals of freedom, justice and equality. Note that my naivety is false not because I know the answer. The reasons are much too complicated to suppose that. Rather, my naivety is false because I know that *asking the question* is not the casual and innocent act I pretend it is. I will discuss why in due course.

To this brief synopsis it is perhaps worth adding a few further comments about the book's structure and aims. As is evident from the foregoing description, I devote a whole chapter—Chapter 1—to explaining how I understand the concept of ideology, but do not offer the same treatment with respect to concept of democracy, or for that matter the concept of international law. The reason for this is that the book in its entirety is an exploration of how the contested meaning of democracy is articulated with the contested role of international law. It is not possible simply to define these terms and on that basis move on to deal with the central issues, for the definition of these terms is itself the central issue. I seek, as intimated, to consider how ideology works to entrench particular meanings, and at the same time to provide a basis for transcending the limitations of those meanings. Ideology thus requires preliminary explication because it frames the contest over democracy's significance within international law. But where democracy and international law are concerned, accounts must be left to enter as the discussion unfolds.

[17] Eagleton 1991, 172.

Secondly, there is the issue of the time-frame of this study. The focus here is on debate during the 1990s over the status and value of an international legal 'norm of democratic governance'. I have not undertaken any systematic reconstruction of relevant historical antecedents, though I believe these certainly merit investigation. The notion that international law can be seen to require democratic government is a recent one. But the question of how democratic ideas and practices affect, and are affected by, the international order is a matter of long-standing—or, at any rate, episodic—interest to international lawyers. As theorists remind us, things often get forgotten or trivialized because they disrupt the coherence of received ideas. To challenge historical narratives is to challenge the ideas to which those narratives lend support. Thus, in the context of efforts to rearticulate current formulations of the norm of democratic governance, valuable critical resources no doubt wait to be uncovered.

A third comment relates to the sources on which my argument relies. One way of gaining 'critical distance' from prevailing interpretations of international law is, as just indicated, through research into international legal history. Another way (which can also serve as a stimulus and aid to the first approach) is by stepping outside the circle of international legal thought, and examining international law in the light of ideas and methods developed in other traditions. 'Pure' knowledge—the effort to 'understand ideas solely in terms of other ideas', international law solely in terms of international law—tends to be self-affirming.[18] If the range of referents is extended, however, what seemed obvious might come to seem strange; what seemed inevitable might come to seem optional; what seemed rational might come to seem arbitrary. In the chapters that follow I seek to attain critical distance in this way, drawing eclectically on writings that include many in which the primary concern is not international law or even law at all, but politics, society, culture, economics, or some other sphere. This manner of proceeding is sometimes labelled 'interdisciplinary' research.[19] But the concept of interdisciplinarity must be used with caution, for it carries the twin dangers of conveying at once too much and too little. By directing energies towards extra-disciplinary sources, it risks signalling that disciplinary failures and omissions are deficiencies which might be 'supplied' from outside. On the other hand, by characterizing recourse to extra-disciplinary sources as exceptional interdisciplinarity, it risks confirming 'pure' knowledge as the norm.

And finally, a personal observation and statement of purpose. When I have mentioned to people that I am working on a book which discusses international law with reference to democracy and ideology, the reactions have been remarkably consistent. This is the sort of project, it seems, which someone might be expected to undertake as part of an effort to win recognition for the contribution of former US President Ronald Reagan. I have gleaned that to write of democracy is already to give some hints of this. To compound the situation by writing also of ideology is to manifest unequivocal allegiance to a reactionary outlook, a hegemonic agenda, a culture of

---

[18] McCarthy 1994, 19.

[19] See, e.g., Slaughter *et al.* 1999, in which the primary focus is on scholarship linking international relations theory and international law.

contentment. It was not always so, of course. Both separately and in combination, the concepts of democracy and ideology have occupied a central place in the work of some of the most radical thinkers the world has known. Karl Marx first brought the two ideas together, but there have been countless others before and since his day who have developed one or both in the service of social transformation. If I dwell on international legal proposals concerning democracy, and if I do so in a way that gives prominence to the notion of ideology, this is because I seek to reawaken a sense of the progressive possibilities which these two concepts—democracy and ideology—*could* help to open up within international law.

Chapter 1

Preface to a Critique of International Legal Ideology

Few concepts come with heavier baggage than ideology. Its tangled history, unedifying role in post-war politics, and plurality of widely diverse meanings, have led many scholars to call for its consignment to oblivion. Because I do not heed this call, I begin with an extended account of how and why—despite the facts just mentioned—I shall use the concept in the chapters that follow.[1] The account is in four parts. The first part sets out the particular conception of ideology I shall employ, and indicates where this conception comes from and how it relates to other familiar notions of ideology. The second part explains why, by the lights of this conception, declarations of the 'end of ideology' cannot be accepted and, indeed, only confirm the persistence of ideology. The third part considers some starting-points that may be used for the analysis of ideology as I understand the term. These correspond to modes in which ideology can often be shown to operate and discursive strategies typically deployed. The final part discusses the aims of ideology critique.

A CRITICAL CONCEPTION OF IDEOLOGY

In everyday language ideology is commonly used to mean something approaching *dogma*. If I say that your position is ideological, what I am generally suggesting is that your position is reached through the unreflective application of received doctrine. While I approach the world with an open mind, and base my judgements on observation and experience, you are just out to vindicate the preconceptions associated with some system of beliefs. This way of using ideology may have polemical value, but it seriously underestimates the extent to which all thought proceeds from preconceptions. In any event, as will come as little surprise, I do not propose to analyse international law in terms of *this* conception of ideology. Let me begin by noting some other conceptions of ideology of which I shall *not* make use. I shall mention six that have, or have at times had, wide currency in everyday or academic contexts.

In the first place, there is the equation of ideology with *'false consciousness'*, that is to say, the condition of being unaware of one's own true situation. This notion of ideology can be traced to the work of Friedrich Engels.[2] For Engels,

---

[1] For a discussion of ideology critique in contemporary international legal scholarship, see Chapter 6.

[2] This conception of ideology is sometimes traced further to the work of Karl Marx. See, e.g., Plamenatz 1979. As will become apparent from the discussion of Marx's work below, the notion of false consciousness indeed has some affinities with one way in which Marx used the term (even if the phrase itself was coined by Engels and never used by Marx). But, as other commentators emphasize, it cannot capture the complexity and subtlety of Marx's ideas about ideology. See Barrett 1991, 5 and McLellan 1995, 16.

Ideology is a process accomplished by the so-called thinker consciously, it is true, but with a false consciousness. The real motive forces impelling him remain unknown to him; otherwise it simply would not be an ideological process. Hence he imagines false or seeming motive forces.[3]

The depiction of ideology in terms of ignorance and self-delusion has attracted much criticism, especially in recent decades. Today the concept of false consciousness is widely regarded as an unsatisfactory basis for a theory of ideology, on the grounds that it arrogantly and unjustifiably presumes that someone else can know my own motivations and interests better than I do.

Secondly, ideology is linked with *class consciousness*. This understanding was first put forward by Lenin.[4] In *What Is To Be Done?* Lenin uses the term ideology to refer to a body of thought appropriate to, or expressing, the situation of a particular class. 'The only choice', he writes, 'is: either bourgeois or socialist ideology'.[5] In making this point, Lenin stresses that socialist ideology, though it expresses the consciousness of the working class, cannot be expected to develop spontaneously. Rather, it must be elaborated 'consciously' by ideologues, that is to say, by intellectuals, or indeed by workers acting in this context 'as socialist theoreticians'.[6] Lenin's way of approaching ideology profoundly influenced Marxist theory and practice, but presumably has limited significance in post-communist times.

A third notion of ideology associates the concept with a *world-view*. By 'world-view' is generally meant a framework of beliefs, values and concepts about central issues of life that define the outlook of an historical epoch or a social group. In the 1930s Karl Mannheim developed an ambitious account of ideology along these lines, as part of an effort to establish a 'sociology of knowledge'.[7] In Mannheim's work particular ideas are set within the larger context of 'thought-systems' or 'intellectual worlds'. In order to understand ideology, it is necessary—he believed—to go beyond the level of individual false consciousness and try to reconstruct 'the characteristics and composition of the total structure of the mind' of the relevant epoch or socio-historical group. Ideology thus directs attention to a person's 'total *Weltanschauung* (including his conceptual apparatus) . . . as an outgrowth of the collective life of which he partakes'.[8] While the project of uncovering total structures of mind is not generally part of contemporary theoretical agendas, the association of ideology with world-views retains resonance, both in everyday language and in academic writing.[9]

Fourthly, ideology is identified with the idea of a *political tradition*. To study ideology in this sense is to study systems of beliefs, values and concepts that are geared to the elaboration of particular political programmes and reflected in the actions of particular political movements. This usage of ideology appeared with the emergence of the discipline of political science, and continues to circulate widely. One commentator

---

[3] Letter from Engels to Mehring (1893), quoted McLellan 1995, 16.
[4] A more subtle variant can be found in the work of Georg Lukács. See Lukács 1971.
[5] Lenin 1988 (1902), 107 (emphasis omitted).   [6] Lenin 1988 (1902), 107 n. and chap 2, *passim*.
[7] Mannheim 1997 (1936).   [8] Ibid. 49–50.
[9] See, e.g., Geuss 1981, 9–11, where this is included as one of the key usages of ideology.

neatly captures the usage, with the observation that it is 'exemplified by the tendency to think of ideologies in terms of "isms" '.[10] Thus, scholars analyse the 'ideologies' of liberalism, conservatism, socialism, communism, fascism, and so on.[11] Given the subject of this book, I should also mention one 'non-ism' commonly subsumed under the category of ideology in this sense: democracy.

In a fifth conception ideology is understood sociologically, as a form of *'social cement'*. This notion was developed in the 1960s and 1970s by French Marxist philosopher Louis Althusser.[12] It became extremely influential among Marxist theorists, and continues to inform post-Marxist perspectives. Althusser used the concept of ideology to focus attention on the production of social cohesion, through processes by which people come to understand themselves as independent actors, but yet also come to 'know their place' in society. In his account, ideology refers to the everyday practices, rituals and institutions that serve to constitute individuals as social subjects and hold together social structures. In his words, it points to 'the way [individuals] live the relation between them and their conditions of existence'. Althusser was particularly interested in the institutionalized dimensions of ideology. He coined the phrase 'ideological state apparatuses' to denote those institutions which work, partly in the public domain but mostly in the private domain, to back up 'repressive state apparatuses' and stabilize social formations.[13]

Finally, ideology is linked with *culture,* in one of the many senses of that term. This conception of ideology emerged in the context of efforts by anthropologists in the 1970s to emphasize that the study of cultures is an interpretative activity, concerned with the analysis of meaning, rather than simply an empirical one, concerned with the recording of data. For Clifford Geertz, ideology refers to the process by which symbolic forms are used to make the modern world intelligible, absent the certainties of traditional societies.[14] Through this process are provided 'the authoritative concepts that render [the world] meaningful, the suasive images by means of which it can be sensibly grasped'.[15] Ideology in this sense is less a matter of pursuing power or reinforcing repression than a way of coping with the sources of social, psychological and cultural strain. It appears as a response to 'a loss of orientation . . . [or] an inability, for lack of usable models, to comprehend the universe . . . in which one finds oneself located'.[16]

Of these various conceptions of ideology, at least some patently hold considerable enduring appeal. But however useful they may be for other purposes, in the context of this book a different conception will aid analysis. I shall use ideology to refer to the *' ways in which meaning serves to establish and sustain relations of domination'.* I take this formulation from the work of John Thompson in the early 1990s,[17] though the general notion of ideology involved has quite wide currency, and is also explicated in the

---

[10] Thompson 1990, 5.   [11] See, e.g., Ball and Dagger 1995.
[12] See Althusser 1969 and 1994.
[13] Concerning 'ideological state apparatuses', see Althusser 1994.   [14] Geertz 1993, chap. 8.
[15] Ibid. 218.   [16] Ibid. 219.   [17] Thompson 1990, 56 (emphasis in original).

work of other contemporary theorists.[18] There are two key terms in Thompson's definition. One is 'meaning'. By this Thompson intends ideas—but ideas conceived in terms of the broad range of forms through which they are communicated. Thus, in referring to meaning, he points to the utterances, texts, actions, and images through which significance is generated, conveyed, received and appropriated. Thompson is a social theorist, who is interested in the way meaning is communicated through everyday social practices, and in particular through the mass media. In the context of an enquiry into international legal meaning, a variety of symbolic forms could be considered. Of these, texts will form the principal focus of my analysis.

The other key term in Thompson's definition is 'relations of domination'. This refers to social relations which are structured in ways that entail differential levels of access to collective resources (social opportunities, economic goods, etc.) and, in turn, inequalities of 'power'. 'Power' is understood here as the capacity 'to make decisions, pursue ends or realize interests'.[19] Thus, relations of domination exist insofar as individuals, by virtue of their location within a social structure, enjoy unequal capacities to participate in decisions that affect them, pursue ends of their choice and realize their own interests. Thompson explains:

We can speak of 'domination' when established relations of power are 'systematically asymmetrical', that is, when particular agents or groups of agents are endowed with power in a durable way which excludes, and to some significant degree remains inaccessible to, other agents or groups of agents . . .[20]

Among the most enduring and significant systematic asymmetries of power in the modern world are those indexed to divisions of class, sex, and ethnicity and to divisions between nation-states. In the sense in which I shall use it, ideology refers, then, to the relationship between meaning and relations of domination. Or rather, it does not just refer to any relationship. It refers specifically to the ways in which meaning helps to ground, support, and perpetuate relations of domination.

This way of understanding the concept of ideology differs from those mentioned at the beginning of this chapter in a number of respects. To elucidate these, it is worthwhile noting two distinctions commonly drawn by theorists of ideology. In the first place, a distinction is drawn between neutral and critical conceptions of ideology.[21] The notion of ideology as a political tradition and the notion of ideology as a symbolic cultural system are examples of neutral conceptions. To designate a phenomenon ideology in either of these senses is to maintain an evaluatively neutral posture with respect to it. The analyst uses the term simply to describe the phenomenon, and perhaps also to explain it, but does not seek to suggest that it is either good or bad. By contrast, Thompson's formulation is a critical one. To speak of the operation of ideology in his sense is to imply a critical or oppositional perspective. The analyst

---

[18] See, e.g., Eagleton 1991 and Barrett 1991.   [19] Thompson 1990, 59.   [20] Ibid.

[21] See, e.g., Geuss 1981. (Geuss makes a threefold distinction between descriptive, pejorative, and positive conceptions. The third category is small; Lenin's conception is a rare example.) See also Eagleton 1991, 2 *et seq.*

uses the term as part of an effort to expose injustice and promote emancipatory change. Indeed, Thompson puts forward his formulation with a view precisely to countering what he takes to be a trend towards the 'neutralization of the concept of ideology'.[22] (Insofar as this trend is manifested in academic writing, it stands—as Thompson notes—in stark contrast to the dominance in everyday language of the unambiguously pejorative sense of ideology as dogma.)

A second distinction commonly drawn by theorists of ideology is between conceptions of ideology that have epistemological concerns—concerns about truth and falsity—and conceptions of ideology that have sociological or political or ethical concerns—concerns about the production or function of ideas in social life.[23] Engels's notion of ideology in terms of false consciousness is an instance of a conception with epistemological concerns. False consciousness implies an understanding of reality that does not correspond—or, at any rate, does not fully correspond—to the available empirical evidence. By contrast, the preoccupations animating Thompson's formulation are political and ethical, rather than epistemological. From the perspective of his formulation, the problem with ideology is not that it involves error, but rather that it is instrumental to injustice. As will be discussed later, ideology in this sense may, and generally does, entail mystification, in the shape of processes through which the character of relations of domination is masked. To this extent illusion may come into play. But, if so, the illusion is not a simple mistake or failure to grasp empirical reality. It is as much part of that reality as are the relations of domination which the illusion serves to sustain.

In asserting the role of ideology as a critical tool and in developing his account of that role, Thompson seeks to renew and reformulate an approach to ideology with deep roots in the concept's history.[24] These roots can be found, above all, in the writings of Karl Marx. In one sense the roots of virtually all notions of ideology can be traced to Marx. Marx did not invent the term; it had been coined at the end of the eighteenth century by the *philosophe* Antoine Destutt de Tracy as the name for a proposed 'science of ideas'.[25] But it was Marx who first developed the concept as an analytical tool, and who put ideology on the map of theoretical enquiry. The notion of ideology articulated by Thompson draws more from Marx than simply impetus, however. Its roots lie in Marx's writings in the much more specific sense that it takes from those writings an awareness that ideology can serve as a critical (rather than neutral) concept, in connection with political and ethical (as distinct from epistemological) concerns. It is worth briefly noting the source of this awareness in Marx's work.

Marx's contribution to the conceptualization of ideology is complicated and contested. One reason for this is that, as many commentators explain, he employed the

---

[22] Thompson 1990, 44 (emphasis omitted).

[23] See, e.g., Geuss 1981, 13 (in which these issues are characterized as involving different sorts of 'falsity'). See also Eagleton 1991, chap. 1.

[24] Recently published histories of the concept of ideology include Eagleton 1991 and McLellan 1995.

[25] *Idéologie* was to refer to a new discipline dedicated to the systematic study of all ideas, in the manner of scientific enquiry into the natural world. On de Tracy and his quaint, but short-lived, project, see Kennedy 1978.

term in a number of different senses—some mutually compatible, others seemingly not—and never sought to synthesize these into a coherent definition or theory of ideology.[26] At least four usages can be discerned. In an initial usage Marx linked ideology with the *'idealist' philosophy* of the Young Hegelians. Ideology refers in this context to the assumption—which Marx ascribes to the Young Hegelians—that ideas determine social reality and that, accordingly, by rethinking ideas, one can achieve social transformation. Marx insists that this is a delusion. In his famous image, these philosophers see 'men and their relationships . . . upside down, as in a *camera obscura*',[27] for '[i]t is not consciousness that determines life, but life that determines consciousness'.[28] It follows that social change is not just a matter of changing ideas, but of changing the material conditions which generate those ideas.

Secondly, Marx used the concept of ideology in connection with the claim that there exists in every society a set of *dominant ideas*, expressing and promoting the interests of the ruling class. These dominant ideas produce social coherence, he argued, inasmuch as they come to be accepted and internalized by members of the subordinate class. In his words:

[i]n every epoch the ideas of the ruling class are the ruling ideas, that is, the class that is the dominant *material* power of society is at the same time its dominant *intellectual* power . . . The dominant thoughts are, furthermore, nothing but . . . the dominant material relations conceived as thoughts, in other words, the expression of the social relations which make one class the dominant one . . .[29]

Here ideology refers to the 'illusion that the dominance of a particular class is only the dominance of certain ideas'.[30] 'Ideologues' are those members of the ruling class who are actively engaged in the intellectual labour of elaborating ideas which secure ruling class interests.[31]

Thirdly, Marx deployed the concept of ideology to focus more generally on the *mystifications through which ideas help to establish and maintain class domination*. In this sense ideology directs attention to the role of ideas in masking economic conditions, making them seem what they are not. Marx's most celebrated illustration of this relates to the mystifications of the labour market. With tongue in cheek, he writes that relations of production—apparently marked by exploitation and inequality—are in fact

a very Eden of the innate rights of man [where the owner of money and the free labourer] contract as free agents, . . . exchange equivalent for equivalent, . . . [and where each party] disposes only what is his own, . . . and looks to himself only'.[32]

At the same time, however, it is this very contradiction that enables 'men [to] become conscious of this conflict [between the material productive forces of society and the

---

[26] There is a voluminous literature on Marx's contribution to the concept of ideology. Recent discussions include Thompson 1990, 33 *et seq*; Eagleton 1991, 70 *et seq*; Barrett 1991, chap. 1; and McLellan 1995 chap. 2.

[27] Marx (O'Malley) 1994, 124.   [28] Ibid. 125.   [29] Ibid. 145 (emphasis in original).

[30] Ibid. 147.   [31] Ibid. 145.   [32] Marx (Tucker) 1978, 343.

existing relations of production] and fight it out'.[33] Thus, ideology both masks economic conditions and provides the context in which consciousness may begin to grasp those conditions.

Finally, Thompson argues that there is a further usage latent in Marx's work in which, more generally still, the sole issue is the *functionality of ideas to class domination*.[34] Here there is a recognition that ideas may help to establish and maintain class domination even without masking economic conditions, simply by orientating social life towards conservation rather than change. Thompson illustrates this 'latent' sense of ideology by reference to Marx's discussion in the *Eighteenth Brumaire of Louis Bonaparte* of the role of tradition in shaping the course of French history during the turbulent period 1848–51. Marx observes how, even (or rather, especially) in the midst of a period of revolutionary crisis, tradition is at work, constraining change or directing it in particular ways.

Tradition from all the dead generations weighs like a nightmare on the brain of the living. And just when they appear to be revolutionising themselves and their circumstances, . . . that is when they nervously summon up the spirits of the past . . .[35]

For Thompson there is implicit in this discussion a notion of ideology that calls attention to the role of ideas (in this case, beliefs about the meaning and value of past practices) in sustaining class domination by encouraging the stabilization of actuality and discouraging its transformation.

The notion of ideology articulated by Thompson takes relatively little from the first and second of these four Marxian usages. The first usage arises from an extreme form of materialist determinism. However much the Young Hegelians may have exaggerated the role of ideas in shaping material reality, Marx seriously underrated that role when he maintained that material conditions determine consciousness. The second usage is also flawed. The claim that there exists in every society a set of 'dominant thoughts', which produce social coherence by co-opting subordinate classes, neglects the possibility and actuality of popular resistance. The 'dominant ideology thesis'—as it was later to be called—underestimates the extent to which members of subaltern groups have independent agency, beyond the control of ruling classes. At the same time, the thesis also overestimates the extent to which ruling cultures are themselves determinate and unified and hence capable of being straightforwardly internalized, even if subordinate classes were the passive recipients of ideas which the thesis suggests them to be.[36] Both these shortcomings are to a degree recognized in the third and fourth senses in which Marx used the concept of ideology, and it is from these that Thompson's definition largely draws. But Thompson's formulation extends these usages in two main ways. In the first place, as noted, it re-frames ideology in terms of *meaning*, rather than specific ideas (pursuing what may be the implications of the fourth, 'latent' conception in this regard). Secondly, the formulation refocuses ideology in terms of *relations of domination*, as distinct from simply class

---

[33] Marx (Tucker) 1978, 5.   [34] Thompson 1990, 40 *et seq.*
[35] Marx (Carver) 1996, 32.   [36] See Abercrombie *et al.* 1980.

domination. As is widely acknowledged today, Marx's approach to domination was too one-dimensional. While class remains, of course, an important dimension of the asymmetrical structure of social relations, there are other dimensions as well of at least equal importance.

It is, then, a *critical* conception of ideology, rooted in *political and ethical* concerns, which I shall use in this book. Whatever the merits or demerits of other conceptions of ideology, for my purposes the value of the concept lies in its capacity to bring out, and invoke scrutiny of, the way meaning can sustain domination. In Thompson's summary:

> The concept of ideology, according to the formulation proposed here, calls our attention to the ways in which meaning is mobilized in the service of dominant individuals and groups, that is, the ways in which the meaning constructed and conveyed by symbolic forms serves, in partic-ular circumstances, to establish and sustain structured social relations from which some indi-viduals and groups benefit more than others, and which some individuals and groups have an interest in preserving while others may seek to contest.[37]

THE 'END OF IDEOLOGY' IDEOLOGY[38]

I have indicated how I shall use the concept of ideology, which of the many available (and potential) conceptions I shall employ. But why use it at all? The view is widely held that the concept of ideology has lost whatever pertinence or usefulness or pur-chase on the world it may once have had; that the 'end of ideology' has been reached. Claims to this effect are not new. Indeed, the tradition of theorizing about the 'end of ideology' is today almost as well established as the tradition of theorizing about ideology itself. As I shall show in this section, however, these claims proceed from a different notion of ideology from that which informs this book, and in no way estab-lish the end of what I shall discuss.

The 'end of ideology' was initially announced in the 1950s and 1960s by Edward Shils, Daniel Bell, Seymour Lipset, and others.[39] By this these scholars meant that there was no longer any room in modern societies for projects of revolutionary change. In Bell's words, ideology as a way of 'mobilizing emotional energy' and '[con-verting] ideas into social levers' had 'come to a dead end'.[40] On the one hand, expe-rience of fascism, Nazism, and Stalinism had demonstrated that programmatic political doctrines only lead to disaster. Both in the West and in Eastern Europe, intellectuals—who, in the analysis of Shils and the others, had assumed a central role in developing and promoting programmes of radical political transformation—had come to realize the naivety of their position, and to appreciate the value of more mod-est, pragmatic approaches to social change. On the other hand, a consensus had emerged that established political institutions in Western societies offer the soundest basis for social progress. If the old ideologies had become 'meaningless, some old

---

[37] Thompson 1990, 72–3.

[38] I borrow this phrase from Eagleton 1991, 4.

[39] Shils 1955; Bell 1962; Lipset 1964.

[40] Bell 1962, 401, 400, 393.

verities are not—the verities of free speech, free press, the right of opposition and of free inquiry'.[41] In consequence, potential sources of social conflict and of revolution-ary passion had been largely defused. Thus, the events of the two decades between 1930 and 1950 meant 'an end to chiliastic hopes, to millenarianism, to apocalyptic thinking—and to ideology'.[42]

As one observer sardonically puts it, this thesis was ' "disproven" dramatically by the sixties, only to "come true" in the seventies and eighties'[43]—and, one might add, *a fortiori*, in the nineties. In the late 1980s and early 1990s Francis Fukuyama advanced the claim that the 'the end of history' had been attained.[44] A 'worldwide liberal revolution' was underway, he argued,[45] following the 'total exhaustion of viable systematic alternatives to Western liberalism'.[46] What this marked was 'not just the end of the Cold War, or the passing of a particular period of postwar history, but the end of history as such: that is, the end point of mankind's ideological evolu-tion and the universalisation of Western liberal democracy as the final form of human government'.[47] Like the earlier 'end of ideology' theorists, Fukuyama expected that ideologies would retain appeal in non-industrialized societies and that, even in devel-oped societies, ideologies might occasionally resurface. In general, however, ideolog-ical competition was a thing of the past.

It is obvious that in these claims ideology means something very different from that which I intend by the term. It is employed in a manner that comes close to the every-day sense of ideology as dogma recalled at the beginning of this chapter. Ideology is used to denote a comprehensive system of ideas about politics and society that is rigid, inflammatory and utopian (or rather, dystopian). For Shils, Bell, and Lipset this apparently equates to communism and, perhaps, socialism. For Fukuyama the term has a similar, if slightly broader, resonance. Insofar as 'history' continues in the devel-oping world, the most significant ideology is, as he sees it, Islamic fundamentalism. Depending on the context, such a usage may point to the instrumentality of mean-ing to prevailing power relations, but equally it may point to an effort to transform such power relations. Either way, dogma does not operate with anything like the sub-tlety—and the effectiveness—of ideology in the sense in which I use the term.

The arguments to which I have so far referred were put forward by theorists of the Right. But from the 1970s onwards radical thinkers also began to assert the obsoles-cence of ideology. This is another way in which the end of ideology was to ' "come true" ' after the 1960s.[48] In an interview conducted in the mid-1970s Michel Foucault expressed the view that ideology had lost its pertinence for three interrelated reasons.[49] In the first place it stands 'in virtual opposition to something else that is supposed to count as truth'. To posit ideology is to presume the existence, or

[41] Bell 1962, 406.   [42] Ibid. 393.   [43] Jameson 1991, 159.
[44] Fukuyama 1989, 1989/90, and 1992. The first article in the series contained a question mark ('The End of History?'), dropped in the later book. Fukuyama's thesis will be discussed further in Ch. 2 below.
[45] Fukuyama 1992, ch. 4.   [46] Fukuyama 1989, 3.   [47] Ibid. 4.
[48] Jameson 1991, 159. This is actually the main way Jameson had in mind. (The bulk of this book appeared as articles before 1989.)
[49] Foucault 1980, 118.

possibility, of an alternative account that correctly represents reality. Yet there can be no such account, for reality is not unitary but differs according to where one stands. Secondly, the concept of ideology predicates a notion of human beings as 'subjects', confronting a distinct object domain. Yet, again, this is misleading, for subjectivity is not a pre-given basis for action and knowledge, but rather a product of interaction in the world and, especially, of power relations. And thirdly, the notion of ideology allocates ideas and symbolic forms to 'a second position [in relation] to something which functions as its infrastructure, as its material economic determinant, etc.'. As has come widely to be acknowledged, however, economic relations are not the sole determinant of history, and ideas and the symbolic forms through which they are expressed belong not just to a superstructure, but are partly constitutive of social conditions.

Here too, it is clear that what is said to be obsolete is something different from what I associate with ideology. None of Foucault's concerns implicates the conception I adopt. Patently he has in mind a conception of ideology which is rooted in orthodox Marxist historical materialism, and which depends on claims about the inaccuracy of the ideas involved. As indicated, I sidestep claims about the material basis of ideas. I also bracket epistemological claims, focusing instead squarely on the relationship between meaning and power. The relationship between meaning and power is, as it happens, one of the central preoccupations of Foucault's work.[50] If he insists that the study of ideology has reached a dead end, this is mainly because he assumes that ideology is necessarily concerned with falsity and cannot afford a basis for historical-political inquiry into 'how effects of *truth* are produced'.[51] In his words, by 'freeing myself of the old concept of ideology, which permitted playing reality against false interpretations of reality . . . [my critics] say that . . . my discussion [becomes] no more than a reactionary echo, which would do no more than confirm things as they are'. In fact, he explains, his project is precisely to unsettle the state of things, by showing, on the one hand, how 'effects of truth' are produced and, on the other hand, how those effects can become 'implements within possible struggles'. He seeks to decipher 'a layer of reality in such a way that the lines of force and the lines of resistance come forth; the points of resistance and the possible points of attack; the paths marked out and the shortcuts'. In short, it is 'the reality of possible struggles that I wish to bring to light'.[52] These remarks leave no doubt that Foucault's rejection of the concept of ideology is quite compatible with the concept's continued use in the manner proposed in this book.

The concept of ideology has also come under attack—from both Right and Left—on other grounds.[53] But, as in the case of the arguments I have mentioned, the target is always a notion of ideology that is different from the one I shall use. My point, however, is not just that declarations of the end of ideology do not declare the end of what I propose to analyse. It is that such declarations actually confirm the persistence

---

[50] His work on this subject is briefly discussed in Ch. 6 below.
[51] Foucault 1980, 118 (emphasis added). On this, see, further, Ch. 6.
[52] Foucault 1989, 261.   [53] See, e.g., Rorty 1994 and Baudrillard 1994, 12–13.

of what I propose to analyse. Of course, in the arguments advanced by Shils, Bell, Lipset, and Fukuyama ideology is said to have 'ended' in a different sense from that in which Foucault suggests that it has 'ended'. The former purport to describe a social-historical development; the latter refers to redundancy or exhaustion on theoretical grounds. None the less, the thrust of both sets of arguments is that the concept of ideology has no further role. Yet, if ideology calls attention to, and prompts critical reflection on, the ways in which meaning helps to stabilize relations of domination, then surely the ideological manœuvre *par excellence* is to dismiss ideology.[54] No idea could stabilize relations of domination more effectively than that. It follows that efforts to dismiss ideology should make us more alert than ever to the concept's enduring pertinence. In seeing ideology out by one door, theorists secure its re-entry by another. [55] This is especially the case where the 'end of ideology' belongs to a more general depoliticization of issues, as in the work of Fukuyama and his precursors. But it may even be the case where, as in the work of Foucault, analysis of the relationship between meaning and power continues outside the context of ideology critique. The very gesture of renouncing the concept of ideology may have a certain ideological import, particularly against the background of corresponding moves by conservative theorists.

In the face of ongoing assault on the concept, John Thompson is one of a number of scholars writing in the 1990s—among them also Terry Eagleton and Slavoj Žižek—who have sought to renew the study of ideology. Motivating this effort is an awareness that the supposed end of ideology does not signal that meaning has ceased to serve as a force for defending the social *status quo*. On the contrary, as noted here, the proclaimed demise of ideology only seems to demonstrate the continuing vigour of meaning as such a force. From this perspective, what is utopian/dystopian is not so much the interest in ideology as the evocation of a 'post-ideological' world. This point is neatly captured in a heading that appeared in a British newspaper: 'Big Brother is bleeping us—with the message that ideology doesn't matter'.[56]

IDEOLOGICAL MODES AND STRATEGIES

If ideology refers to the ways in which meaning serves to establish and sustain relations of domination, then the study of ideology is directed to highlighting those ways. Clearly, meaning may support domination in an infinite number of ways. In looking for the operation of ideology, where does an analyst begin? To provide starting-points for analysis, theorists of ideology have identified a number of common ideological manœuvres (of which, as just indicated, the 'end of ideology' is one). In describing

---

[54] On the ideological character of 'end of ideology' arguments, see Eagleton 1991, xii–xiii and 4–5.

[55] On this point, see Žižek 1994*a*, 17.

[56] *The Guardian*, 4 July 1998, Saturday Review, 8 (title of a review by Stefan Collini of P. Davison (ed.), *The Complete Works of George Orwell*, in which Collini delivers a timely reminder that Orwell's real name was Blair).

these manœuvres, Thompson draws a distinction between the general modes through which ideology typically operates and the particular discursive (or other symbolic) strategies which ideology typically deploys.[57] The latter refer to the ways in which meaning capable of operating as ideology is mobilized; the former to the ways in which meaning, thus mobilized, may come to sustain relations of domination. Five principal modes of operation are often regarded as characteristic of ideology: legitimation, dissimulation, unification, reification, and naturalization.[58] In the paragraphs that follow I consider each of these modes in turn, indicating what they involve and how they might serve to sustain dominant power. I also note some of the discursive strategies commonly associated with them. In doing so, I highlight examples of these modes and strategies discussed by Marx. Since, as noted earlier, the conception of ideology involved here draws on Marx's writings, it is not surprising that his account of the operation of ideology remains instructive.

By *legitimation* is meant the process by which authority comes to seem valid and appropriate. As Max Weber observed, ruling power generally depends not on forcible imposition, but rather on the consent and support of those subject to it, whether for reasons to do with tradition and habit or with the personal qualities of leaders or (as he proposed was more common in the modern world) with the legality of the rules laid down.[59] Without doubt, legitimation is one of the most effective ways of establishing and maintaining relations of domination. If subaltern individuals and groups can be encouraged to regard their subordination as justified, their complicity can be engaged in perpetuating that subordination. As Eagleton puts it, the 'most efficient oppressor is the one who persuades his underlings to love, desire, and identify with his power; and any practice of political emancipation thus involves that most difficult of all forms of liberation, freeing ourselves from ourselves'.[60] Ideology almost invariably operates in this mode, and the various other modes of operation of ideology which I shall discuss can be thus understood in most cases as specific forms of legitimation. A number of characteristic legitimating strategies are, however, worth noting at this point.[61] One is *rationalization*. Social and political arrangements may be legitimated through the construction of a chain of reasoning of which they are the logical conclusion. In this way it is made to seem as if there are good reasons why things are as they are, with the result that change becomes irrational. Another common legitimating strategy is *normalization*. Legitimacy may be conferred on a particular set of arrangements by making them seem normal. Different arrangements thus come to appear as deviations from the proper state of things or, at any rate, as exceptions which prove the validity of the rule. Thompson highlights yet another legitimating strategy, which he refers to as *'narrativization'*. This involves the telling of stories

---

[57] Thompson 1990, esp. 59–60 and 292–3.
[58] The account that follows is adapted from the (largely overlapping) accounts of Thompson and Eagleton. See Thompson 1990, 60 *et seq.*, and Eagleton 1991, ch. 2.
[59] Weber 1958, 78–9.
[60] Eagleton 1991, xiii–xiv. I take up below Eagleton's point about emancipation from ourselves.
[61] The majority of discursive strategies mentioned here are discussed in Thompson 1990, 61 *et seq.*

which set contemporary conditions in the context of a history. By means of such stories, social and political arrangements may be made to seem worthy of respect because
they are venerable. Or they may be made to seem so because they represent the culmination of history, that is to say, because they represent progress.

A second mode in which ideology frequently operates is *dissimulation*, whereby
relations of domination are obscured, masked or denied. One discursive strategy associated with this mode of operation is straightforward *inversion*. Domination may be
sustained by being made to seem its opposite. Marx's discussion of the capitalist
labour market recalled above illustrates how this may occur. Labour relationships
characterized by inequality and exploitation appear as the outcome of free exchange
on a footing of equality and mutuality.

The exchange of commodities of itself implies no other relations of dependence than those
which result from its own nature. On this assumption, labour-power can appear upon the market as a commodity, only if, and so far as, its possessor, the individual whose labour-power it
is, offers it for sale, or sells it, as a commodity. In order that he may be able to do this, he must
have it at his disposal, must be the untrammelled owner of his capacity for labour, i.e., of his
person. He and the owner of money meet in the market, and deal with each other as on the
basis of equal rights, with this difference alone, that one is buyer, the other seller; both, therefore, equal in the eyes of the law.[62]

Another discursive strategy which may be deployed in this connection is *displacement*,
that is to say, the transfer of attributes belonging to one person or object to another.
Thompson calls attention to an example of this which can likewise be found in
Marx's writings. In the *Eighteenth Brumaire of Louis Bonaparte*, Marx highlights how,
by identifying himself with Napoleon, Louis Bonaparte sought to encourage the sum-
moning up of the 'spirits of the past', and in this way to forestall revolutionary
change.[63] Eagleton notes a further strategy through which ideology may operate in
the mode of dissimulation. Ideology can frequently be seen to involve a ' "performative contradiction", in which what is said is at odds with the situation or act of utterance itself'.[64] The 'end of ideology' ideology is an example of this.

Ideology often operates, thirdly, through a process of *unification*, in which social
relations come to appear coherent and harmonious, and cleavages are made to seem
non-existent, or, at any rate, irrelevant. This may help to sustain relations of domination because, if social divisions no longer count, then the systematic asymmetries
indexed to those divisions may likewise seem no longer to count. Awareness of the
extent to which individuals suffer oppression on the grounds of class, sex, ethnicity,
etc. may be occluded. Thus, Žižek characterizes ideology in terms of the imaginary
resolution of social cleavages, the repression of social conflict.[65] The discursive strategy most often associated with this mode of operation of ideology is *universalization*.
Marx called attention to this strategy, highlighting the way it serves to confer illusory
unity on societies and thus to mask differential levels of social power. '[U]nder the

---

[62] Marx (Tucker) 1978, 336–7.   [63] Thompson 1990, 62. See Marx (Carver) 1996, 32.
[64] Eagleton 1991, 24.   [65] See Žižek 1994*a* and *b*.

rule of the bourgeoisie', he observes, 'the concepts of freedom, equality, etc. . . . take on the form of universality'. For, in order to establish its dominance, a social class must

represent its interests as the common interests of all members of society; that is to say, in terms of ideas, to give its thoughts the form of universality, to present them as the only reasonable ones, the only ones universally valid . . . [T]he revolutionising class presents itself . . . not as a class, but as representative of the entire society; it appears as the entire body of society opposed to the single dominating class.[66]

Through the universalization of social and political institutions, those institutions may be made to seem impartial, inclusory, and rooted in considerations of mutual interest. A further strategy commonly deployed to secure the imaginary unification of social formations is *simplification*. By means of a reductive account of social life, the character and significance of heterogeneity, and the unevenness and complexity of social processes may be removed from view.

A fourth mode in which ideology typically operates is *reification*. Georg Lukács developed this concept to refer to a process by which human products come to appear as if they were material things, and then to dominate those who produced them.[67] Through reification men and women cease to recognize the social world as the outcome of human endeavour, and begin to see it as fixed and unchangeable, an object of contemplation rather than a domain of action. The roots of this concept lie in Marx's account of the 'fetishism of commodities', in which he explains how

a definite social relation between men . . . assumes, in their eyes, the fantastic form of a relation between things . . . Man's reflections on the forms of social life . . . [begin] with the results of the process of development ready to hand before him. The characters that stamp products as commodities, and whose establishment is a necessary preliminary to the circulation of commodities, have already acquired the stability of natural, self-understood forms of social life, before man seeks to decipher, not their historical character, for in his eyes they are immutable, but their meaning.[68]

Reification, then, may help to build and support relations of domination by making those relations seem eternal, rather than historically specific, and necessary, rather than contingent. Among the discursive strategies through which meaning may be mobilized to this end are a range of *figurative devices*. Discussion may, for instance, be structured in terms of particular metaphors, geared to representing social practices and institutions as static, ahistorical, and unalterable. Or it may be structured in terms of synecdoche, where a part is made to stand for a whole or vice versa, or in terms of metonymy, where an attribute is substituted for the referent itself. Through the use of synecdoche and metonymy relationships may be made to seem abstract, and their social and historical specificity masked. Also employed to reify social relations are, as Thompson highlights, certain *syntactic devices*. The passive voice may, for

---

[66] Marx (O'Malley) 1994, 146.   [67] Lukács 1971, 83 *et seq.*
[68] Marx (Tucker) 1978, 321, 323–4.

example, be used to depict social processes as events or facts, independent of the actors involved in them. Likewise verbs may be turned into nouns, thus tending to minimize awareness of the extent to which action and interaction are in issue.[69]

Finally, ideology can often be seen to operate in the mode of *naturalization*, whereby existing social arrangements come to seem obvious and self-evident, as if they were natural phenemona belonging to a world 'out there'. Thus, as in the process of reification, historical products begin to appear forces of nature. In this mode, as Eagleton puts it, 'a ruling ideology does not so much combat alternative ideas as thrust them beyond the very bounds of the thinkable'.[70] Domination is stabilized by making it impossible to imagine more symmetrical social relations. For Žižek ideology serves to this extent as a 'generative matrix that regulates the relationship between visible and non-visible, between imaginable and non-imaginable, as well as the changes in this relationship'.[71] Marx illustrates how this matrix may work by reference to the doctrine of the division of powers between monarchy, aristocracy, and bourgeoisie. In particular historical circumstances, he observes, this doctrine has come to seem, not a political decision, but an 'eternal law'.[72] One very common discursive strategy deployed to confer self-evidence is the *assumption* of that which requires demonstration. In this way we may be encouraged to take the world for granted, rather than to approach it in terms of choices. We may come to see it as an objective domain to which we must adapt, rather than a political one defined through struggle and negotiation. Thus, for instance, concepts which are contested may be treated as predetermined; practices which are problematic may be treated as given; institutions which are open to debate may be treated as beyond question. Another discursive strategy frequently deployed to naturalize existing social arrangements is the use of *dichotomous reasoning*. Alternative social arrangements, insofar as they are considered, may be presented in terms of stark oppositions, in which actuality and its polar opposite appear as the only options. By ruling out more moderate, intermediate possibilities, change may be made to seem unfeasible and actuality thus confirmed.

A number of points arise from this discussion of ideological modes and strategies. One relates to a distinctive, though not necessary, feature of the operation of ideology, as I use the term. Mystification is generally involved.[73] While legitimation may occur without mystification, ideology mostly works to support relations of domination by, so to speak, covering their tracks. To clarify this aspect further, it may be helpful to revisit the distinction highlighted earlier between conceptions of ideology that have epistemological concerns and conceptions of ideology that have sociological or political or ethical concerns. I indicated that the one adopted here is of the latter kind, and in this respect differs from the notion of ideology as false consciousness.

---

[69] Thompson 1990, 66.   [70] Eagleton 1991, 58.   [71] Žižek 1994a, 1.
[72] Marx (O'Malley) 1994, 145.
[73] Thus, at the end of an historical survey of the concept of ideology Michèle Barrett concludes there is 'a useful set of meanings that the term ideology can capture well; they cluster around processes of mystification'. Barrett 1991, 166–7.

As I suggested then, however, from this it does not follow that illusion plays no part. Insofar as there is mystification, illusion may indeed be involved, but it is not a simple case of error or ignorance of social reality. I may be perfectly aware that labour relations involve exploitation and inequality, and yet still act as if they do not. In doing so, I may cynically accept this situation.[74] But that would be relatively unusual; most people do not behave cynically most of the time. More likely, I will be troubled by my bad faith, and will look forward to the day when employment relationships are no longer exploitative and unequal. What I may be unaware of, however, is the impact of acting *as if* labour relations were based on free exchange among equals. I may not fully realize the extent to which my pretence itself helps to perpetuate asymmetries in the sphere of labour, by keeping alive the idea that those asymmetries do not exist, or are unalterable, or are legitimate. According to Žižek, this is where, with ideology, illusion comes in.[75] The mystification lies not in unawareness of social reality, but in unawareness of the extent to which actions (or utterances, texts, images, etc.) and the ideas expressed through them serve to shape social reality. For, as Thompson explains, the symbolic forms through which meaning is generated do not simply 'articulate or obscure social relations or interests which are constituted fundamentally and essentially at a pre-symbolic level; rather symbolic forms are continuously and creatively implicated in the constitution of social relations as such'.[76]

But there is also another, deeper level at which the illusion involved differs from simple error or ignorance of social reality. In contrast to the assumption that underlies the notion of ideology as false consciousness, no assumption is made here that there is a truth about social reality which anyone with a sound command of the available empirical evidence could know. On the contrary, the possibility is denied of grasping reality from a single, Archimedean point. The illusion is precisely the failure to register this, the failure to recognize the extent to which reality is experienced variably, rather than uniformly. But if an 'absolute' notion of truth is eschewed here, in which the world appears accessible to anyone sufficiently well informed, so too is a 'relative' one. To be sure, a 'perspectival' account of this kind is often equated by its critics with relativism. However, it is in fact quite different. Terry Eagleton captures the difference vividly.

[T]o claim that all knowledge springs from a specific social standpoint is not to imply that any old social standpoint is as valuable for these purposes as any other. If what one is looking for is some understanding of the workings of imperialism as a whole, then one would be singularly ill-advised to consult the Governor-General or the *Daily Telegraph*'s Africa correspondent, who will almost certainly deny its existence.[77]

What is illusory, then, is the assumption that the world appears the same from all vantage points, and that one vantage point is as suitable for all purposes as every other. In

---

[74] A theory of 'cynical reason' and 'enlightened false consciousness' is put forward by Peter Sloterdijk. See Sloterdijk 1988.

[75] I adapt slightly Žižek 's (psychoanalytic) account here, but (if I understand it correctly) retain the main thrust. Žižek 1994*b*, 314–16.

[76] Thompson 1990, 58.   [77] Eagleton 1991, 97.

this sense the conception of ideology I employ may be seen to have epistemological concerns, but those concerns proceed from a different notion of knowledge than one in which falsity is understood as simple inaccuracy or non-correspondence with reality. As I shall discuss further in Chapter 6, they proceed from an approach that connects epistemological issues with ethical and political preoccupations, knowledge with justice and power.

Another matter arising out of the foregoing discussion of ideological manœuvres concerns the interrelation of the various modes and strategies. Patently, there is considerable overlap among the five modes of ideology I have mentioned and the strategies associated with them. All of the modes could be expressed partly in terms of the others. Indeed, as noted, each is arguably a form of legitimation. And all of the discursive strategies with which I have linked each mode can equally be deployed to support other modes. At the same time, though they may usefully be separated for analytical purposes, the various modes and strategies rarely, of course, work independently. Rather, they tend to act in mutually reinforcing combinations.

A related issue concerns the status of the particular modes and strategies I have discussed in relation to the analysis of ideology. As indicated, these modes and strategies are put forward simply as starting-points for understanding the operation of ideology. They in no way exhaust the forms through which meaning may serve to sustain dominant power. Ideology may, and does, operate in innumerable other ways, including ways that are incompatible with the manœuvres I have described. Thus, for instance, while ideology commonly operates in the mode of unification, it also operates in the mode of fragmentation, stabilizing relations of domination by making opposition seem alien and disparate.[78] Conversely, the manœuvres I have discussed by no means necessarily and invariably operate as ideology. Dichotomous reasoning may, for example, serve to buttress asymmetrical social relations, but it may also be deployed to challenge them. In order to establish which in the event it does, an investigation is necessary into the particular circumstances in which the reasoning becomes significant.

This last point delivers an important reminder that the operation of ideology cannot fully be grasped through the analysis of discursive forms. As Thompson stresses, one cannot simply 'read off the characteristics and consequences of symbolic forms by attending to the symbolic forms alone', in the manner of structuralist approaches.[79] While certain common ideological strategies can be identified, it must be recognized that no ideological strategy is ever 'ideological as such';[80] what counts is the way the strategy works in practice. Žižek illustrates this point by highlighting the extent to which ideology deploys opposed strategies in different contexts. To support relations of domination is sometimes to make things seem simple, sometimes complex; sometimes to make things seem ahistorical, sometimes contingent.[81] If certain common ideological strategies may be identified, there is nonetheless a sense in which these strategies subvert themselves. The most effective vehicles for ideology

---

[78] For a discussion of fragmentation as an ideological *modus operandi*, see Thompson 1990, 65.
[79] Ibid. 291.   [80] Ibid. 67.   [81] Žižek 1994*a*, esp. 3–5.

are, of course, those for which we are precisely not looking out. It follows that, while formal analysis can lead to tentative or preliminary conclusions about the operation of ideology, firmer conclusions depend on research into the contexts in which those forms come to matter. I highlight this as a qualification to the conclusions I reach in this book, for here analysis is largely limited to discursive forms.

THE CRITIQUE OF IDEOLOGY

In introducing the conception of ideology that informs this book, I mentioned a distinction between neutral and critical conceptions of ideology. I noted that the conception I use belongs to the latter category. Analysis of the ways in which meaning serves to establish and sustain relations of domination is motivated not just by a desire to describe and explain the world, but by a desire to criticize and change it. The analyst takes up the study of ideology in this sense not just out of intellectual curiosity or professional interest, but from a sense of injustice.[82] To clarify further the function of ideology as a critical tool, I discuss in this section the concept of ideology *critique*.

Marx, as is well known, attached much importance to the distinction between 'critique' (or, as it is sometimes called, 'immanent critique') and mere 'criticism'. His understanding of this distinction is explained by Seyla Benhabib in the following terms:

While criticism . . . stands outside the object it criticizes, asserting norms against facts, and the dictates of reason against the unreasonableness of the world, critique refuses to stand outside its object and instead juxtaposes the immanent, normative self-understanding of its object to the material actuality of this object.[83]

Criticism, then, judges an object by reference to external criteria. Critique, on the other hand, judges the object by reference to its own standards, that is to say, by reference to the criteria by which it judges itself. In this way critique escapes the challenge which criticism faces: what authorizes the critical criteria used? by what criteria are *they* adjudged valid? In Marx's words, criticism entails 'the designing of the future and the proclamation of ready-made solutions'.[84] Criticism criticizes facts for their failure to correspond to imposed standards; it invents blueprints and seeks to change the world to fit them. In contrast, 'we [who practice critique] do not attempt dogmatically to prefigure the future, but want to find the new world only through [critique] of the old'.[85] Critique involves 'bringing out the true significance underlying [actuality]', pushing it to 'go beyond its own confines'.[86] Put differently, it consists in 'enabling the world to clarify its consciousness, in waking it from its dream about itself'.[87]

---

[82] On this issue, see further Ch. 6.   [83] Benhabib 1986, 32–33.
[84] Marx (Tucker) 1978, 13.   [85] Ibid.   [86] Ibid. 14.
[87] Ibid. 15.

Marx's account of the concept of critique was later taken up and reformulated in the 1930s and 1940s, in the context of an effort by members of the Frankfurt School of Social Research to develop a general method of 'ideology critique'.[88] The contributions of Max Horkheimer and Theodor Adorno are especially important in this regard.[89] For Horkheimer the critique of ideology serves to '[confront] the existent, in its historical context, with the claim of its conceptual principles, in order to criticize the relation between the two and thus transcend them'.[90] This has a negative dimension, in that critique involves 'negation' of ideological pretensions. But, for Horkheimer, the critique of ideology also has a positive dimension, in that, through these negations, the 'relativity' of actuality by reference to an essential 'theoretical whole' is brought into focus. The existent comes to appear only one among many possible realizations of that whole. In this way, alternatives—the further possibilities that remain unfulfilled in actuality—come into view; 'relative truths [are salvaged] from the wreckage of false ultimates'.[91] Horkheimer thus follows Marx in conceiving ideology critique as a process of revealing the truth partly concealed in actuality, waking the world from its dream about itself and bringing it to consciousness of how far that dream is from realization.

In the work of Adorno, however, the concept of critique underwent a significant shift. Benhabib highlights that, for Adorno (and, under his influence, later on for Horkheimer as well), ideology critique is not a simple matter of bringing out a truth partly concealed in actuality, for—as he sees it—there is no such truth.[92] Far from presenting as a 'theoretical whole', ideology is a contradictory, indeterminate, and conflicted affair. The principles and claims that constitute the world's 'dream about itself' have no fixed essence, but rather are constantly defined and redefined, negotiated and renegotiated, appropriated and reappropriated. It follows, in Adorno's account, that one cannot anticipate the content, or indeed count on the beneficence, of the unfulfilled possibilities that will be revealed through the practice of negation. As Benhabib explains, Adorno denies that 'there is an immanent logic to the actual that is emancipatory'. And if there is no such logic, then critique can give no 'guarantees' that its own effects will be emancipatory. Or rather, it can guarantee that its effects will be emancipatory only insofar as it insists on keeping the future open and refusing to give guarantees. Adorno thus 'rejects the logic of immanence, while preserving immanent critique'.[93] From this perspective, ideology critique cannot be understood in terms of a gradual narrowing of the gap between claims and actuality. Rather, its significance lies in loosening the imaginative grip of actuality, and expanding the prospects for creative engagement with claims.

What are the implications of these points as regards the character and aims of the critique of ideology, as I use that term? From Marx we learn that ideology critique is

---

[88] Leading studies of this include Jay 1973; Held 1980; Geuss 1981; and Benhabib 1986.

[89] I draw here on the account in Held 1980, 183 et seq. Horkheimer's views on the distinctiveness of 'critical' approaches will be discussed further in Ch. 6 below.

[90] Horkheimer 1947, 182.   [91] Ibid. 183.   [92] See Benhabib 1986, 171 et seq.

[93] Ibid. 173 (emphasis omitted).

geared to promoting social change, not by advancing blueprints for the future, but by encouraging investigation of the resources of the past. Rather than pressing new principles, critique insists on the principles to which social systems already claim to subscribe: equality, freedom, democracy, and so on. In doing so, it aims to show how these principles can be understood to point beyond existing social arrangements, beyond existing relations of domination. In this way ideology critique seeks to push actuality to consider its own further possibilities and transcend its current confines. Thus, as Marx suggests in his discussions of the labour market (cited earlier), ideology is at one level self-confirming, but at another level contains the seeds of its own undoing. If the sphere of labour is made to seem a 'very Eden of the innate rights of man', this masks economic conditions, while also providing a context within which those conditions can be changed. The very contradictions involved in ideology are what enable 'men [to] become conscious of [class] conflict and fight it out'.[94] Horkheimer provides further insight into the methods of ideology critique. The characteristic manœuvre, he explains, is negation. The notion, for instance, that social reality is a unified, harmonious whole is turned into the notion that it is not; the notion that relations of domination are a natural state of affairs is turned into the notion that they are not; the notion that power relations are structured symmetrically is turned into the notion that they are not, and so on. By calling attention to the modes through which ideology operates, the critic unsettles particular meanings and shifts them onto a larger domain of alternative possibilities. The important caveat which Adorno then registers is that those possibilities come with no emancipatory guarantees attached. Once the mystifications through which meaning supports relations of domination have been exposed, no progressive logic will begin to unfold, propelling domination towards emancipation, actuality towards ideals. For in issue here are not simple finishing-lines, decided and accepted in advance. The question of what counts as emancipation (and therefore also domination) and what is constituted by ideals (and therefore also actuality) remains—and must remain—permanently open. As Adorno highlights, only in ideology is it closed.

To return, then, to the distinction between critique and criticism, ideology critique seeks to criticize ideology without adopting the external, Archimedean standpoint of criticism. At the same time, in criticizing ideology, it also refuses the internal 'self-understanding' of ideology itself. Instead, Eagleton explains, ideology critique proceeds from awareness that ideology is never a seamless monolith; it is always 'inherently contradictory, comprising at once beliefs and interests wholly "internal" to it, and other forms of discourse and practice which run counter to its ruling logic'. The critical challenge is to find points of strain and contradiction through which an existing self-understanding might be led to 'surpass itself'.[95] The critique of ideology, accordingly,

seeks to locate itself neither wholly inside nor wholly outside the given system, but, so to speak, in that system's very internal contradictions, in the places where it is non-identical with itself,

---

[94] Marx (Tucker) 1978, 5.   [95] Eagleton 1991, 171.

in order to elaborate from them a political logic which might ultimately transform the power-structure as a whole.[96]

Žižek , for his part, characterizes this standpoint as an 'empty place', which allows the critic at once to 'occupy' ideology and to maintain 'critical distance' from it.[97] He offers a pyschoanalytic interpretation of the function of ideology critique, in which the focus of attention is 'repressed social antagonism'.[98] As Eagleton recalls, ideology critique has long been understood in psychoanalytic terms. His own account of legit-imation mentioned above suggests that emancipation may indeed involve, in some sense, 'freeing ourselves from ourselves'. But then, he also notes, critique 'presumes that nobody is ever wholly mystified'; otherwise how could 'critical distance' arise, and resistance occur?[99] At any rate, ideology is not so much a matter of failing to 'see through' the rationalizations and mystifications from which asymmetries of power draw support. Rather, as observed earlier, it is a matter of acting *as if* one fails to see through them. To quote Eagleton again:

Ideology . . . [is] not just a matter of what I think about a situation; it is somehow inscribed in that situation itself. It is no good my reminding myself that I am opposed to racism as I sit down on a park bench marked 'Whites Only'; by the action of sitting on it, I have supported and perpetuated racist ideology. The ideology, so to speak, is in the bench, not in my head.[100]

Ideology critique, then, seeks to come in at the level of meaning—whether commu-nicated through actions, words, images, or some other symbolic form—and help in turning contradictions into resources for emancipatory claims.

CONCLUSIONS

Let me now try to sum up how and why I use the concept of ideology in this book. The term 'ideology', though it first appeared in late eighteenth century France, was taken up and relaunched by Karl Marx, in the context of an effort to expose the con-tradictions of bourgeois societies and the conservatism of 'idealist' philosophers. The word then entered the language of politics and of everyday life, becoming a fairly crude instrument for discrediting an opponent's position. At the same time, ideology passed into the vocabulary of social theorizing, mostly within, but also beyond, the Marxist tradition. There it was to be deployed all too often for simplistic and mis-leading criticism. Or neutralized to the point where it came close to being emptied of distinctive content. Or yet, abolished: the concept which Marx had developed as a tool for the critique of capitalism was later to be identified with communism, and pronounced dead upon the latter's demise.

   Small wonder, perhaps, that many believe the abolitionists are right, even if their reasoning is held to be wrong. At best an anachronism, the concept of ideology seems

---

[96] Eagleton 1991, 172.   [97] See Žižek 1994a, 17.   [98] See ibid. 25.
[99] Eagleton 1991, xiv (emphasis omitted).   [100] Ibid. 40.

more probably a liability. With so many meanings, and so many of them problematic, the word appears best jettisoned as an analytical category. After all, as one commentator points out, 'old meanings adhere'.[101] And yet, there is also another story to be told. The concept of ideology has served, at least in the hands of some, as a powerful instrument for analysing the functionality of meaning to power. It has provided unparalleled insight into the ways in which words and other meaningful forms can help to make historically specific power relations seem natural, inevitable, immutable, justified, or non-existent. It has offered a means for directing attention to issues that remain as vital and urgent today as they ever were. While there is much that is unsatisfactory in the legacy of this contested term, there is a great deal that is valuable as well. Rather than ditching the concept, better surely to refocus, resharpen, and renew it. That, at any rate, is the perspective of Thompson, Eagleton, and Žižek, on whose work I have relied so heavily in this discussion. And that is the perspective which I adopt in the chapters to come.

These things said, I do not seek to insist too strongly on the word 'ideology'. For my purpose what counts is the distinctive terrain of enquiry to which this concept gives access. Thompson defines this terrain when he characterizes the study of ideology as the 'study [of] the ways in which meaning serves to establish and sustain relations of domination'.[102] Thus, I use the concept to analyse international legal processes through which asymmetrical power relations are legitimated, obscured, denied, reified, naturalized, or otherwise supported. To be sure, this sort of enquiry is more usually associated with the work of sociologists and political scientists seeking to show how, in everyday life or in the political domain, meaning works to reproduce differential capacities to participate in decision-making, pursue ends and realize interests. But the attempt to elucidate links between meaning and power has no less pertinence for all other spheres of social practice, of which international law is obviously one. With this in mind, I take up ideology critique in the succeeding chapters to investigate how moves to promote democracy through international law may serve, on the one hand, to stabilize systematic asymmetries of power and, on the other, to suggest ways of transforming those asymmetries.

[101] Barrett 1991, 168.   [102] Thompson 1990, 56 (emphasis omitted).

Chapter 2

International Law and the 'Liberal Revolution'

Should international law seek to universalize democratic politics? Does it already do so? What challenges are confronted in such an endeavour? And why until recently did these questions command so little serious attention? Let us dwell for a moment on this last issue. Why have international lawyers been so reticent in broaching the topic of democracy and its universalization? Part of the answer lies presumably in the relative novelty of democracy as a widely endorsed principle of political organization.[1] The democratic concept of self-rule on a footing of equality among citizens is, of course, extremely ancient, going back to fifth century BC Athens and beyond. But, as political theorists are fond of reminding us, the character of democracy as a form of mass politics, and its identification with legitimate political authority, are signally recent phenomena. While democracy assumed its modern shape as national representative government in the eighteenth and nineteenth centuries, participation in elections was long confined to a narrow section of society, defined by class, race and sex. It was not until the twentieth century, indeed well into the twentieth century, that universal suffrage became the norm. And if by then democracy had come to be associated with desirable and praiseworthy politics, that too marked a change.[2] Long after its 'reinvention' in the eighteenth century, democracy remained at best an ambiguous term, still carrying Plato's association with mob rule; to call someone a democrat was very possibly to insult the person. A more favourable connotation began to predominate in liberal societies by the beginning of the twentieth century, though it was only following two world wars fought in its name that democracy was firmly established as the byword for political legitimacy we now recognize.

Another part of the explanation for international lawyers' reticence with respect to democracy can be traced to the history of international law itself. In the course of its emergence as a distinct discipline, international law was repeatedly detached from other disciplines or domains to which the issue of constitutions in general, and later democracy in particular, were held more appropriately to belong. Thus, for the early jurists the 'forms of government' raised questions of practical politics, not law. Grotius wrote that 'the superior excellence of this or that form of government' should not be reflected in the law of nations, as this was a matter 'in regard to which different men hold different views'.[3] This point was reinforced when in the eighteenth and nine-

---

[1] There are many available histories of democracy. I have relied principally on Held 1996 and the collection of essays in Dunn 1992.

[2] For instructive historical surveys of the usage of the word 'democracy', see Williams 1983, 93 and Hanson 1989.

[3] Grotius 1964 (1646), 29 (Prol., para. 57) and 104 (Bk 1, ch. 3, VIII, 2). See also Textor 1916 (1680), ch. 1, 5: the forms of government belong to the realm of 'politics' and 'statesmanship'; the 'Law of Nations,

teenth centuries the law of nations became international law, a system of law regulating relations between sovereign states. Since the interstate domain—however its character was conceived—had no government, questions pertaining to the forms of government were relevant to the national domain alone.[4] It followed that, even if the topic did belong to law, it belonged to national law, not international law. Vattel accordingly observed that a nation's constitution is a matter 'of purely national concern'.[5] Still further was the point reinforced when in the nineteenth century international legal scholars became preoccupied with defending their discipline against charges that, in the absence of institutionalized sanctions for non-compliance, it could count only as 'positive morality', not as law. The lack of enforceable sanctions would not disqualify international law as law—they insisted—provided it was confined to rules that nation-states had manifestly made and accepted through their conduct in international relations. On the question of the organization of public power, there was no evidence that sovereign states had accepted international legal rules. At most, prescriptions concerning the forms of government might belong to the realm of what the law ought to be, and were not to be confused with what the law is. Woolsey thus affirmed that 'the law of nations preserves an entire indifference to constitutions, so long as they do not prevent the fulfilment of obligations'.[6] Even as the idea took root that democratic security is an international responsibility, international legal agnosticism with respect to the forms of government still remained in place. This aspect of early twentieth century liberal internationalism was taken to engage instead the new discipline of international relations. Oppenheim, accordingly, reaffirmed that under international law every state possesses 'the faculty of adopting any Constitution it likes and of changing such Constitution according to its discretion'.[7]

The boundaries—between politics and law, national law and international law, law and positive morality etc.—through which scholars have defined the distinctive terrain of international law have not, of course, remained stationary. In the decades following the Second World War, the protection of human rights was brought within the scope of international legal regulation. But if human rights were now clearly a legal issue, the question of the forms of government continued to be treated as largely a political or at any rate non-legal issue. Despite the close connection understood to exist between democratic politics and the protection of human rights, general international law was held to preserve its official indifference to constitutions.[8] Again, the explanation for this is very familiar. In the divided world of the post-war years, some very illiberal forms of politics claimed the title of democracy. As the term had by then

on the other hand, does not similarly deal with these matters, but presupposes in interstate affairs a definite form of State on either side'.

[4] On this aspect, see further Ch. 4.   [5] Vattel 1916 (1758), 19 (Bk 1, ch. 3, para. 37).
[6] Woolsey 1860, 87. Some of the most eminent international legal scholars of this period were also prominent anti-democrats, e.g. Sir Henry Maine.
[7] Oppenheim 1905, 403.
[8] Regional international law contrasts with general international law in this respect. Human rights instruments adopted within the framework of the Council of Europe and Organization of American States were explicitly linked to a commitment to democratic government.

become a synonym for legitimate politics, no bloc was prepared to concede such coveted ground to any other. Thus, totalitarian rule was consolidated in the Soviet Union and elsewhere under the banner of 'people's democracy'. Decolonization ended one form of heteronomy, only subsequently to see it replaced all too often by 'one party democracy'. And in Latin America military juntas installed government by decree for the pretended purpose of 'safeguarding democracy'. Concerned that the word was becoming drained of all significance, Western governments worked to resist moves to link democracy with the human rights guarantees of the 1948 Universal Declaration of Human Rights, the 1966 Human Rights Covenants and other texts of international (as distinct from regional) scope.[9] Relatively few references to democracy survive in the final drafts, especially of the Covenants. Supervisory organs, set up to monitor observance of human rights instruments, likewise put to one side the question of the relationship between human rights and democracy.

Following the demise of communist regimes and related developments in national and international practice, however, some scholars have begun to question this tradition of international legal neutrality with respect to constitutions, and to argue that international law should now, and to an extent already does, come out on the side of democratic political arrangements. For these scholars an emergent 'norm of democratic governance' belongs in today's international law. In this chapter I outline this claim, and highlight some of the critical comment it has attracted. It will be instructive to begin by recalling something of the context in which the claim was advanced. With this in mind, the first part of the chapter returns to the contention of Francis Fukuyama, mentioned in Chapter 1, that the end of the Cold War marks the 'end of history as such'. While that assertion proved unsurprisingly controversial, the general account of contemporary circumstances which went with it reflects—in exceptionally clear fashion—an influential analysis. For Fukuyama, as for other observers, a 'worldwide liberal revolution' occurred in the twentieth century's closing decades, and one consequence is to transform the basis on which international security should rest. Rather than depending on the balance of power, our hopes for peace should henceforth be pinned to the spread of democratic government. The second part of the chapter takes up the arguments concerning the 'norm of democratic governance', and shows how, through these arguments, scholars are seeking to pursue in international law the implications of the developments related by Fukuyama and others. The final part of the chapter sets out some of the misgivings to which these international legal arguments have given rise. Inasmuch as the proposed norm is grounded in the twin claims that a worldwide liberal revolution is underway and that this opens up the

---

[9] One representative argued, for instance, that popular sovereignty was a 'political principle rather than a human right, a theoretical concept rather than a human concept': see statement of Mr Sandifer (USA), citing this as the reason for abstaining on what became article 21, para. 3 of the Universal Declaration of Human Rights. See UN Doc. A/C.3/SR.134 (1948). Another representative objected that democracy 'currently embraced two diametrically opposed concepts': see statement of Mr Whitlam (Australia), referring to liberal and Marxist-Leninist conceptions, in the context of debate about what became article 21 of the International Covenant on Civil and Political Rights. See UN Doc. E/CN.4/SR.169 (1950), 10 (para. 41). On the concern that democracy was losing all meaning, see further Orwell 1954, 168–9 and Parry 1969, 141.

prospect of a 'democratic peace', scepticism is expressed with regard to both these claims. In later chapters I shall add some further misgivings, using the concept of ideology to bring them into focus.[10] On the other hand, I shall also seek to defend the belief animating the proposed norm, that international law can and should act as democracy's advocate. Despite the various concerns to be raised, I shall thus draw back from concluding that the effort explicitly to promote democratic politics through international law should be dropped, and instead shall consider in due course an alternative way in which this effort might be carried forward.[11]

THE LIBERAL REVOLUTION AND THE DEMOCRATIC PEACE

In writings published between 1989 and 1992 Fukuyama argues that the collapse of communism in Eastern Europe confirms a worldwide consensus in favour of liberalism as the basis for economic and political life.[12] A crisis of authoritarianism, already evident in the changes which took place in Southern Europe in the 1970s and Latin America in the 1980s, has combined with a crisis of socialist central planning to set in train a 'liberal revolution' that brings with it both capitalism and democracy.[13] Fukuyama recognizes, of course, that, while almost every society now has some form of capitalist economic structure, not all authoritarian regimes have given way to democratic ones. He observes that the 'liberal revolution has left certain areas like the Middle East relatively untouched'.[14] He also acknowledges that not all the new democracies which have been established can be regarded as secure. Relapse into dictatorship cannot be ruled out, and setbacks will undoubtedly occur. But, he contends, these points should not obscure the reality that, for a very large part of the world, there is today no other political tradition 'with pretensions to universality that is in a position to challenge liberal democracy, and no universal principle of legitimacy other than the sovereignty of the people'. Thus, '[w]hat is emerging victorious is . . . the liberal *idea*', even if liberal practice lags behind.[15]

Fukuyama urges us to see this development as more than simply a temporary upswing in the fortunes of liberal democracy. When a long historical view is taken, he contends that a pattern becomes apparent: though the progress of democracy has not been smooth or even, there has nonetheless been a pronounced secular trend towards democratic political arrangements. Against this background, he proposes that the 'current liberal revolution takes on special significance'. It 'constitutes further evidence that there is a fundamental process at work that dictates a common evolutionary pattern for *all* human societies—in short, something like a Universal History of mankind in the direction of liberal democracy'.[16] It is in this sense that Fukuyama

---

[10] See Chs. 3 and 4 below.   [11] See Ch. 5 below.
[12] See Fukuyama 1989, 1989/90 and, esp., 1992, ch. 4.   [13] Fukuyama 1992, ch. 4, *passim.*
[14] Fukuyama 1992, 45.   [15] Ibid. 45 (emphasis in original).
[16] Ibid. 48. Fukuyama explains this by reference to certain claims about human nature and, in particular, the human desire for 'recognition'. See ibid., Part III.

intends his claim that the world has reached 'the end of history as such'.[17] For him
recent events demonstrate that historical change should be seen as oriented to a particular goal, and the goal to which it should be seen as oriented is liberal democracy.
He does not seek to argue that there will be no further events, no further conflict, and
no further diversity. Nationalism and religion, in particular, appear to him likely
sources of future violence. More generally, he is conscious that many societies have
not yet begun, or have scarcely begun, to democratize, and face turbulent times in
doing so. In his words, 'the vast bulk of the Third World remains very much mired
in history'.[18] What he does seek to argue is that, at the level of ideas, the struggle is
over. After centuries of contestation over the principles to govern the organization of
political life, 'only one competitor [is left] standing in the ring'.[19] 'Western liberal
democracy [has emerged] as the final form of human government.'[20]

      And if this is so, then for Fukuyama important consequences follow for inter-
national relations.[21] The pessimistic tradition known as realism or *Realpolitik*, which
(in one form or another) has dominated the theory and practice of international relations in the United States in the post-war period, and has also had influence elsewhere, needs urgent reassessing. Fukuyama recalls that in realist analyses insecurity is
the starting-point for international politics. The international order is conceived as an
anarchic realm in which states are permanently under threat from one another. In this
realm the central factor determining the likelihood of war breaking out is held to be
whether the 'power' of states is 'balanced' or not. If power is balanced, aggression will
not pay, and peace will be likely to endure. From this perspective, the bipolar structure of the Cold War years is the decisive factor that explains the lack of a third world
war in the second half of the twentieth century. As Fukuyama sees it, realism was an
understandable approach to international politics at a time when the world was
indeed an insecure place, in which polities of diverse stripes—fascist, communist, liberal, etc.—coexisted in precarious relations of hostility, mistrust and fear.[22] And it
played a beneficial part in counteracting exaggerated faith in what could be achieved
through international institutions. In the post-Cold War era, however, its usefulness
has declined considerably, both as a description of actuality and as a presciption for
policy.

      In Fukuyama's analysis, a key weakness of realism which accounts for its inefficacy
in contemporary conditions is its assumption that only exogenous factors count in
international relations; that states interact according to a logic which is unaffected by
their own internal political arrangements.[23] This led realism to miss the implications
of the fact that, while insecurity prevailed across the world as a whole, peace remained
secure within one subgroup of states: liberal democracies. The abidingly pacific relations among such states cannot be explained, he contends, in terms of the balance of

---

[17] Fukuyama 1989, 4.   [18] Ibid. 15.   [19] Fukuyama 1992, 42.
[20] Fukuyama 1989, 4.   [21] See Fukuyama 1992, chs. 23–26.
[22] That said, he does, however, consider the character of realism as a 'self-fulfilling prophecy'. See ibid.
247.
[23] Evoking John Burton's celebrated metaphor, Fukuyama refers to this as the 'billiard ball' model. See
Burton 1972, 28 *et seq.*

power, since in many cases there has existed a profound imbalance of power. Rather, the lack of mutual hostility among such states must be linked to their liberal democratic constitutions. Taking this into account, the end-of-century liberal revolution portends a peace that will arise 'out of the specific nature of democratic legitimacy'.[24] Fukuyama expects that power politics will continue to characterize relations involving states that are not liberal democracies—those which, in his terminology, are still 'in history'. But he infers from the point just highlighted that, within the expanding circle of 'post-historical' liberal democracies, realist tenets rooted in notions of insecurity, distrust, self-help, militarism and so on, retain little enduring pertinence. More than that, 'if the post-historical world behaves as differently from the historical world as postulated here, then the post-historical democracies will have a common interest both in protecting themselves from external threats, and in promoting the cause of democracy in countries where it does not now exist'.[25] Fukuyama does not advocate recourse to military intervention, but he does argue that democracies should work together to preserve and extend the sphere of democratic nations. If international organizations are to be the vehicle for this, he contends that they will need to be reshaped as a distinctively 'liberal international order'. Indeed, he remarks, such an order already began to emerge 'willy-nilly during the Cold War under the protective umbrellas of the organizations like NATO, the European Community, the OECD, the Group of Seven, GATT, and others that make liberalism a precondition for membership'.[26]

In elaborating these claims, Fukuyama makes reference to both speculative and empirical writings which seem to support the connection he posits between liberal democratic national constitutions and peaceful international relations. Since this same literature is invoked in the international legal arguments to be discussed below, it is worthwhile pausing at this point to note some of the principal contributions involved. Among the speculative writing, the key work is Immanuel Kant's *Perpetual Peace*.[27] As is well known, Kant argues in this text that perpetual peace might be established if three conditions are met.[28] The first is that every state should have a 'republican' constitution. It is generally assumed that this corresponds in present-day terms to a liberal democratic constitution (whether or not the polity is a 'republic' in the modern sense of that word).[29] Kant reasons that such a constitution is likely to discourage warfare because a government that is accountable to citizens will not be quick to take a decision for which citizens will have to pay dearly (as soldiers, taxpayers, etc.). The second condition is that, having put in place their republican constitutions, states should join together to form a 'pacific federation', that is to say, an alliance under which the parties agree to refrain from waging war against one another.

---

[24] Fukuyama 1992, 279.   [25] Ibid. 278.   [26] Ibid. 283.
[27] Kant (Reiss) 1991.   [28] Ibid. 98 *et seq.*
[29] By 'republican' constitution, Kant explains that he means a constitution which respects the 'principle of *freedom* for all members of society (as men); . . . the principle of *dependence* of everyone upon a single common legislation (as subjects); and . . . the principle of legal *equality* for everyone (as citizens)': ibid. 99). Though he drew a sharp distinction between such a constitution and a 'democratic' political order, this is because his conception of democracy was, of course, a pre-modern one.

As Kant envisions it, an alliance of this kind might begin with only a small number of parties, but would be likely to '[extend] gradually to encompass all states and thus [lead] to perpetual peace'.[30] The final condition is that the pacific federation should be underpinned by a body of 'cosmopolitan law' directed to safeguarding 'the right of a stranger not to be treated with hostility when he arrives on someone else's territory'.[31] The basis for this is the notion that 'the peoples of the earth have . . . entered in varying degrees into a universal community, and it has developed to the point where a violation of rights in *one* part of the world is felt *everywhere*'.[32] Kant adds that facilitating commercial interdependencies, or at any rate links, between citizens of different nations will promote peace because 'the spirit of commerce . . . cannot exist side by side with war'.[33] Internationalists have long attended to Kant's second and third prerequisites for perpetual peace. Particularly compelling in the aftermath of the twentieth century's two world wars, these ideas are reflected in the League of Nations, the Kellogg–Briand Pact, the United Nations and the GATT. Indeed, they inform the whole enterprise of modern international law and international institution-building. But what of Kant's first prerequisite, that every state should have a republican constitution? And what of his assumption that the recommended pacific federation would be a federation of states so constituted?

Even before the events of the late 1980s international relations scholars began to argue that these aspects of Kant's proposal had been wrongly overlooked. Studies were initiated to investigate whether historical research might not corroborate the postulated link between republican/liberal democratic constitutions and international peace.[34] The results of one such study are reported in a celebrated article by Michael Doyle, published in 1983.[35] Based on an analysis of international wars since 1817, Doyle argues that a separate 'zone of peace'—in effect, a Kantian 'pacific federation'—has in fact been established among states with liberal constitutions. He defines such constitutions as those characterized by a commitment to four key institutions: juridical equality among citizens and the protection of fundamental civil rights; representative legislatures which derive their authority from the consent of the electorate; recognition of private property rights; and a free market economy, in which economic decisions are shaped predominantly by the forces of supply and demand.[36] Doyle's claim is that, while there have been repeated wars among non-liberal states, and between liberal and non-liberal states, liberal states have remained at peace with one another throughout this period. As new states have become liberal democracies, they too have developed peaceful relations with other liberal democracies. Thus, the zone of peace has steadily expanded as the number of liberal democratic states has increased. He emphasizes that this evidence does not warrant the general conclusion that liberal democracy produces peace. 'Domestic republican restraints do not end war. If they did, liberal states would not be warlike . . .' Yet, he

---

[30] Kant (Reiss) 1991, 104.   [31] Ibid. 105.   [32] Ibid. 107–8 (emphasis in original).
[33] Ibid. 114 (emphasis omitted).
[34] For a survey of relevant literature, see Brown, M. *et al.* 1996, 374 *et seq.*   [35] Doyle 1983.
[36] Ibid. 207–8.

observes, this 'is far from the case'.[37] In their relations with non-liberal societies, liberal democracies appear to be exceptionally war-prone: attitudes are often characterized by an 'extreme lack of public respect or trust', and tensions escalate easily into violence.[38] On the other hand, the inference is, in Doyle's view, warranted that liberal democratic states are likely to avoid wars with other liberal democratic states, and that to this extent liberal societies are 'fundamentally different' from non-liberal ones.[39] In his words, '[n]o one should argue that such wars are impossible; but preliminary evidence does appear to indicate that there exists a significant predisposition against warfare between liberal states'.[40] The scope of this predisposition, and the reasons for it, continue to be debated.[41] In its broad lines, however, the 'democratic' or 'liberal' 'peace' is spoken of as a 'fact'[42] and 'as close as anything we have to an empirical law in international relations'.[43] It is an empirical law which, according to Fukuyama and other analysts, deserves renewed attention today: with the events of 1989, an unprecedented opportunity has arrived to set about—as one scholar puts it—'grasping the democratic peace'.[44]

THE DEMOCRATIC NORM THESIS

Against this background, international legal scholars began to propose that the time had likewise arrived to revise their discipline's traditional impartiality on the subject of political systems. Instead of simply taking states as it finds them, international law should be seen to require democratic government. I shall refer to this as the 'democratic norm thesis', though it should be noted immediately that the argument is by no means a unitary one. Rather, it is made up of various contributions which bear certain 'family resemblances' to one another, but which also exhibit differences and are not all, in fact, framed in terms of a democratic norm (or 'norm of democratic governance') as such. In the succeeding paragraphs I outline some of the main claims involved. To make the discussion manageable, I shall deal separately with claims in which the emphasis is on reflecting the impact of political developments (and, in particular, the occurrence of a *world-wide liberal revolution*) and claims in which the emphasis is on reflecting the impact of academic developments (and, in particular, the emergence of evidence concerning a *democratic peace*).

International Law and the Liberal Revolution

The move to reconsider international law's approach to constitutions in the light of political changes was initiated by Thomas Franck. In a path-breaking article published in 1992, Franck advanced the contention that a 'norm of democratic

---

[37] Ibid. 230.   [38] Ibid. 326.   [39] Ibid. 235.   [40] Ibid. 213.
[41] See Brown, M. 1996.   [42] See Russett 1993, ch. 1.
[43] Levy 1988, 662.   [44] Russett 1993.

governance' (or 'right to democratic governance') is emerging under international law.[45] His idea was later taken up and refined by others, among them Christina Cerna, James Crawford, Gregory Fox, and Georg Nolte.[46] The norm these scholars have in mind would imply, in the first place, that the legitimacy of governments is judged by international—rather than purely national—criteria. Secondly, it would entail that those criteria stipulate democracy; that is to say, only democratic governments will be accepted as legitimate. And thirdly, it would establish that democratic governance is a human right, subject to international protection through appropriate procedures of monitoring and enforcement. Conceived in this way, a norm of democratic governance would alter received international legal doctrines in a number of fundamental respects. Whether a government is recognized for international purposes as the representative of the state would depend not just on whether the government wielded control over the state's territory, but on whether it was a democratic government. The norm would also modify accepted notions of sovereignty. Instead of being tied solely to coercive power, sovereignty would become linked to political legitimacy, as it is in national contexts. In Fox's words, 'popular sovereignty'—sovereignty that resides with citizens—would replace 'state sovereignty'—sovereignty that resides with states, whether governed with the consent of citizens or not.[47] Finally, the norm of democratic governance would challenge assumptions about human rights. The notion that internationally recognized human rights do not presuppose any particular political system could no longer hold. Cerna observes that 'by becoming a party to a human rights instrument, a state agrees to organize itself along democratic lines'.[48] The norm would make democratic organization a universal right, enforceable against all states, whether or not they have become parties to human rights treaties.

How has such a norm come to 'emerge'? Franck traces the evolution of the norm of democratic governance through a series of overlapping phases of international rule-making and rule-implementation, a series of 'generations' or 'building stones' which helped it take shape.[49] As he explains it, the process began in the period following the First World War, with efforts to articulate and implement a principle of collective self-determination.[50] The plebiscites, popular consultations and commissions of inquiry that were mandated at the Versailles Peace Conference in connection with the re-drawing of European boundaries laid the groundwork for the notion that 'a people organised in established territory [has the right] to determine its collective political destiny in a democratic fashion'.[51] At the same time, the holding and organization of these plebiscites initiated an important body of practice. This was later supplemented

---

[45] Franck 1992. A revised version of the article appears in Franck 1995, ch. 4. See also Franck 1994. For earlier discussion of this theme, see Steiner 1988.

[46] See Cerna 1995; Fox 1992*a*; Crawford 1994; Fox & Nolte 1995. See also Panel Discussion, *Proc. Am. Soc. Int. L.* (1992) 249–71.

[47] Fox 1992*a*.   [48] Cerna 1995, 295.   [49] See Franck 1992.

[50] Franck also refers to earlier articulations of the concept of self-determination, as forming part of the norm's pre-history.

[51] Franck 1992, 52.

when self-determination assumed relevance outside Europe, as the legal basis for decolonization. The next stage in the development of the norm occurred after the Second World War, with the international legal recognition of human rights. With this came the idea that all human beings have certain rights which international law should protect. In the context of an eventual entitlement to democratic governance, Franck calls particular attention to the recognition of rights to free expression, thought, assembly, and association. These rights are affirmed in the Universal Declaration of Human Rights, adopted by the United Nations General Assembly in 1948, and also feature in the 1966 International Covenant of Civil and Political Rights and in regional human rights treaties. In support of these and other human rights, a huge array of international and regional institutions and procedures has been created, variously helping to clarify the scope of human rights, hold governments to their correlative obligations, and secure remedies for abuses.

Finally, Franck contends, the edifice has reached completion, and the norm of democratic governance has begun to 'emerge', as a result of a post-Cold War consensus that governments must be the result of periodic and genuine elections. To be sure, he observes, the right to vote and stand for election was included in human rights instruments well before the 1980s and 1990s. The Universal Declaration of Human Rights and the International Covenant on Civil and Political Rights, along with certain regional treaties, contain provisions to the effect that 'everyone shall have the right to take part in the conduct of public affairs' and 'to vote and be elected at genuine periodic elections'.[52] Yet, at the time they were drafted and for decades thereafter, these provisions could hardly be said to express entitlements acknowledged in every country, or even in most countries. The proclaimed right to vote and stand for election was not accompanied by general acceptance of the idea that governments must be subject to popular recall. The decisive change, in Franck's assessment, is that that acceptance now exists. A substantial majority of states has begun to practice electoral democracy or, at any rate, some 'reasonably credible version' of it.[53] The United Nations General Assembly has started to adopt resolutions which presuppose the existence of a 'principle of periodic and genuine elections'.[54] And the United Nations and other organizations have established an expanding programme of election-related activities, including the provision of technical assistance to governments holding elections and the monitoring of elections with a view to verifying the extent to which they are free and fair.[55] The result, as he memorably writes, is that:

[The global democratic] entitlement now aborning is widely enough understood to be almost universally celebrated. It is welcomed from Malagache to Mongolia, in the streets, the universities and the legislatures, not only because it portends a new, global political culture supported

[52] Universal Declaration of Human Rights, art. 21; International Covenant on Civil and Political Rights, art. 25.
[53] Franck 1992, 64.
[54] The first such resolution was UN GA Res. 43/157 (18 Dec. 1988).
[55] In addition to the United Nations, the Organization for Security and Cooperation in Europe and Organization of American States have been particularly active in this field.

by common rules and communitarian implementing institutions, but also because it opens the stagnant political economies of states to economic, social and cultural, as well as political, development.[56]

In Franck's account, then, the principle of self-determination and the international protection of human rights gave support for democratic claims. But the lack of consensus over elections blocked the emergence of any customary law norm in this regard. With the end-of-century turn to electoral politics, that barrier has fallen. No longer can all forms of government be held equal under international law. In contemporary conditions a new doctrine is more consistent with the evidence, the doctrine that democratic governance is the only lawful option. Other scholars likewise contend that the entitlement to democratic governance, affirmed in the Universal Declaration and in human rights treaties but long 'honoured more in the breach than the observance', has finally entered the corpus of universal international law.[57]

As these arguments make clear, the notion of 'democratic governance' involved here is one which has as its 'keystone' the holding of periodic and genuine elections. Thus, the expressions 'norm of democratic governance', 'entitlement to participatory electoral process', 'right to political participation' and 'right to free and open elections' are used with relative interchangeability. A right to democratic governance is an entitlement to 'participate in the selection of one's own national government'.[58] Franck explains:

The term 'democracy', as used in international rights parlance, is intended to connote the kind of governance that is legitimated by the consent of the governed. Essential to the legitimacy of governance is evidence of *consent to the process by which the populace is consulted* by its government.[59]

All those concerned acknowledge that this is a limited conception of democracy. As Franck puts it, '[t]his definition is not ambitious, it is not necessarily unambiguous, and it is almost certainly not the one an American would prefer'. But, given the diversity of polities and traditions in the world, and given the inbuilt resistance of the states system to the international regulation of national affairs, he contends that this conception, or something like it, 'probably represents the limit of what the still frail system of states can be expected to accept and promote as a right of people assertable against their own, and other, governments'.[60] Fox reasons that the right to periodic and genuine elections must be seen as the 'master' democratic right because this is the entitlement upon which the protection of other democratic rights depends. In any event, he remarks, it is the aspect most readily protected internationally. Whereas international organizations can monitor and evaluate elections, it 'is much more difficult to stay in a country after elections, for the long haul, to monitor all institutions of government and attempt to secure key elements of democracy: to make sure there is no political corruption, to ensure that all classes are included in the institutions of power, and so forth'. It follows that elections 'must not end the push to a democra-

---

[56] Franck 1992, 90.
[58] Fox 1992*a*, 542.
[57] Both Crawford 1994, 7 and Cerna 1995, 290 use this phrase.
[59] Franck 1994, 75 (emphasis in original).
[60] Ibid.

tic society, but they are an essential first step'.[61] With this in mind, Fox and others devote considerable attention to clarifying the applicable standards for a free and fair election: who should be entitled to vote; who should be entitled to stand; what should count as equality of arms among candidates; how the ballot should be organized; and so on.[62]

Finally, there is the question of the measures that might be used to enforce compliance with the entitlement to democratic governance. Again, the concern is to ensure that elections are free and fair, but it is also to ensure that elections are held in the first place, and that those elected are installed in office and allowed to remain there until the end of their terms. For Franck, the norm's validity is clear; if he qualifies it as 'emerging', this is because of doubts about the adequacy of existing supervisory procedures. In his analysis, the democratic entitlement will lack full 'coherence' until enforcement measures are put in place which are both consistent in their application and compatible with other international rules (such as the principle of non-intervention).[63] To this end he suggests a number of initiatives, to supplement mechanisms already operating within the framework of human rights. One proposal is that programmes of electoral assistance and verification by international and regional organizations should be strengthened and extended, and that governments of long-standing democratic commitment should help to promote election-monitoring by volunteering to have their own elections observed. Another initiative is concerned with the situation of elected governments which are overthrown. Franck does not consider that unilateral action is justified, but he does urge that, in the event of a coup, the United Nations—acting with relevant regional organizations—should be prepared to take or authorise action to restore the elected government, even, if necessary, involving the use of force. A third recommendation is that ongoing sanctions should be implemented against governments which fail to comply with the democratic entitlement. In addition to economic sanctions, he raises the possibility that undemocratic regimes might be denied the benefit of collective security arrangements (such as those under Chapter VII of the UN Charter and regional pacts) in the circumstances of foreign intervention. Thus, just as elected governments would be assured of collective assistance in the event of their overthrow, so conversely they would receive privileged protection in the event that their country is invaded.

Cerna, writing in 1995, offers a somewhat less qualified account than Franck of the status of the democratic entitlement, on the ground that some of these measures have

---

[61] Fox 1992*b*, 270–1.

[62] See, e.g., Fox 1992*a* and Fox & Nolte 1995. In the latter article the question is raised of candidates who are committed to replacing the democratic system with an autocratic order. (The authors have in mind the case of Algeria, in particular.) Fox and Nolte point out that the issue should not just be whether an election is free, fair, and genuine, but whether it is conducted in a way which ensures that free, fair, and genuine elections can continue to be held at periodic intervals in the future. They observe that safeguarding the system of electoral democracy as a whole is widely held to justify excluding candidates who are committed to the establishment of a non-democratic political order. The right to 'be elected' should thus be understood as a right to candidature in elections in general, but not necessarily to candidature in any particular elections.

[63] See Franck 1992 and 1994.

in fact been put in place.[64] The United Nations, the Organization of American States and the Organization for Security and Cooperation in Europe have indeed enlarged their election-related activities, and each has created a special office to support and promote those activities. The OAS has established, and on several occasions invoked, a procedure whereby collective measures (including non-recognition and trade sanctions) can be adopted in the event of a coup in a member state. The OAS has also taken the further step of amending the OAS Charter to permit a state whose democratically elected government has been overthrown to be suspended from membership of the Organization. And the UN Security Council has shown itself willing to authorize force to assist an elected government which is overthrown.[65] Fox recommends a further sanction. The United Nations and other international organizations should refuse to accept the credentials of governments other than those elected in free and fair elections. Only democratically elected governments should be allowed to represent states.[66] Crawford has reservations about this idea, but puts forward the alternative proposal that elected governments should be permitted to reopen transactions entered into by their dictatorial predecessors, and third parties dealing with the latter should be required to accept the risk of this occurring.[67]

International Law and the Democratic Peace

I have so far been discussing arguments aimed at bringing international law into alignment with international practice. In summary, the claim is that consensus has emerged around liberal democracy, in consequence of which a norm of democratic governance must now be acknowledged and (in a more focused way than hitherto) enforced. During the same period, another set of arguments began to be put forward, leading to a similar conclusion but starting out from a concern to bring international law into alignment with international thought. The most important writings on this theme are by Anne-Marie Slaughter and Fernando Tesón. For both these scholars, international legal doctrine is flawed by a failure to take adequate account of the democratic peace.

Slaughter recalls that the idea of a link between national representative government and peaceful international relations is a fundamental tenet of the liberal internationalist tradition of international thought.[68] She notes that this idea draws inspiration from Kant's sketch for perpetual peace, and that it has recently received support in empirical research. Doyle and others have shown that a separate zone of peace has in fact arisen among liberal states, a zone which has steadily grown as the number of liberal states has increased. She remarks that, 'although the causes for this phenomenon are complex, they rest on a positive claim that liberal states differ fundamentally from nonliberal states, and that these differences translate into different behavior patterns

---

[64] See Cerna 1995 for discussion of the developments noted in this paragraph.
[65] The Council did this when it authorized military intervention in Haiti in 1994.
[66] Fox 1992, 597 et seq.   [67] Crawford 1994, 22–3.
[68] See Slaughter (Burley) 1990, 1992a, 1992b, 1992c, 1993, 1995.

in the international realm'.[69] The record of hostilities between liberal and non-liberal states leaves no doubt that liberal states are not inherently pacific. But they do not wage war against one another. Based on her own research, Slaughter argues that the liberal zone of peace is accompanied and reinforced by a 'zone of law'. In presenting this argument, she approaches the definition of liberal and non-liberal states in the same way as Doyle:

'Liberal' states, for these purposes, are defined broadly as states with juridical equality, constitutional protections of individual rights, representative republican governments, and market economies based on private property rights. 'Nonliberal' states, by contrast, are defined as those states lacking these characteristics.[70]

Her contention is that transnational disputes involving only liberal states are more readily resolved through judicial procedures than is the case where non-liberal states are involved. A key reason is that courts of liberal states cooperate with one another, and take into account each other's national interests, in a way that courts of non-liberal states, and courts of liberal states confronted with disputes involving non-liberal states, do not. Transnational cooperation at the level of the executive and legislative branches of government is also greater among liberal states than among non-liberal states or between liberal and non-liberal states.[71]

For Slaughter, the central lesson to be learned from these points is that the prospects for peace would be best if all states embraced not just market economics but also liberal democracy. In her words, '[o]ur hopes for international order should be pinned on our hopes for democracy'.[72] Yet, she observes, the 'full import of Kantian liberal internationalism as a framework for political and legal analysis cannot be explained in the language of traditional international law'.[73] For under traditional international law no distinction is made between liberal states and non-liberal ones. The issue is simply whether a state exists as a sovereign state or not, and that is a matter of whether there is a government with control over a permanent population in a defined territory and, perhaps, whether other states recognize its independent statehood. The representative character or otherwise of the system of government is not relevant. As in the realist tradition of international political analysis, a state's internal political structure is detached from its international political status. Slaughter urges that this approach must change. Instead of '[sacrificing] the values of universalism . . . to the realism of recognizing that States in the international system inhabit very different worlds', international law should commit itself to the construction of a 'world of liberal states'.[74] In the first place, the issue of governmental legitimacy should be brought within the purview of international law. The idea should be abandoned that this is an exclusively national issue. Secondly, international law should accept as legitimate only liberal democratic governments. It should stipulate that a legitimate government—one that has a right to exercise sovereign authority—is not just any government that wields factual power; it is a liberal democratic one. Slaughter

---

[69] Slaughter 1992*a*, 395.   [70] Slaughter 1992*b*, 1909.   [71] See Slaughter 1992*b* and 1995.
[72] Slaughter 1992*a*, 403.   [73] Ibid. 395.   [74] Slaughter 1995, 538.

comments that these changes are, indeed, already underway, and one indication of this can be found in the work of Franck and others concerning the emergence of an entitlement to democratic governance.

Tesón argues, in a similar vein, that international law should connect sovereign authority with political legitimacy.[75] The insights of Kant, backed up by historical evidence analysed by Doyle and others, show that 'if international law validates tyrannical governments as legitimate members of the international community, it interferes with the purpose of achieving peaceful cooperation needed to meet pressing global challenges'.[76] For him, however, what is at stake is not just international order and the capacity to meet global challenges. Also in question is the extent to which justice is achieved in the international domain. Analysts have tended to foster a bifurcated approach or 'double paradigm', according to which questions of justice are central to national law and politics, but peripheral to international law and politics. Against this, Tesón counterposes a 'Kantian theory of international law' in which national conceptions of justice inform international conceptions of legitimacy. He contends that, since government is a form of delegated power, and since the delegation entails representation or agency in international affairs, the 'agency relationship should itself be subject to international scrutiny'. 'Individuals who claim to represent a nation but have in fact seized power by brute force should not be accepted as members of the community that makes the law'. For '[t]here is every reason to extend these common sense notions of justice to international relations and include them in a definition of international legitimacy'.[77]

Tesón's 'Kantian theory' is accompanied by a series of practical proposals designed to help in realizing his approach to international legitimacy. In the first place, he endorses the proposal put forward by Franck and Fox that the UN and other international organizations should change their rules to admit only states with liberal democratic governments, and to allow only such governments to participate. Secondly, he also shares Franck's view that, in the event of a coup, the UN should be prepared to take or authorize forcible action to restore the elected government. Unlike Franck, and unlike also Slaughter,[78] he considers that unilateral action involving force might even be justified in extreme circumstances. Thirdly, he proposes that the law of treaties might be modified to reflect the illegitimacy of non-liberal governments; such governments might, for instance, be deprived of the competence to create binding obligations in their own favour. Fourthly, he suggests that diplomatic law might also be changed, so as to deny diplomatic status to representatives of non-liberal regimes. Finally, he maintains that the circumstances in which international law imposes on states a duty of non-recognition should be extended to include the non-recognition of, or at any rate refusal of dealings with, non-liberal governments.

In outlining the claims comprising the 'democratic norm thesis', I have distinguished between those for which the point of departure is the occurrence of a worldwide liberal revolution and those which for which the point of departure is the

---

[75] Tesón 1992. [76] Ibid. 97. [77] Ibid. 98. [78] Slaughter 1992a, 404.

democratic peace. The former are mostly concerned with the status or validity of the
norm of democratic governance. The latter bear primarily on the norm's justification
or value. But, of course, this is just an analytical distinction, reflecting a difference of
emphasis. In fact, both sets of claims are at once descriptions of evidence that a norm
is emerging, prescriptions for promoting compliance with the norm, and evaluative
assertions about why such a norm represents a desirable development.[79] Just as in the
work of Fukuyama, so too in the work of the international legal scholars discussed
here, the world-wide liberal revolution and the democratic peace co-occur, as mutually reinforcing arguments. Thus, Franck infers the emergent entitlement to democratic governance from changes that 'portend a new global political culture'. But he
also seeks to justify the entitlement on the ground that it supports 'the [international]
community's most important norm: the right to peace'; referring to Kant and his
modern interpreters, Franck observes that 'one way to promote universal and perpetual nonaggression . . . is to make democracy an entitlement of all peoples'.[80]
Conversely, Slaughter calls for international law to take seriously the correlation
between democracy and peace. But she also writes of historical processes that lead
'towards an age of liberal nations', and celebrates the occurrence of a 'Revolution of
1989 [which] liberated millions of people. *Millions*'.[81] To this extent, though the
proponents of the democratic norm thesis dissociate themselves from Fukuyama's
'smug [exaltation] at the "end of history" ',[82] they join him in evoking the advent,
with the new millennium, of a new era of peace and good government. If this sounds
like millenarianism, it is a distinctively secular millenarianism that does not anticipate
the return of Christ, but does find signs that the 'universalisation of Western liberal
democracy' may now be in view.[83]

THE DEMOCRATIC NORM THESIS IN QUESTION

The notion that a worldwide liberal revolution has occurred and the idea that democracy is correlated to peace are today the subject of a very substantial critical literature.[84] The effort to relate these claims to international law has itself attracted rather
less critical comment. But the democratic norm thesis has not gone wholly unchallenged, and in this section I review some of the principal objections that have been
raised. In doing so, I also touch upon some of the concerns that have been expressed
with respect to the underlying claims on which the thesis rests.

---

[79] For some general observations about the relationship between description and evaluation in international legal argument, see Ch. 6 below.
[80] Franck 1992, 88.   [81] Slaughter 1992*a* and 1990, 1 (emphasis in original).
[82] Franck 1990, 601. See also Franck 1995, 141.
[83] On this theme, see Marks 1997*a* and (for a brief summary) Marks 1997*b*.
[84] See Burns 1994 and Brown, M. *et al.* 1996, and the references cited below. For critical perspectives
on the 'worldwide liberal revolution', see further Chs. 3 and 4 below.

The 'Liberal Revolution' in Question

Responding to accounts of the emergence of an international legal norm of democratic governance, Thomas Carothers cautions: 'one must be careful not to be starstruck by the trend toward democracy'.[85] He observes that, while such a trend is evident in Europe and Latin America, there is limited evidence of a shift in the direction of liberal democratic politics in the Arab world, and in Africa and Asia. At any rate, the record in these latter regions is much more mixed. To gloss over this is to engage in a 'facile universalism' that significantly overstates the level of consensus around liberal democracy.[86] Once the more complex reality is taken into account, it becomes unclear whether state practice can support the conclusion that a norm of democratic governance is emerging. In Carothers's words, 'we must be hesitant about postulating a customary law norm for democracy. The fact is that many nations do not practice democracy and do not ascribe to it as an aspiration'.[87] Brad Roth likewise finds evidence lacking that 'liberal-democratic legitimism' is taking root in general international law.[88] He characterizes the norm as a 'drive to impose a specific liberal-democratic world view that has yet to find general acceptance'.[89]

This points to a further concern. Even if there were sufficient evidence of liberal-democratic legitimism taking root, these and other scholars have doubts that go beyond the status or validity of the proclaimed norm, and pertain to its desirability. By dividing the world into liberal and non-liberal states, the democratic norm thesis opens the way—they fear—for 'harm in the name of good'.[90] This is an apprehension that cannot forget all the other notorious divisions of history—between citizen and barbarian, Christian and heathen, occidental and oriental, developed and underdeveloped—and all the 'just wars' and 'civilizing missions' which these divisions have helped to justify. For Carothers, '[a]dvocacy of a democratic norm actually highlights [the] West versus non-West division and the tension in international law concerning the fact that it is, at root, a Western system that Western countries are seeking to apply to the entire world'.[91] Insofar as economic sanctions are used to enforce the norm, considerable short- and medium-term suffering is, moreover, likely to be caused to ordinary people, along with serious long-term damage to the socio-economic base of developing states. Carothers recalls the problematic logic which has so often rationalized '[destroying a country's] economy in the name of helping [it] politically'.[92] Insofar as enforcement by military intervention remains a possibility, Roth notes the corresponding logic, according to which one can establish a (democratic) peace by breaching it. He remarks that such an approach is 'chillingly akin to those long-discredited calls for peace through victory that resulted only in endless war, whether "hot" or "cold"'.[93] For him, a norm of democratic governance carries with it the danger of making international law 'the plaything of interventionist powers'.[94]

[85] Carothers 1992, 262.   [86] Ibid.   [87] Ibid. 264.
[88] Roth 1997, 363 *et seq.* See also Roth 1996.   [89] Roth 1997, 368.
[90] Carothers 1992, 266.   [91] Ibid. 264.   [92] Ibid. 266.
[93] Roth 1997, 369.   [94] Roth 1996, 236.

Martti Koskenniemi too warns of the 'risk of imperialism'.[95] A norm of democratic governance is apt to serve simply as a 'call for contextual management of far-away societies in reference to Western-liberal policies'.[96] It follows that the norm will always be

suspect as a neo-colonialist strategy. It is too easily used against revolutionary politics that aim at the roots of the existing distributionary system, and it domesticates cultural and political specificity in an overall (Western) culture of moral agnosticism and rule by the market.[97]

The 'Democratic Peace' in Question

In addition to these concerns about the supposed liberal revolution, a further set of reservations centres on the concept of the democratic peace. Some critics take issue with the adequacy and interpretation of the evidence involved. They argue that the case for the democratic peace simply does not fit the facts; that the historical record cannot support the existence of a liberal zone of peace, or at any rate cannot support the particular correlation asserted between democracy and peace or the particular explanations given for that correlation.[98] Other critics express reservations about the scope of the claims that are made, even accepting those claims at their most far-reaching. The conceptions of war and peace involved suffer, they contend, from a number of important limitations. One limitation is reflected in the disparity between relations among liberal states and relations between liberal and non-liberal states. While liberal states are believed likely to avoid war with other liberal states, those states are not held to adopt an especially peaceful posture towards non-liberal states. Indeed, Doyle observes that relations between liberal and non-liberal states may be especially aggressive. For Chris Brown, the problem is that little attention is given to the implications of this. He points out that we do not know whether liberal states would have remained peaceful *inter se* if they had not perceived common threats outside their 'zone of peace'. It follows that a 'key issue here is the relationship between liberal and non-liberal states'.[99] Koskenniemi likewise raises the possibility that the establishment of a liberal zone of peace is a function, not so much of the liberal democratic character of the states concerned, but rather of the continuation of conflict between liberal and non-liberal states. He speculates that 'war has not been absent but has been externalized—wars by proxy'. And if this is so, then, he observes, 'the causal link is not between democracy and peace but between imperialism, development and peace—with the implication of underdevelopment and war *au delà*'.[100]

A second limitation is reflected in the fact that, while liberal democracy is said to induce peaceful relations among liberal states, no claim is made that democracy prevents civil war. Of course, there could be no empirical case for the proposition that democracy secures civil peace. This means that, even putting aside the question of relations between liberal and non-liberal states, the thesis of the democratic peace

[95] Koskenniemi 1996, 231.   [96] Ibid. 233.   [97] Ibid. 234.
[98] See, e.g., the essays in Brown, M. *et al.* 1996, Part II.   [99] Brown, C. 1996, 40.
[100] Koskenniemi 1996, 234.

leaves out of account the whole phenomenon of civil conflict. Calling attention to this omission, Roth finds little reason to imagine that democracy will 'be the solution to or the prophylactic against civil strife'.[101] Yet civil strife is today the most prevalent form of armed conflict, affecting larger numbers of people and posing a more serious danger than international military engagement. Or is contemporary war more complicated than that? A final limitation of the democratic peace is reflected in the changing character of armed conflict, the increasing difficulty of disentangling international from internal conflict and war from peace. In a study of 'new wars' Mary Kaldor highlights that much contemporary conflict arises out of the break-up of states, and revolves around ethnicity, religion, and other focal points of 'identity politics'; support frequently comes from overseas diasporas, along with foreign governments and foreign advisers; state actors are often hard to distinguish from non-state actors; fighting is commonly sporadic, scattered within and across borders, and focused to a large extent on civilian targets.[102] Is this peace or war? Civil war or international war? The boundaries between these categories—like those between violent crime and armed conflict, public aims and private aims, combatants and civilians—are becoming blurred. Kaldor concludes that:

the prognosis is grim. The breakdown of the distinction between war and peace, the reprivatization of violence, implies more or less continuous geographically pervasive low-level violence, ranging from individual criminality to organised warfare.[103]

Far from holding out the prospect of perpetual peace, contemporary conditions may thus suggest the prospect of perpetual war. The central point, at any rate, is that, even if liberal democracy promotes peace in the manner claimed, it is a 'peace' which remains compatible with wide-ranging violence, within and across national boundaries. To curb this violence, it cannot suffice to promote democratic government—or anything else—at national level. 'The only way to re-establish legitimate control of violence', writes Kaldor, 'is at a transnational level'.[104]

CONCLUSIONS

This chapter has drawn together and described, under the collective label of the 'democratic norm thesis', a series of arguments in which the contention is put forward that a right to democratic governance and a democratic standard of international legal legitimacy now belong in international law. The premise of these arguments is that, on the one hand, non-liberal conceptions of political organization (including those which styled themselves as democracy, such as 'one-party democracy' and 'people's democracy') have given way to a widespread consensus in favour of liberal democracy. On the other hand, evidence has come to light to back up Kant's account of the link between political arrangements within states and peaceful rela-

---

[101] Roth 1997, 369.   [102] Kaldor 1997.   [103] Ibid. 30.   [104] Ibid.

tions among states. To the proponents of the democratic norm thesis, these developments are the cue to reconsider international law's attachment to the realist notion that sovereignty is merely a function of factual power, and shift international legal doctrines to the centre of efforts to grasp the democratic peace.

I have highlighted a number of misgivings that have been expressed with respect to these claims. Some of these arise from empirically based doubts about the extent to which the claims are well-founded. Others stem from normative concerns about the extent to which the democratic entitlement would be a desirable development, if it were, or were in the future to become, part of international law. Within the latter category, I have noted arguments about the problematic character of the 'democratic peace' and anxieties about the interventionary action which a democratic norm might justify. But there is another set of concerns about the value of the democratic entitlement, to which I have not yet referred. Carothers recalls that 'analyses of the norm of democracy tend to focus on elections as the crucial element of democracy'. Yet 'elections are underdeterminative of democracy', a 'necessary but not sufficient condition'. He comments that, while 'democratic norm advocates are well aware of this, . . . they nonetheless tend to slip into a very election-oriented view'.[105] Koskenniemi also raises the question of the notion of democracy that informs the democratic norm thesis, but frames the problem in a more general way. He states that his most fundamental difficulty with the thesis lies in the 'initial positioning of the author him/herself, as possessing a transparent view of the essential meaning of democracy . . .'.[106] He observes that a characteristic of contemporary political debate is that all sides claim to represent 'true' democracy. It follows that, to understand what is at stake, one must uncover the 'contexts of life from which "democracy" takes these contrasting meanings'.[107] How, then, does the democratic norm thesis slip into such an 'election-oriented view'? What are the consequences of doing so? And what is the 'context of life' from which democracy takes this particular meaning?

[105] Carothers 1992, 264.   [106] Koskenniemi 1996, 234.   [107] Ibid. 232.

Chapter 3

Limits of the Liberal Revolution I:
Low Intensity Democracy

Writing in the United States in the 1940s Joseph Schumpeter famously defined democracy in the following terms:

the democratic method is that institutional arrangement for arriving at political decisions in which individuals acquire the power to decide by means of a competitive struggle for the people's vote.[1]

Schumpeter's avowed aim was to get to grips with what democracy really means in contemporary conditions. He believed that a transition would soon occur from capitalism to socialism, and considered that the best way of theorizing democracy for these challenging times was to cut away the ethical fat of earlier theories, and formulate a slimmed-down, up-to-date account of democratic politics.[2] His starting-point is the observation that in modern industrialized societies the scale and complexity of the issues confronted are such that not only is Athenian-style 'direct' democracy impossible. The notion that the people govern themselves *indirectly*, through representatives who meet to give effect to the popular will, is equally inapposite. In contemporary conditions public decision-making power is not, and cannot be, vested in the people. Instead, such power is entrusted to politicians. The role of the people is not to 'decide issues', but 'to produce a government'.[3] Schumpeter concludes that modern democracy is best conceived not so much as an idea or ideal of self-rule and political equality, but as a distinctive method of producing governments.

What characterizes this method and legitimizes the governments produced is the procedure of periodic competitive elections. Thus, Schumpeter explains, in order to understand modern democratic politics, 'we must start from the competitive struggle for power and office', just as in the 'theory of economic activity in commercial society . . . we start from propositions about profits'. Politicians can be understood as entrepreneurs, vying for custom and its rewards. Political parties are like 'trade associations' or 'department stores', working to organize the relation between supply and demand. And citizens can be compared to consumers, making their selections in the political market.[4] It follows that a realistic account of democratic politics must put aside romantic notions about citizenship and popular sovereignty, emancipation and social justice, and place at its centre the selection of representatives and the competitive struggle for office. While every citizen must have the right to take part in elec-

---

[1] Schumpeter 1987, 269.
[3] Ibid. 282, 269.
[2] Ibid. See Preface to the First Edition 1942, 409.
[4] Ibid. 282–3 (and ch. 22, *passim*).

toral processes, Schumpeter remarks that one feature of his account is that it gives proper recognition to 'the vital fact of leadership'.[5] '[E]veryone is free to compete for political leadership', he observes, only 'in the same sense in which everyone is free to start another textile mill'.[6] Another feature of the account is that it elucidates the link between democracy, rights and the rule of law. 'If, on principle at least, everyone is free to compete for political leadership . . ., this will in most cases though not in all mean a considerable amount of freedom of discussion *for all*. In particular it will normally mean a considerable amount of freedom of the press'.[7] And freedom of the press, together with other fundamental freedoms, cannot be protected unless public power is organized within a framework set by law. Thus, the institution of periodic elections must go hand in hand with the necessary institutions for securing respect for the rule of law and constitutional guarantees of civil and political rights.

Schumpeter's analysis plainly touches on some notable features of political life in liberal democratic societies. But it also has signficant limitations, highlighted in writing from many different traditions. On the one hand, critics take issue with the claim that he offers a realistic depiction of democratic politics, whether in his own time or thereafter. Where, they ask, is the role registered of organized interest groups and civil society associations in influencing the terms of collective life? Perhaps more importantly, where is the role registered of businesspeople, bureaucrats, and experts? How can multipartyism and periodic elections deliver control over public decision-making when public decision-making in part occurs, and is profoundly shaped by activities occurring, outside parliaments? Even insofar as public decision-making occurs inside parliaments, to what extent do contemporary electoral processes provide a basis for accountability? To what extent do political parties act as channels for collecting citizens' demands and conveying them to political authorities? To what extent is the arena of political competition a free market? According to some theorists, Schumpeter's portrayal of decision-making structures and electoral procedures is scarcely less idealized than the ideal he purports hard-headedly to reject. For all his concern to modernize democratic theory, he remains in thrall to venerable fictions about liberal institutions that bear uncertain relation to contemporary arrangements. On the other hand, critics also take issue with the notion that democracy *should* be defined in a way which reflects the actuality of democratic politics. While recognizing that empirical referents are indispensable, they insist that such referents cannot exhaust analysis. For much of the value of the democratic concept lies in its function as a tool for criticizing prevailing arrangements and promoting change, and the exercise of that function depends on our holding on to the ideals of self-rule and political equality. From this perspective, the ethical dimensions of democracy are not superfluous fat to be trimmed away, but a vital part of what distinguishes democracy from other, more authoritarian approaches to political organization. Rather than encouraging us to reconcile ourselves to high levels of citizen passivity, weak

[5] Ibid. 270.   [6] Ibid. 272 and 272, n 6.   [7] Ibid. 271–2 (emphasis in original).

structures of accountability and systematic inequalities among citizens, democracy should thus serve as a force for enhancing popular participation in decision-making processes, developing a vigorous and vigilant public sphere, and redressing asymmetries of access to social goods and opportunities.

In the decades since Schumpeter presented his definition of democracy, the limited character of that definition has become very widely acknowledged, and even in some respects self-evident. Today few would seek to defend his analysis as an adequate account of democracy's contemporary significance. Yet if we shift our focus from debates about political life in liberal democratic countries to initiatives for the promotion of democracy in post-communist and developing states, a striking incongruity appears. That same inadequate account, or something very like it, frequently informs those initiatives. The notion of democracy which Schumpeter framed for one expected transition is now being recycled for use in the context of another (albeit inverse) set of transitions. What are we to make of this state of affairs? Some analysts have sought to capture it with the expression 'low intensity democracy'.[8] At one level, this expression names the relatively superficial—'low intensity'—model of democracy that often shapes political change in post-communist and developing countries. The effect of such a model is to concentrate attention on forms and events, and correspondingly to shift the emphasis away from relationships and processes. In turn this serves to reduce the justification for challenging the existing order, and thus to weaken the impetus for radical social and political change. A measure of democratization occurs, while deep-rooted structural transformation is pre-empted. At another level, the expression 'low intensity democracy' also hints at the larger context of this phenomenon, by alluding to the American strategy of containment known as 'low intensity warfare'. According to that strategy nationalist and revolutionary movements in the Third World were fought less through conventional military engagement than through political, economic, and psycho-social methods, combined with rebel-style operations carried out by local proxies.[9] For these analysts, the contemporary agenda of democracy promotion shares with 'low intensity warfare' the goal of influencing developments in Third World (and now, ex-communist) countries so as to moderate popular demands and foster open markets. Indeed, in some contexts it is simply a rearticulation of that same strategy. From this perspective, low intensity democracy is as much a form of intervention on the side of those resisting the redistribution of power and resources as low intensity warfare. As the analysts explain:

By evoking the American counterinsurgency catch-phrase 'Low Intensity Conflict', it is our intention to show that perhaps more than at any time in the recent past, it is now that the struggle to define 'democracy' has become a major ideological battle.[10]

What message is there here for international legal scholars? Continuing the discussion of proposals for a norm of democratic governance introduced in Chapter 2, and drawing on the account of ideology presented in Chapter 1, this chapter considers the

---

[8] Gills *et al.* 1993.   [9] On low intensity warfare, see Klare and Kornbluh 1989.
[10] Gills *et al.* 1993, 3.

place of the democratic norm thesis in the ideological battle just referred to. The first part of the chapter outlines in greater detail the argument as to the prevalence, and consequences, of a 'low intensity' model of democracy in activities concerned with political reconstruction. The second part examines the bearing of this argument for the democratic norm thesis. If democracy is indeed being promoted in ways that constrain democratic change in post-communist and developing countries, and if the democratic norm thesis pulls with that trend rather than pushing against it, this invites us to reflect on the ambiguity of contemporary moves to promote democracy through international law.

PROMOTING DEMOCRACY, CONSTRAINING DEMOCRACY

The claim that in recent years processes of democratization have been informed by a distinctive kind of 'low intensity' democracy is put forward in a series of writings published during the 1990s. In the discussion that follows I rely principally on two accounts: one by Barry Gills and collaborators; the other by William Robinson.[11] Both accounts include detailed studies of democratic reconstruction in particular countries.[12] These case studies attest to the fact that each national history is unique. At the same time, however, they also suggest the existence of some general patterns and trends. A conception of democracy tends to prevail, they show, in which certain institutions—above all, the holding of periodic multiparty elections and the official separation of public powers—are taken largely to suffice. A signally undemanding standard is set with regard to more far-reaching objectives, such as enhancing respect for human rights, social justice, and civilian control of the military. At any rate, the standard set is considerably less demanding than that which underpins political life in 'actually existing democracies'. Thus, for instance, democratization may be seen as compatible with the maintenance, in practice, of a veto on the part of the military over legislative action. Or it may be seen as compatible with continuing restrictions on the activities of trade unions. But if democratic reconstruction is not oriented to the reproduction of Western political practices, neither is it designed to capitalize on the distinctive democratic possibilities offered by non-Western experiences and traditions. Rather, its significance lies in providing some of the institutions and procedures associated with modern democracy, while leaving established centres of power substantially intact. 'Low intensity democracy' is one of a number of phrases that have been coined to highlight the relative formality of this conception of democracy. Others include 'cosmetic democracy' and 'façade democracy', as well as expressions

[11] The work by Gills is an introductory essay to a work which contains contributions from a number of scholars. The co-authors of this introductory essay are Joel Rocamora and Richard Wilson. See Gills *et al.* 1993; Robinson 1996.

[12] In the case of Gills *et al.*: Guatemala, Argentina, the Philippines, and Korea. In the case of Robinson: the Philippines, Chile, Nicaragua, and Haiti.

which eschew reference to democracy altogether.[13] Whatever label is used, the broad lines of the analysis are the same. In the words of Gills and his co-authors:

Democracy seems to be sweeping the globe, driving before it both communist party dictatorships and rightist military regimes on every continent . . . Yet . . . [a]lthough they may have formally instituted some of the trappings of Western liberal democracies (for example, periodic elections), in a real sense these new democracies have preserved ossified political and economic structures from an authoritarian past. Not only have they not come close to operating a political structure modelled on actual Western liberal democracies, this is not part of a long-term agenda for the future.[14]

How is the prevalence and respectability of low intensity democracy to be explained? And what are its consequences for the prospects of democracy in post-communist and developing countries? This section takes up these two questions in turn.

Democracy Promotion and Economic Liberalization

In setting out the reasons why low intensity democracy is held to be so prevalent, it will be valuable to begin with brief reference to two precursors of the analysis developed by Gills and Robinson. One is the critique of imperialism elaborated by Lenin and others. The other, for which Lenin's critique itself served as a precursor, is the tradition of international thought known as 'world-system theory', developed most notably by Immanuel Wallerstein.

Whereas Marx appears to have assumed that capitalist relations of production are everywhere the same, such that a unity of interest exists among the workers of the world, Lenin argued that at the beginning of the twentieth century this assumption could no longer be sustained.[15] Monopoly capitalism had, through imperialism, developed an uneven international structure, involving the exploitation by a small number of rich countries of the world's poor. In consequence of this structure, not only could capitalists prosper at the expense of workers. Capitalists in rich countries could also mitigate the tensions generated by capitalist production by improving the lot of their own workers without losing profit themselves. Workers in such countries could be made to prosper at the expense of the inhabitants of less developed regions. The situation of proletariat and bourgeoisie is thus not identical in all countries, but differs, depending on a state's location in the international hierarchy. It followed for Lenin that capitalist economic relations must be viewed in international perspective. Likewise international politics must be viewed in economic perspective; international political life, as much as the political life of individual countries, is shaped by capitalist forces. In the study of international politics, not just the interaction of states, but also the interaction of classes, has to be considered.

---

[13] Robinson generally refers to it (borrowing Robert Dahl's alternative) as 'polyarchy', or more specifically 'peripheral polyarchy', though he sometimes uses the term 'low intensity democracy'.
[14] Gills *et al.* 1993, 3.   [15] Lenin 1964, 185 *et seq.*

More than half a century later, this approach was taken up and reformulated by Immanuel Wallerstein and others, under the banner of 'world-system theory'.[16] The expression 'world-system' refers here to a system for the distribution of power and resources which is large enough to operate as a self-sufficient, self-propelling unit, even if it is not necessarily world-wide in scope. Wallerstein considers that the modern world-system is the capitalist economy. He holds, moreover, that this is the first world-system in history which *is* in fact world-wide in scope. From its origins as a much more localized system of production and exchange, the capitalist order has expanded to the point where today its arena is the entire globe. Pursuing Lenin's line of thought, Wallerstein maintains that the modern world-system is based on a structural differentiation of the world into core, periphery and—he adds a third category—semi-periphery. The division between core and periphery is also replicated within states. Wallerstein explains that, though these concepts are intended to have geographical significance, they are primarily relational. The relation between core and periphery is the relation between, on the one hand, the more monopolized and hence more profitable links in the chain of production, and, on the other, the less monopolized, less profitable links in that chain. Semi-peripheral regions are conceived as intermediate zones, where a mixture of core-like and peripheral activities occur and where efficient administrative structures are in place, yet labour costs remain relatively low. The central feature of this structure is that wealth is transferred from peripheral sectors to core ones.

By characterizing the global economy as a system, Wallerstein intends to convey the idea that it affects all relationships within it, as well as all changes to those relationships. In particular, it affects political outcomes. Both within states and among them, politics must be seen to confront tensions between economic forces—tensions between national and transnational classes and between national and transnational capital. Wallerstein does not claim that international capital necessarily prevails. That is to say, he does not seek to argue that economics determines politics, as in some Marxist approaches. Rather, his contention is that the capitalist order imposes structural constraints which frame political choices.[17] That said, the general thrust of world-system theory is certainly to emphasize the pre-eminent role of global capital in shaping collective life. As critics are quick to point out, however, the dynamics of world politics cannot be grasped solely in economic terms; even multiaxial accounts inevitably simplify. Without doubt, world-system theory does not offer as complete an explanation of world politics as some of its practitioners may suppose. But, of course, it is one thing to observe that capitalist logics cannot account for the whole complex reality of international political life; quite another to suggest that those logics do not account for a part of that reality, even a part of considerable import. After discussing critical responses to Wallerstein's approach, and after acknowledging that charges of determinism against him may to a certain extent have validity, Steve

[16] See, among many works, Wallerstein 1974, 1980, and 1996. I draw here on the helpful account of Wallerstein's work in Hobden and Wyn Jones 1997.
[17] McGrew 1992b, 17 stresses this.

Hobden and Richard Wyn Jones put forward an intriguing suggestion. '[R]ather than attempt to defend Wallerstein against charges of determinism as if this were a major weakness', they write, 'it may be more valuable for students of world politics to consider whether he is actually right.'[18]

This, perhaps, is the spirit in which Gills, Robinson, and their collaborators approach the task of explaining the prevalence and respectability in the 1980s and 1990s of a low intensity model of democracy as the basis for democratic 'transition'. At any rate, their contention is that low intensity democracy cannot adequately be understood unless account is taken of the role of transnational economic forces. How so? As noted earlier, United States policy is seen as a significant factor, both in certain particular cases and in relation to more general trends. In 1982 President Ronald Reagan declared that his Administration had embarked upon a 'campaign for democracy', and called for allies to join in making this a 'crusade for freedom that will engage the faith and fortitude of the next generation'.[19] The announcement came at a time when authoritarian regimes were on the brink of collapse. Especially in the Latin American region which Reagan quite probably had primarily in mind, counter-authoritarian moves were well underway. Inasmuch as this new campaign for democracy expressed a decision to 'change horses' and support these moves, it also served to constrain change by steering democratic reconstruction in the direction of low intensity democracy. For Gills and co-authors a key objective was to encourage 'stable viable "democratic" regimes that could pre-empt more radical change by incorporating broad popular forces in electoral participation, yet guarantee continuity with the anti-communist and anti-reformist traditions of their military predecessors'.[20] In a similar vein, Robinson writes that the 'promotion of "low-intensity democracy" is aimed not only at mitigating the social and political tensions produced by elite-based and undemocratic status quos, but also at suppressing popular and mass aspirations for more thoroughgoing democratization of social life in the 21st century international order'.[21]

If the United States led the way in promoting low intensity democracy, these analysts observe that other international initiatives reflect a similarly ambiguous approach. A major reason, they hold, is that governments and inter-governmental agencies respond in this regard not just to pressures from particular national constituencies, but also to pressures from powerful transnational forces. In Robinson's words, 'the United States (more precisely dominant groups in the United States) is assuming a leadership role on behalf of a transnational hegemonic configuration', a configuration made up of 'Northern elites and their Southern counterparts'.[22] From this perspective, low intensity democracy is linked, on the one hand, to the goal of stabilizing existing positions in the global distribution of power and resources. It meets the immediate needs of anti-authoritarian crisis, easing tensions, and restoring order. Yet it does so in a manner that forestalls far-reaching structural change in

[18] Hobden and Wyn Jones 1997, 135.
[19] Speech to the British Parliament, 8 June 1982, Reagan 1983, 742, 745 and 748.
[20] Gills *et al.* 1993, 8.   [21] Robinson 1996, 6.   [22] Ibid. 12, 72.

peripheral and semi-peripheral regions. Thus, the concentration in these regions of relatively low wage, low profit, less monopolized economic activities is not endangered. On the other hand, low intensity democracy is linked as well to the project of expanding the reach of global markets and eliminating remaining barriers to the transnationalization of capital. It facilitates the penetration and consolidation of capitalist relations of production in peripheral and semi-peripheral regions. Policies of economic liberalization, structural adjustment, exchange deregulation, and so on, have greater legitimacy when pursued by elected governments than when imposed by unelected regimes. In this sense, as Gills explains, 'the new formal democratisation is the political corollary of economic liberalisation and internationalisation'.[23] The 'campaign for democracy' and what some analysts have called the 'crusade of market fundamentalism' belong to the same holy war.[24]

If low intensity democracy and its economic counterpart have purchase within some post-communist and developing countries, these analysts well recognize that the reasons for this are complex and variable, and cannot be reduced to any simple equation. In highlighting the significance of considerations arising from core economic interests, the scholars do not minimize the importance of other factors, whether exogenous or endogenous. In parts of Central and Eastern Europe, for instance, post-communist reconstruction was seemingly informed by the idea that the new society was to be the opposite of the old. In place of the all-determining plan, overblown bureaucracy and omnipotent state, there were to be no macroeconomic planning, few large-scale institutions, and a minimal state. What the theorists of low intensity democracy seek to bring into focus is the way international initiatives, both by individual governments and by inter-governmental agencies, interact with such ideas and the debates and struggles in which they are implicated. The aim, in other words, is to show how moves to 'promote democracy' operate to endorse certain policy orientations and check others, encourage certain logics and inhibit others, support certain factions and weaken others. Hence the contention that low intensity democracy is to be understood against the background of 'low intensity warfare'. With it comes a new approach to counter-revolutionary intervention and hegemonic power for a new, democratic age.

Beyond Low Intensity Democracy

The discussion so far has concentrated on the question why a relatively formal model of democracy frequently informs processes of democratic reconstruction. Let us now turn to consider the consequences or impact of such a model. For, although 'democracy promotion' is supposed to foster stable governments, Gills and Robinson propose a different assessment. According to their analysis, low intensity democracy builds a highly fragile structure. In this regard a key factor is the point mentioned above, that low intensity democracy is the political corollary of economic liberalization and

[23] Gills *et al.* 1993, 4.
[24] On the 'crusade of market fundamentalism', see Amsden *et al.* 1994, 4.

internationalization. As is widely recognized, neo-liberal economic reform tends to exacerbate disparities between rich and poor, both within states and among them. As economies are opened to the forces of transnational capital, and as states are dedicated to servicing those forces, asymmetries in the distribution of material and cultural resources become magnified. The hardships of restructuring fall most heavily on less privileged sections of society; yet liberalization precludes the implementation of social and economic policies—agrarian reform, industrial planning, expanded programmes of education and training, etc.—which might help to correct this. With heightened social polarization comes escalating social tension, the response to which—these analysts find—is frequently the blocking off of even those restricted avenues for challenging state policy created by low intensity democracy. Thus, after an initial loosening of political repression, repressive measures are re-introduced. Gills concludes that low intensity democracy 'may "work" in the short term, primarily as a strategy to reduce political tension, but is fragile in the long term, due to its inability to redress fundamental political and economic problems'.[25] More than that, low intensity democracy is fragile due to its tendency, in conjunction with neo-liberal economic restructuring, to deepen fundamental political and economic problems. Robinson likewise holds that the 'neo-liberal model . . . generates the seeds of social instability and conditions propitious to the breakdown of [low intensity democracy]'.[26]

Against such a limited approach to the entrenchment of democracy in post-communist and developing states, both these scholars counterpose an alternative geared to linking political transformation with socio-economic justice. Under the title 'popular democracy', Robinson describes a democratic model which 'conjoins representative government to forms of participatory democracy that hold states accountable beyond the indirect mechanism of periodic elections'. He envisions such a model as a 'tool for change, for the resolution of such material problems as housing, health, education, access to land, cultural development, and so forth'.[27] Popular democracy 'begins with respect for human rights, civil liberties, the rule of law, and elections', but, rather than treating these as 'democracy in itself', regards them as ' "pre-conditions" for processes of democratization, which unfold to the extent that structures are developed which allow for . . . the direct participation of majorities in their own vital affairs'.[28] Robinson highlights the importance for democratic consolidation of effective political institutions, civilian control of the military and, more generally, the nurturing of democratic values. But he also stresses the need to redress barriers in the socio-economic domain, the need to democratize the structures and institutions of civil society.[29] Gills and co-authors also describe a form of democracy which includes the protection of fundamental rights, respect for the rule of law and effective civilian control of the military, but additionally encompasses far-reaching redistributive change, as well as devolution of power to regions and localities.[30]

---

[25] Gills et al. 1993, 27.   [26] Robinson 1996, 344.   [27] Ibid. 57.
[28] Ibid. 58.   [29] Ibid. 58, 344–5.
[30] In place of Robinson's term 'popular democracy', he uses the phrase 'participatory progressive democracy', but the gist of his proposal is the same. Gills et al. 1993, 29; see also 28–33.

Informing these proposals is a long tradition of democratic thought, carried forward in the second half of the twentieth century through such concepts as 'participatory democracy', 'strong democracy', 'discursive democracy', 'deliberative democracy', and 'communicative democracy'.[31] The shared starting-point for these concepts, as for the concept of popular democracy, is a belief that, contrary to Schumpeter's definition quoted at the beginning of this chapter (and reflected also in low intensity democracy), democracy cannot be understood simply as an 'institutional arrangement for arriving at political decisions in which individuals acquire the power to decide by means of a competitive struggle for the people's vote'.[32] Instead of repudiating the democratic principle of *rule by the people on a footing of equality among citizens*, an adequate account of contemporary democracy must reaffirm and renew that principle. The challenge of ensuring that collective decision-making is subject to popular control, and of overcoming asymmetries in the distribution of citizenship rights and opportunities, must remain firmly in view. From this perspective, a number of points deserve particular emphasis.

In the first place, democracy cannot be conceived purely as an 'institutional arrangement', organizational form or checklist of procedures. Rather, it must be understood as an ongoing process of enhancing the possibilities for self-rule and the prospects for political equality, against a background of changing historical circumstances. Nor, secondly, can democracy be grasped simply as a 'method of government'. While modern democracy is incompatible with forms of political organization developed for small city-states, the institutions of representative government can and must coexist with expanded opportunities for involvement by ordinary citizens in public affairs. The Rousseauian notion of democracy as a form of society retains pertinence, if not for the reasons of self-realization that he had in mind, then at least on the prudential ground that active citizenship is necessary to ensure that those who rule do so in the interests of all and not just in their own interests. Thirdly, political legitimacy cannot be approached as a matter of episodic procedure. The fact that parliaments are subject to periodic popular recall is not, of itself, sufficient to justify public power. Democracy demands that state authority be required to justify itself to the citizenry on a continuing basis. To enable this, a democratic polity must include a vigorous 'public sphere', that is to say, an arena distinct from the institutions of the state in which citizens can come together to define collective goals, shape public policies and evaluate governmental activity. Fourthly, political equality must be seen to require more than the constitutional guarantee of civil rights. Universal suffrage has not put an end to inequalities in the capacity of citizens to exercise and influence state power, because that capacity is affected by disparities in society. Subordinate socioeconomic status tends to reinforce, and be reinforced by, political marginalization. Efforts to ensure political and civil rights must thus go hand in hand with moves to secure respect for social, economic, and cultural rights. Finally, the homogeneity of the democratic 'people' cannot be assumed. Since the social disparities which affect

[31] See respectively, e.g., Pateman 1970; Barber 1984; Dryzek 1990; Habermas 1996; Young 1996.
[32] Schumpeter 1987, 269.

participation in public processes are systematically correlated (*inter alia*) to divisions of gender, ethnicity, and other group affiliation, political equality must not be understood in terms of (a particular) identity. Rather, it must be approached in terms of the need to ensure that differences among citizens do not operate as disadvantages. Democracy must be conceived as requiring that all citizens have the chance to participate in decision-making which affects them.

As noted at the beginning of this chapter, the limitations of Schumpeter's definition are today quite widely accepted. This is reflected in the fact that each of the points just mentioned informs democratic practice in liberal societies, albeit, of course, in varying ways, to varying degrees and with varying counterpoints. What is significant about the argument of Robinson and Gills is the claim that these ideas must likewise inform democratic practice in 'transitional' societies. In Robinson's words, '[s]tability in the emergent global society, I submit, enjoys a correlation not with [low intensity democracy] but with popular democracy'.[33] Yet the prospects for popular democracy remain poor insofar as low intensity democracy continues to be promoted.

The possibility of achieving social stability in the South . . . is dependent upon greater socio-economic equalities within and between nations in the world system, which in turn depends on the extent to which popular democratization advances around the world *against the efforts to curtail popular democracy via the promotion of [low intensity democracy]*.[34]

In this connection Robinson highlights the contrast between the coercive methods of low intensity warfare and the consensual methods of low intensity democracy, the shift in emphasis from force to ideology. Thus, he calls attention to the way low intensity democracy is rationalized as a model for democratic transition, on the ground that the 'only way to assure "democracy" is to accept the boundaries of the possible, and the "possible" is [low intensity democracy]'. Demands which go beyond low intensity democracy are 'deferred as "trade-offs" necessary to assure the end of authoritarianism'.[35] One such trade-off—the 'equity trade-off', as Robinson calls it—is the postponement of social justice. The guarantee of civil and political rights is presented as the means by which social justice will eventually be achieved. Another trade-off is the postponement of fully civilian government. Concessions to the military, typically including maintenance of existing military structures and non-prosecution of human rights abuses, are presented as the means by which civilian rule will ultimately be consolidated. Robinson's investigations suggest, however, that these supposedly 'transitional' trade-offs tend to 'become a structural feature of the post-authoritarian political landscape'.[36]

Reinforcing this logic is what Robinson refers to as low intensity democracy's 'electoral fixation'.[37] On the one hand, low intensity democracy identifies democratic citizenship with participation in elections. On the other hand, it attaches overriding importance to the form of elections. What counts is that elections should be free and fair, in the sense that all citizens are legally entitled to vote and stand for election, and

[33] Robinson 1996, 345.   [34] Ibid. (emphasis in original).   [35] Ibid. 64.
[36] Ibid. 65.   [37] Ibid. 59 (emphasis omitted).

that the ballot is conducted correctly and without procedural irregularities. Thus, the extent to which social and material conditions affect the opportunities for political participation is made to appear irrelevant. The real inequality of influence among citizens is masked by the formal equality of participation among voters.[38] Robinson also highlights one further move geared to legitimating low intensity democracy. This is the idea that democracy, however limited, is surely preferable to authoritarianism and dictatorship. His rejoinder is as follows:

To place the issue in this light is tantamount to claiming that the juridical equality which African Americans enjoy in the late twentieth century is preferable to the juridical discrimination of earlier times (it *is*, of course, preferable), and that this alone is grounds to dismiss a political or theoretical discussion of contemporary racism in US society.[39]

Gills gives even shorter shrift to the notion that low intensity democracy is at least an advance on authoritarian rule. With low intensity democracy, he writes, a form of 'cosmetic democratisation' is legitimised, such that 'democracy . . . is in danger of . . . serving as a euphemism for sophisticated modern forms of neo-authoritarianism'.[40]

INTERNATIONAL LAW AND LOW INTENSITY DEMOCRACY

One need not accept the explanation advanced by Gills and Robinson for the prevalence of low intensity democracy, indeed one need not concede that the matters they identify play any part at all in accounting for this phenomenon, to see the force of these theorists' concerns. Where democracy differs little in substance from authoritarian rule, while enjoying significantly greater legitimacy, pressing questions arise as to the basis and consequences of that legitimacy. These questions have particular pertinence in view of the wide gap between aspiration and actuality that characterizes many of the reconstructions of the 1980s and 1990s. What Gills, Robinson and others bring into focus is the way this gap is sustained by a profoundly ambiguous approach to democratic reconstruction. Low intensity democracy celebrates worldwide liberal revolution, yet reins in democratic ambitions. It proclaims the universalization of Western political forms, yet posits a distinct, 'beginner's' model of democracy. It encourages moves to end dictatorial rule, yet limits political restructuring and checks socio-economic change. Whether or not these analysts are right that—in the words of Gills and his co-authors—'[t]his "crusade" for democracy is the new ideological agenda of global capitalism',[41] some kind of 'ideological agenda' seems to be in play. The drive to promote democracy is also a drive to constrain democracy, against the efforts of those seeking to transform relations of domination by insisting on the link between democratization and change in the structures of power and wealth.

What then of moves to promote democracy through international law? In the paragraphs that follow I argue that the democratic norm thesis entails a similarly

[38] See ibid.   [39] Ibid. 11 (emphasis in original).   [40] Gills *et al.* 1993, 21, 5.   [41] Ibid. 7.

ambiguous approach to democratic reconstruction. To this end, I draw on the discussion of ideological modes and strategies presented in Chapter 1. Before proceeding, one point noted in that chapter merits re-emphasis. To assert the operation of ideology is not to assume a cynical attitude on the part of those involved. There can be little doubt that those associated with the democratic norm thesis are concerned about the limited character of low intensity democracy, and look forward to the day when that spare notion of political democracy is supplemented by a (new or, as the case may be, renewed) commitment in post-communist and developing countries to social democracy and pluralist democracy, as it is (to some extent, at least) in most Western countries.[42] What counts, however, is that they act *as if* low intensity democracy were adequate or, at any rate, necessary, rational and normal—or so I shall suggest. It is this 'acting as if' which is the focus of ideology critique. Recall Eagleton's story about taking a seat on a bench marked 'Whites Only'. Reminding yourself as you sit down that you are opposed to racism has little significance for, as he puts it, the racist ideology is in the bench, not in your head.[43] Robinson restates this point with specific reference to 'democracy promotion':

Ideology . . . should not be confused with deliberate falsehood. It is not necessary to assume a conspiracy among scholars in the service of hegemony. . . [W]hat is pertinent is not the subjective status or conscious intent . . . but the objective significance of the scholarship in question, independent of its agents, in the ideological rationalization of the new political intervention as the "promotion of democracy" and in the provision of technical solutions for effectively carrying out this intervention.[44]

With this in mind, let us now return to the democratic norm thesis, to consider some of the strategies through which it contributes to the diffusion of low intensity democracy. I shall begin by highlighting a series of specific strategies, engaging all five of the modes of operation of ideology discussed in Chapter 1. I shall then try to elucidate in a more general way how subsisting inequalities are thereby sustained.

Legitimating Low Intensity Democracy[45]

An initial set of ideological strategies is geared to *justifying* the identification of democracy with low intensity democracy. Thus, the democratic norm thesis *rationalizes* the promotion of low intensity democracy on grounds that recall the argument rehearsed by Robinson: the 'only way to assure "democracy" is to accept the boundaries of the possible, and the "possible" is [low intensity democracy]'.[46] Where international law is concerned, the crucial factor is said to be that elections can be monitored by international observers. As Fox remarks, '[i]t is much more difficult to stay in a country after elections, for the long haul, to monitor all institutions of government and attempt to secure key elements of democracy: to make sure there is no political corruption, to ensure that all classes are included in the institutions of power,

---

[42] I take these terms from Beetham 1995, 32.   [43] Eagleton 1991, 40.
[44] Robinson 1996, 43–4.   [45] See further Marks 1999.   [46] Robinson 1996, 64.

and so forth'.[47] He concludes that '[e]lections . . . must not end the push to a democratic society, but they are an essential first step'.[48] The premise of this argument is that priority should go to that which can most readily be monitored by international observers. One might equally hold, however, that priority should go to that which strengthens the public sphere as a forum for political debate and initiative. Or that priority should go to that which makes most difference to marginalized and vulnerable groups. Or that, since democratic life is not uniformly, but variably, experienced, any form of verification must take into account the diversity of social standpoints from which democratic progress is to be assessed. By ordering democracy according to the criterion of monitorability by international observers, the democratic norm thesis helps to make low intensity democracy seem the logical focus of international legal efforts to promote democratic reconstruction.

Also helping to justify a focus on low intensity democracy is the strategy which John Thompson refers to as *narrativization*. In one form of narrativization, particular arrangements are made to seem worthy of respect because they represent the culmination of history. As noted in Chapter 2, Thomas Franck sets his claim that a norm of democratic governance is emerging in the context of a history which begins with the principle of self-determination, develops with the post-war project of protecting the right to freedom of expression and related human rights, and reaches its apogee in the early 1990s with the widespread turn to electoral politics and the accompanying growth of international procedures of electoral assistance and monitoring. Through this history the idea is put forward that the holding of elections represents the highest stage of normative progress. Low intensity democracy appears as the outcome of a process that began long ago, and recently achieved its completion with the acknowledgement—no longer in mere lip service, but now as an accepted legal commitment—that governments must be the result of free and fair elections. As also noted in Chapter 2, the democratic norm thesis rests not only on arguments about a worldwide 'liberal revolution', but on arguments about a 'liberal peace' as well. The strategy of narrativization is likewise evident in these latter arguments. Anne-Marie Slaughter sets her call to recognize a norm of democratic governance in the context of a history which is characterized by an expanding zone of liberal states. For this purpose the definition of a liberal state closely corresponds with low intensity democracy, revolving as it does around juridical equality and the constitutional protection of civil rights, representative government, and a market economy based on private property rights. In this way low intensity democracy comes to appear as the measure of progress towards the eventual inclusion of all states within the liberal zone. And since in Slaughter's account the inclusion of all states within the liberal zone raises the possibility of perpetual peace, low intensity democracy comes in turn to appear as a mark of progress towards that larger goal.

One further strategy of justification is worth noting. Low intensity democracy is *normalized* as democracy's 'general rule'. If the experience of 'actually existing democracies'

---

[47] Fox 1992*b*, 270.   [48] Ibid. 271.

is acknowledged to be rather different, the logic of the arguments developed in support of the democratic norm thesis is that deviations from low intensity democracy must nonetheless be regarded as exceptional. By according a central place to the production of governments through multiparty elections, the democratic norm thesis postulates a vision of normal democratic politics in which parliaments are where public decision-making takes place; elections, if free and fair, assure the accountability to citizens of public power; and political parties mediate between citizens and the state. This, of course, is a familiar archetype of democratic politics. But it fails to capture many, equally familiar, features of contemporary political life: the constraints affecting parliamentary politics in liberal democratic societies; the stage-managed character of contemporary electoral processes; the emergence of political parties as power blocs in their own right; the significance of civil society as an arena of political agenda-setting and action. The norm's transcendence in the countries that supposedly exemplify it does not, however, entail a revision of what counts as normal. Rather, the resulting disparity serves to reinforce the notion that a developmental gap separates democratic countries from those engaged in democratic reconstruction. The latter are invited to proceed step by step, beginning with a model of democracy that bears, at best, questionable relation to the realities and possibilities of contemporary politics.

In the first place, then, the identification of democracy with low intensity democracy is justified using strategies of rationalization, narrativization, and normalization. A second set of ideological strategies legitimates low intensity democracy by *masking* or obscuring the extent to which citizenship is compromised by asymmetrical power relations. One notable example of this involves an 'electoral fixation' of the kind highlighted by Robinson. In the democratic norm thesis self-rule is equated to the opportunity to participate in elections and, in turn, the opportunity to participate in elections is assessed by reference to the form of elections. Thus, proponents of the thesis give detailed consideration to the procedural requisites for a 'free and fair' election: who should have the right to vote; who should have the right to stand as a candidate; what should be done to ensure fair election campaigning; how the ballot should be organized; and so on. They devote little attention, however, to the question of whether the social and economic conditions exist for effective participation by all citizens. Yet social and economic inequalities translate into differential capacities to exercise and influence political power. To make these inequalities appear as equalities is to *invert* the true situation. Citing Ralph Miliband, Robinson observes that equality of influence 'is in fact an illusion. The act of voting is part of a much larger political process, characterized . . . by marked *inequality of influence.* Concentration on the act of voting itself, in which formal equality does prevail, helps to obscure the inequality, and serves a crucially important legitimating function'.[49] Robinson concludes that the electoral fixation is an ideological manœuvre, which shields domination beneath a veneer of formal equality and procedural correctness. Another way in which asymmetrical power relations may be masked is through the strategy referred

[49] Robinson 1996, 59 (emphasis in original), citing R. Miliband, *The State in Capitalist Society* (New York: Basic Books, 1969), 194.

to in Chapter 1 as *displacement*. Gills points to the use of this strategy when he warns that democracy is in danger of serving as a euphemism for neo-authoritarianism: the legitimizing attributes of the former are being transferred to the latter. The possibility must likewise be considered that the democratic norm thesis provides assistance in clothing intervention on the side of new forms of authoritarianism in the more acceptable attire of democracy promotion.

A third set of ideological strategies legitimates low intensity democracy by means of an imaginary resolution of social and political antagonisms. Through strategies of *unification* the various cleavages around which relations of domination are articulated are made to seem non-existent, with the consequence that efforts to transform those relations come to appear unnecessary. One unifying move was touched upon in the preceding paragraph. The democratic norm thesis insists on the importance in democratic reconstruction of constitutional guarantees of the right to vote and stand for election, along with rights to freedom of expression, freedom of assembly, and other such civil rights. In doing so, however, it detaches the need to protect these rights from the issue of how economic deprivation and social marginalization affect opportunities for political participation. The *universalization* of civil and political rights thus serves to confer an illusory wholeness on the divided social body. Universal suffrage, together with universal civil rights, appear as the hallmarks of political institutions that are impartial and inclusory. The gap between low intensity democracy and popular democracy is imaginatively closed. In this way, societies engaged in democratic reconstruction are encouraged to start by putting in place certain institutions and constitutional guarantees, and leave for later questions about how to provide the conditions in which those guarantees can be made meaningful for all citizens.

Another unifying strategy is what was referred to in Chapter 1 as *simplification*. By presenting social life in reductive terms, attention may be drawn away from the unevenness and complexity of social processes. In the democratic norm thesis a notion of democracy is put forward in which individual rights, but not group-oriented rights, assume central importance. Though the need for group-oriented rights is certainly acknowledged, especially in the case of some societies where political transformations have been accompanied by inter-communal conflict, this is compromised by an account of democratic politics which is predicated on relative national homogeneity. Political life is envisioned as unfolding as if the only relevant differences between citizens are contingent differences of interest, belief and opinion. Thus, democracy is depicted in terms of citizens voting in national elections, political parties competing for power, parliaments reaching decisions, and courts upholding the rule of law, on the footing that identity and culture are not in issue. National identity is posited as prior to democratic politics, rather than as partly determined through it. Put differently, the setting for democracy is portrayed as one in which the relation between nation and state is settled and unproblematic. And if this is so, then there is no need for group-oriented protection. All that is necessary is to ensure that current majorities do not become entrenched, and for that individual rights, reinforced by non-discrimination guarantees, will generally suffice. Minority and other group rights thus come to appear as exceptional measures to deal with pockets of resistant heterogeneity. Insofar as this fails to capture the extent to which a more pluralistic conception of democratic life is gaining ground in liberal societies, then yet again societies engaged in democratic reconstruction are encouraged to democratize by reference to ideas which (albeit to varying extents) have been left behind in 'actually existing democracies'. A conception of democracy that is premised on national homogeneity becomes the modernizing medicine for 'primitive' societies, not yet secure or mature enough to experiment with the 'politics of difference' and of 'recognition'.

A fourth set of ideological strategies operates in the mode of *reification*, whereby human products come to appear as if they were pre-given objects, to be grasped, embraced, contemplated, and/or discussed, but not shaped and changed. Reifying devices mask the extent to which particular ideas and arrangements reflect moments in an ongoing history of struggle among social forces. As noted in Chapter 1, this effect is often secured through the use of particular *figurative devices*. In the democratic norm thesis, as in international argument more generally, discussion of democracy is structured according to a characteristic metaphor. Democracy is commonly figured as a place. Thus, in a passage quoted above, Fox writes of the first step 'to a democratic society'.[50] Franck takes note of the 'nearly global move towards democracy'.[51] Cerna discusses the implications of 'the existence of a democratic form of government'.[52] In these and other statements democracy is a destination, rather than a journey; a state of being, rather than a project; a point in space, rather than a process over time. Democratic reconstruction comes in this way to seem a matter of putting in place a set of institutions, operationalizing a transition from one condition to another. This is reinforced by the use of *syntactic forms* that tend to play down the historicity of democratic processes. Instead of being rooted in contestation over social self-definition, the use of passive and adjectival forms makes democracy appear as the realization of an event. Thus, discussion focuses on the fact that governments have 'become democratic or [are] preparing to hold elections'.[53] Or it concentrates on the need to enhance the acceptability of procedures by which democratic processes can 'be monitored'.[54]

A final set of ideological strategies is perhaps the most effective. Whereas democracy is a profoundly contested concept, low intensity democracy is *naturalized* as the sole notion of democracy that requires consideration. Other possibilities, such as popular democracy, are moved outside the sphere of contemplation. To recall Eagleton's phrase, alternatives are not so much combatted as 'thrust . . . beyond the very bounds of the thinkable'.[55] In one naturalizing move the democratic norm thesis proceeds on the basis of an *assumption* that, for the purposes of international law, democracy is to be identified with low intensity democracy. The meaning of democracy in this context is made to appear self-evident, so that discussion becomes superfluous. Ideology

---

[50] Fox 1992*b*, 271.   [51] Franck 1990*b*, 621.   [52] Cerna 1995, 295.
[53] Ibid. 312.   [54] Franck 1992, 84.   [55] Eagleton 1991, 58.

here, as Eagleton again puts it, 'offers itself as an "Of course!", or "That goes without saying" '.[56] In another move the meaning of democracy is made to appear a technical or objective issue, a matter of defining one's terms and then using them consistently. The extent to which choices are involved, with implications in the real world of social practices and institutions, is removed from view. Tesón is particularly explicit about this. He writes: 'I wish to avoid terminological debate about the meaning of the words "liberal" and "democracy" . . . A liberal democracy is one in which individual rights are honoured and rulers are appointed by the people'.[57] Another strategy of naturalization involves the use of *dichotomous reasoning*. Through such reasoning low intensity democracy is set against the flattering foil of something very much worse. In Franck's account the contrast is with 'bogus "people's democracy" or outright dictatorship', and with '"dictatorship of the proletariat" and, more recently, . . . forced-march "modernization" '.[58] Fox opposes 'democracies' to 'communist governments . . . military juntas . . . and one party states'.[59] And Slaughter distinguishes 'liberal' from 'non-liberal' states. In her argument, an eventual 'world of liberal states' is the sole alternative to '[sacrificing] the values of universalism . . . to the realism of recognising that States in the international system inhabit very different worlds'.[60] When the choice is either liberal universalism or realist difference, either grasping the liberal-democratic peace or living perpetually on the edge of war, low intensity democracy comes to appear the natural and unanswerable option. By presenting the alternatives in terms of stark oppositions, and ruling out intermediate possibilities, these writings help to sustain a highly attentuated conception of democracy. To count as democratic (and, in turn, to expand the prospects for peace), politics only has to be not dictatorial, not authoritarian, not totalitarian, not non-liberal. In this context the variety of existing democratic forms becomes difficult to register, the inadequacy of those forms even more difficult to assert.

A Two-Track Approach

Claims that a right to democratic governance is, or should be, recognized as a norm of international law reflect a widespread sense among international legal scholars that the political transformations of the 1980s and 1990s were to be the occasion for international law's renewal. Freed from the constraints that had 'deformed' it, 'ensured its ineffectiveness',[61] and kept scholars on the defensive with respect to its 'very existence',[62] international law was now poised to take an active part in the building of a new post-Cold War world. Where before there was stasis, the prospect had finally

---

[56] Ibid. 59.   [57] Tesón 1992, 61 n. 39.   [58] Franck 1992, 47–8.
[59] Fox 1992*a*, 540.   [60] Slaughter 1995, 538.

[61] Reisman 1990, 860. 'The need for international law after the Cold War will be more urgent than during the conflict. In many ways, what is expected of international law will be greater' (866).

[62] Franck 1995, 6. Franck considers that international law has entered a 'post-ontological era. Its lawyers need no longer defend the very existence of international law. Thus emancipated from the constraints of defensive ontology, international lawyers are now free to undertake a critical assessment of its content'.

opened up of an alliance with the forces of change.[63] Or had it? In an essay published in 1991 David Kennedy expresses doubts about the extent to which developments of the period can support such an optimistic assessment.[64] He takes the example of developments in the economic field in Europe, focusing in particular on the differing arrangements in place for the regulation of economic relations within Western Europe and between Western Europe and newly capitalist Eastern Europe. Within the European Community interaction was guided by the 1992 programme for the completion of the internal market; between EC countries and the 'emerging markets' further east dealings were governed by the general regime of international trade. Kennedy's analysis of these two economic 'architectures' is worth briefly noting at this point. Though something of a digression from our immediate concerns, it will provide an illuminating perspective from which to consider the implications of the discursive moves reviewed in the preceding paragraphs.[65]

Kennedy's central argument is that post-1989 economic relations in Europe were shaped by the distinctive account of the developments of 1989 and 1992 respectively which can be found reflected in 'renewalist' writing. In this account the changes in Eastern Europe are to be understood as a completely new beginning, calling for a wholesale recasting of existing arrangements. By contrast, the EC's 1992 pro-gramme—though arguably more of a break with established traditions of inter-national relations—is to be conceived as the continuation or perfection of an ongoing project. In this way the Western European endeavour is made to appear 'ahead', com-pared with the situation of the Eastern nations, which are seen to be standing at or near 'square one'. In Kennedy's words, renewalist commentary had as one of its back-ground assumptions that 'East and West confront the same systemic imperatives at different chronological stages, that the East "lags" behind the West . . .'.[66] A geo-graphical boundary thus became also a chronological boundary, according to which submission to the international trade regime preceded inclusion in the EC's internal market: the former Eastern bloc countries had first to throw their markets wide open before being considered for the more sheltered and structured forms of free trade practised within the Community. For Kennedy this 'suggests a darker side of the renewal story—a side in which relaxation of Western hesitance about allowing the East "in" seems only possible once the conditions of chronological inequality have been stabilized'.[67]

In this regard a key legitimating strategy to which Kennedy calls attention is the strategy of normalization. He observes that international trade law fosters the notion that state intervention to regulate trade is exceptional, while unregulated trade is the norm. Thus, for instance, treaty-based rules against tariffs and quotas, procedures for mitigating swings in commodity prices, and provisions managing exchange rate fluctuations, are presented as exceptional measures which in normal conditions—

[63] Slaughter 1990 exemplifies this outlook.   [64] Kennedy 1991.

[65] I draw here on a more detailed discussion of Kennedy's analysis and of its bearing for the democra-tic norm thesis in Marks 1999.

[66] Kennedy 1991, 374.   [67] Ibid. 379.

characterized by stable and self-regulating trade, commodity exchange, and currency convertibility—are not required. Kennedy's point is, of course, that the modern industrialized societies which supposedly embody this norm have long since departed from it, if they ever adhered to it. In these societies, with their quangos, market-oriented civil services, and private–public joint ventures, private commerce and public regulation are harder than ever to disentangle. Yet, as in the case of low intensity democracy discussed above, the prevailing image of normality remains undented. The disparity between economic relations within the EC and economic relations within the framework of the international trade regime simply serves to reinforce both the sophistication of the insiders and the immaturity of those outside. The former appear as those who, having mastered the rules, may now break them. The latter are those who 'must undertake a long march not only through austerity but through formalism'.[68]

The impact of these ideas can be traced, Kennedy observes, in the economic policies adopted in many Eastern European states during the early 1990s. The particular conception of a market economy articulated in these policies is 'the familiar, if extreme, version of the classic deregulated laissez-faire economics more common to Western fantasy than practice'.[69] He concludes that a two-track approach is in play, at odds with the widely celebrated vision of dissolving divisions and emergent regional unity: '[t]here is a sophisticated track for developed societies, which are understood to need advanced forms of governmental regulatory cooperation to manage their interdependence, and there is a less sophisticated track for determining which participants fall into this category and which do not'.[70] Eastern policymakers and Western advisers alike are advocating for the East an approach to economic and political life which Western societies no longer adopt, and probably never did. As he puts it, Eastern European societies are urged to 'build a form of government and economy at home and interact with the first world in an international economic and political regime animated by ideas about property and the appropriate distinctions between public and private which have long since between abandoned by the more sophisticated players both at home and in their relations with one another'.[71]

While the adequacy or appropriateness for Eastern Europe of a vision of economic organization which Western European societies consider inadequate or inappropriate is open to serious question, Kennedy does not seek to argue that Western European practice is a flawless exemplar either. On the contrary, the problem for him lies not just in what are held to be the early stages of transition, but also in what is held to be the mature stage. The neo-liberalism of the international trade system and the EC's technocratic regime—in which politics has become less a matter of contestation than of managing popular pressures through policy initiatives and ongoing institutional reform—are 'unhappy alternatives'.[72] Kennedy is quite aware that, in Europe, as elsewhere, these are by no means the only alternatives reflected in contemporary arrangements. If he concentrates on two contrasting architectures in the sphere of European

[68] Ibid. 381.   [69] Ibid. 390.   [70] Ibid. 395.   [71] Ibid.   [72] Ibid. 394.

economic relations, his aim is simply to highlight the way assertions of international legal renewal are rooted in ideas that help to sustain existing asymmetries of power and resources, both within states and among them. By bringing into focus the wide gap between universalizing rhetoric and hegemonic reality, and by insisting on the extent to which 'choices and political struggles' are in issue, as distinct from 'natural transitions', he seeks to create impetus and clear space for the exploration of transformative possibilities.[73] In his assessment, one crucial source of such possibilities is the changes in 'our ideas about markets and democracy which have been wrought in the domestic cultures of most modern economies'. He points out that attention to these changes 'would challenge the image of Eastern primitivism' (and, by inference, Western sophistication as well); 'both blocs, after all, have participated in the development of technocratic modernism'. Thus, he writes: '[m]y suggestion is that these two tracks be brought together, and that both sides experience the shock of the new'.[74]

Though Kennedy's primary concern is with the economic dimensions of post-Cold War restructuring, his argument is that renewalist writing posits an analogous ordering where the political dimensions are concerned. In his words, '[j]ust as the economic model of the internal market, with its deep public–private partnerships [contrasts] with the austerity shocks and regulatory abstinence demanded of outsiders, . . . so also [the EC's] vision of a technical industrial policy unmoored from more traditional forms of democratic participation contrasts sharply with the institutional reforms urged on the East'.[75] Informing those reforms is an 'idealized system' not only 'of private property', but also 'of representative democracy'.[76] The thrust of the ideological strategies reviewed earlier in this section (and the reason for this excursus into European economic relations) is to confirm that indeed the same two-track approach which Kennedy identifies with respect to economic architecture applies to the reconstruction of political arrangements. Renewalist commentary, exemplified for our purposes in the thesis that an international legal right to democratic governance should now be recognized, envisions democracy in terms of a sophisticated track for developed societies and a 'long march through formalism' for the rest. In helping to establish low intensity democracy as the democratic standard for 'new democracies', the thesis lends weight to the claim that '[n]ot only have [these societies] not come close to operating a political structure modelled on actual Western liberal democracies, this is not part of a long-term agenda for the future'.[77] As Gills and his co-authors argue, it is not a coincidence that ideological formations in the economic sphere are paralleled in the sphere of democratic reconstruction: 'the new formal democratisation is the political corollary of economic liberalisation and internationalisation'.[78]

What are the implications for processes of democratization? In the first place, policymakers are encouraged to adopt a linear, evolutionary conception of modernization, in which democratic reconstruction is a matter of phased transition to a given goal. One consequence of this is that social goals are treated as pre-set; the only issue

[73] Kennedy 1991, 379.   [74] Ibid. 395–6.   [75] Ibid. 385.   [76] Ibid. 394.
[77] Gills et al. 1993, 3.   [78] Ibid. 4.

is how most efficiently to reach them. Democracy thus comes to appear an affair of means, but not of ends; an activity of technique, but not of agenda-setting. From this perspective, democratic reconstruction can be understood as a set of empirical data which the authorities would be well advised to obtain, consider, adjust to local conditions and eventually operationalize. By making democratic change seem a technical challenge, the democratic norm thesis depoliticizes the meaning of democracy. It fosters the idea, to borrow a phrase, that '[p]olitics, in the sense of choice between rival projects of society' is no longer conceivable.[79] In this way the political significance of low intensity democracy—the extent to which it promotes particular projects of society and obstructs others—becomes obscured from view. Likewise obscured is the existence of different models of democracy, differently articulated with the struggle over public agendas.

Where democratic reconstruction is depicted as a transition, a further consequence is that democratization comes to seem a matter of passing from one political condition to another, quite novel one. Thus, secondly, the democratic norm thesis figures democratic reconstruction as a complete break with the past, such that the societies in question are to be located at or near the beginning of an evolutionary path, with no relevant pre-history. The effect is to detemporalize the process of social change; to make the future seem the negation, rather than the transformation, of the past. To this extent, the democratic norm thesis encourages policymakers to reject their entire inheritance, and fuels the logic, noted in earlier discussion, according to which liberal democracy must be the opposite of state socialism, the minimal state the successor to the totalitarian state.[80] The gloomy prospects of such an approach suggest that, despite—or rather in part because of—this supposition that reconstruction calls for a complete reversal of fortune, the fortunes of 'transitional' societies are not likely to change much at all. To recall Marx's distinction between criticism and critique, democracy becomes in this way a matter of criticism, a case of inventing blueprints and seeking to change the world to fit them. Little room is left for his more promising alternative, in which efforts are directed not to prefiguring the future, but rather to searching for the new world through critique of the old. At the same time, little room is left for awareness of the historical specificity and contingency of existing democratic forms.

Thirdly, the evolutionary path is presented as one in which the democratization of state institutions precedes the democratization of civil society. Thus, the 'official' politics of electoral competition, parliaments, and political parties appears as prior both to the private power of economic undertakings and to the informal politics of citizens' initiatives. Efforts to secure the accountability of business, like moves to engage the participation of social movements, are postponed for later. (In cases where social movements were already key players in political life, this move to downgrade their significance appears as a kind of 'shock therapy', forcing politics into formalized institutional structures.) Correspondingly, civil and political rights appear as prior to

---

[79] Cox 1997, 63.

[80] For discussion of the implications of this in the economic sphere, see Amsden *et al.* 1994, 1–2.

economic and social rights. Debate about the allocation of social goods is initially bracketed, and attention focused on the rule of law, the establishment of free and fair electoral processes and the need to guard against tyrannous majorities. Finally, individual rights appear as prior to group rights. Concerns about the way political processes are skewed in favour of particular groups are put aside, to await a later stage when group difference can be confronted, and norms and procedures elaborated to deal with its political implications. Policymakers, then, are invited to orient themselves to a conception of citizenship and political participation abstracted from informal political processes, socio-economic contexts and membership of particular communities.

This points to a fourth implication of the phased transition identified with democratic reconstruction. Democratic 'substance' comes only—or most quickly—to the fittest survivors of formalism. An initial phase in which democracy is conceived abstractly, by reference to the existence of certain institutional forms, serves as a precondition to a more developed phase in which democracy can be approached more concretely, by reference to the social outcomes produced. Thus, the democratic norm thesis posits a chronology in which at the elementary stage the question is *whether* there is democracy. Either particular institutions, procedures and rights have been put in place, in which case there is democracy. Or they have not, in which case there is still dictatorship, totalitarianism, authoritarian government, or some other form of 'non-democracy'. Understood in this way, democracy is a matter of either–or classification of forms of government. Only once democratizing countries have embraced this conception do they reach the more advanced stage, at which the central question becomes *how democratic* are the processes by which decisions affecting people's lives are taken. Such issues can then arise as: to what extent can all citizens participate in setting the terms of collective life? how much economic deprivation and social marginalization are compatible with the equality of citizens in a democracy? As soon as democracy becomes a matter of degree, it becomes an issue of lived experience.

Finally, and connectedly, democratic change is cast as independent of changes in the organization of economic life. Insofar as the latter have been shaped by policies which, as Kennedy highlights, recall nothing so much as the *laissez-faire* theories of the Scottish Enlightenment, the democratic norm thesis puts to one side the implications for democracy of such policies. In the transition to democracy, free markets and weak states are depicted as forming the taken-for-granted backdrop against which democratizing efforts proceed. The neo-liberal programme that disfavours regulation in the public interest and deters long-term institution-building is made to seem a given of democratic reconstruction, rather than a problem confronting it. The ways in which the free market constrains democratic processes by generating and sustaining systematic inequalities of wealth that serve to entrench systematic inequalities of power are thus placed beyond consideration. In the result, these constraints are effectively ratified, and modernization appears to begin with a phase in which neo-liberal policies assume priority over democratic aspirations, passing only later to a phase characterised by more mixed economies. Once again, however, the rhetoric of 'catching up' may well conceal a reality of 'slowing down'. Analysing developments in Eastern Europe, one group of scholars argues that the consequence of economic liberalization is that 'Eastern Europe has . . . been assigned a place in the international economy roughly comparable to what it occupied in earlier centuries: that of a poor cousin in the division of labour with the rest of Europe'.[81]

To sum up these five points, the impact of the ideological moves reviewed above is to foster the idea that democracy must initially be detached from politics, from history, from society, and from economics. In this account, a phase of formalism is the prerequisite for a more contextualized approach to democratic politics; societies engaged in democratic reconstruction must first renounce the world before they can rejoin it as members of the larger community of democratic nations. The mystification here arises from the fact that formalism remains formal. A norm of democratic governance which confers legitimacy on the basis of only superficial institutional reform risks strengthening repressive forces and correspondingly debilitating oppositional ones. It risks promoting a self-defeating approach to democratic reconstruction, masking continuity as change. But it is not only the initial phase of the postulated evolution that should concern us. As Kennedy emphasizes, the problem lies not just with what is held to be the beginners' track, but also with what is held to be the advanced track. If democracy is a place, rather than a journey, and if 'actually existing democracies' have arrived there, then they appear to have nowhere further to go. Democracy is predicated as a largely irrelevant issue for such societies. All that remains is to safeguard their gains through the protection of human rights. Thus, as Kennedy observes, the 'internationalization of democratic rhetoric has accompanied a domestic displacement of democratic politics'. An 'intriguing migration' of democratic ideas has occurred 'from the metropolis to the periphery'.[82] As if to confirm this, Franck writes that for citizens of some states a norm of democratic governance would 'merely embellish rights already protected by their existing domestic constitutional order. For others it could be the realization of a cherished dream'.[83] The inference, whether intended or not, is that such states are already satisfactory from a democratic perspective; the rest is ornament.

Perhaps, then, it is worth recalling that 'actually existing democracy', in all its diverse forms, is subject to profound, wide-ranging, and in some respects growing, challenge. This is not the place to discuss specific misgivings, but in broad terms the issues revolve around, on the one hand, the pervasiveness of unaccountable power in various arenas and, on the other, the persistence of political exclusion of various sorts. As one analyst puts it, contemporary democratic life is marked by a raft of 'broken promises'.[84] Against the promise of self-rule and political equality stands a reality of oligarchy and technocracy, invisible power and bureaucratic-business domination, individual political alienation and differentiated social opportunity. By encouraging the belief that liberal societies represent the near-pinnacle of democratic achievement, the democratic norm thesis promotes an uncritical, affirmative approach to democratic life which shifts

---

[81] Amsden *et al.* 1994, 5.   [82] Kennedy 1991, 384.   [83] Franck 1992, 50.
[84] Bobbio 1987, 27 *et seq.*

attention away from liberal democracy's manifold broken promises. At the same time, such an approach shifts attention away from the enduring fragility of political institutions that came close to being annihilated only fifty years earlier. It thereby reduces the prospects for redeeming the promises and strengthening the institutions. To this extent, the thesis contains a dangerous inducement to complacency. To be sure, low intensity democracy holds out fewer prospects still of redeeming democracy's promises; the ideas associated with popular democracy find greater reflection in the political life of liberal states than in contemporary approaches to democratic reconstruction. But that is by no means to say, of course, that liberal states, or any of them, incarnate those ideas. Apart from the considerations just alluded to, popular democracy is to be understood as an ongoing process of enhancing self-rule and political equality, against a background of changing historical circumstances. It thus stands as a permanent corrective to the notion that democracy can be conceived as an originary act or foundational moment—a permanent corrective, in other words, not just to low intensity democracy, but to established democratic practices and institutions as well.

CONCLUSIONS

In the 1980s and 1990s more of the world's population than ever before had the 'quintessentially liberal democratic experience of voting in free elections'.[85] What significance should be attached to this development? What are the prospects for realizing the democratic aspirations it raised? What is the impact in this regard of international support for democratic reconstruction? To these questions the theorists of low intensity democracy suggest some unsettling answers. They suggest that moves to support democratic reconstruction may serve to curb democratic aspirations; that free elections may substitute for transformative social and political change. If these theorists are correct, key international agencies are promoting a model of democracy which is geared to providing some familiar features of democratic politics (periodic elections, multipartyism, the rule of law and civil rights), while demobilizing efforts to secure more far-reaching democratization. One way of grasping the features in question is to return to Schumpeter's account of the 'democratic method', presented in the 1940s. Though that account carries little weight today as an analysis of liberal democratic politics, the thrust of the critique of low intensity democracy is that it has been given a new lease of life in the circumstances of post-Cold War political reconstruction.

In this chapter I have argued that the democratic norm thesis falls in with the trend identified by the theorists of low intensity democracy. The proposed norm of democratic governance identifies democracy with the holding of multiparty elections, the protection of civil rights and the establishment of the rule of law. It has international law endorse calls to institute formal or 'political' democracy in post-communist and

[85] Archibugi & Held 1995, 3.

developing countries, but tends to countervail moves to secure the development of social and pluralist democracy. At the same time, it adopts an affirmative approach to 'actually existing democracy', which tends to eclipse awareness of the enduring—and in some respects increasing—deficits of liberal states. Just as Kennedy urges critical scrutiny of the two tracks of European economic life, so, in the light of this analysis, discussion needs to be opened concerning the limits and further possibilities of democratic life, *both* in societies engaged in reconstruction *and* in societies of long-standing democratic commitment. But there is also another arena which is in need of the 'shock of the new' in this sense. Gills and co-authors direct attention to it in the context of their account of popular democracy. The question of democracy in particular states cannot be separated, they write, 'from the question of democracy in the global system as a whole'. The challenge has to be confronted of developing 'a new global participatory politics aimed at the hitherto unaccountable governing institutions of the international system'.[86]

[86] Gills *et al.* 1993, 30.

Chapter 4

Limits of the Liberal Revolution II: Pan-National Democracy

Keywords, Raymond Williams's celebrated 'vocabulary of culture and society', was first published in 1976. A second edition appeared in 1983.[1] Had Williams survived to produce a third edition, we can be fairly confident about at least one revision he would have made. Between 'genius' and 'hegemony' he would surely have interposed a new entry. By the 1990s *globalization* had emerged as a central term of debate about culture and society, especially in their relationship with economy.

The concept of globalization is sometimes used quite specifically to refer to a series of late twentieth-century changes in the organization of economic life. These include the deregulation of financial transactions and attendant growth of global financial markets, the internationalization of production by multinational corporations, and the increasing integration of national economies in world trade. But globalization also has a wider meaning, elaborated by scholars seeking to explore connections between these economic phenomena and concurrent developments in other domains. In this broader sense globalization calls attention to a whole range of processes serving to augment the extent to which the lives of people in different countries are intertwined. To quote Anthony Giddens's influential definition, it denotes the 'intensification of worldwide social relations which link distant localities in such a way that local happenings are shaped by events occurring many miles away and vice versa'.[2] Thus, globalization is employed to refer, *inter alia*, to the enlargement of telecommunications networks, the advent of new technologies for the worldwide dissemination of information, the internationalization of media and entertainment concerns, the generation of global or at any rate transboundary environmental harm and risk, the proliferation of inter-governmental agencies and of transnational pressure groups.

For some observers globalization heralds the establishment of a new global order, in which most important issues are taken out of the hands of national governments and in which the nation-state, accordingly, loses its central role in the organization of social power. More commonly, however, globalizing processes are not understood to signal the demise of the nation-state. But nor are they held to be without consequence for state sovereignty. Rather, globalization is seen to involve a reconfiguration of national sovereignty. What is significant, on this view, is the way global linkages are changing the context in which state functions are exercised. While these functions remain pivotal, and in some fields are assuming increasing salience, so too is the

---

[1] Williams 1983.   [2] Giddens 1990, 64.

impact of activity in other fora. In fundamental respects collective life is affected by decision-making undertaken not only at a national level, but also in a host of non-national settings—other states, international organizations, intergovernmental meetings, regional and inter-regional networks, global markets, and so on.

Whichever of these accounts is accepted, globalization delivers a major challenge to traditional assumptions and approaches on a range of matters. One of these is democracy. On the one hand, globalization puts into question the assumption that democratic politics can be understood solely or largely in terms of the interaction of national forces. The part played by transnational forces in spreading democratic ideas, fuelling democratic claims, and reshaping democratic practices, must be taken into account. On the other hand, and more far-reachingly, globalization also puts into question the assumption that democracy can be achieved through the democratization of national politics. If decisions about collective life are taken not only in national settings, but also in a multiplicity of non-national settings, then democracy will remain compromised unless efforts are made to bring democratic principles to bear on those non-national settings as well. With globalization, then, the conventional approach of democratic theory and practice—proceeding on the basis that the nation-state is democracy's site and state boundaries its limits—stands in urgent need of review.

This chapter considers the implications of these points for discussions about the promotion of democracy through international law. To what extent do those discussions register the significance of globalization? The first part of the chapter outlines in a little more detail the main arguments about what globalization entails and how it affects the prospects for democracy. The second part relates these arguments to international legal debates. In some respects, of course, registering the significance of globalization for democracy is precisely what international legal scholars have in mind when they argue for recognition of a norm of democratic governance. That international forces have a part to play in spreading democratic ideas is the very premise—and intent—of their argument. But what of the more far-reaching idea that efforts to entrench democracy cannot rest content with the democratization of national politics? In proposing a norm of democratic governance, do these scholars intend that global governance, as well as national government, should be democratic? Is it envisioned that the United Nations and other international agencies be democratized? Are democratic principles seen as applicable to decision-making in non-institutionalized inter-governmental settings and in the 'private' sphere of international economic activity? Are the deficits of democracy in global politics held to constrain the possibilities for democracy in national politics? And if, as I shall suggest, the answers to these questions are, on the whole, 'no', does this provide further evidence that the leading accounts of how international law should promote democracy are apt to serve as ideology?

In reviewing the implications of globalization for democracy, it is first necessary to note something of the ways in which globalizing processes can be seen to change the general conditions in which democratic politics occurs. Attention can then shift to the issue of how these changes, in turn, alter the task that confronts those seeking to build a democratic political community.

Globalization

Without doubt, discussions of globalization often suffer, as Jan Aart Scholte observes, 'from over-simplifications, exaggerations and wishful thinking'.[3] To avoid these weaknesses, a few points merit highlighting at the outset. One concerns the pattern of the processes involved. While in some accounts globalization is associated with an overall trend towards convergence, for most analysts it is more accurately understood as a 'dialectical process',[4] in which homogenization goes hand in hand with differentiation, integration with fragmentation, centralization with decentralization, universalization with particularization.[5] To be sure, transnational networks foster the circulation of cultural forms. But this in no way spells the end of global cultural diversity, for as those forms circulate, they get appropriated in different ways—reinterpreted in the light of local circumstances, mixed with local traditions, or yet rejected in favour of a re-assertion of local uniqueness.

Another aspect worth emphasizing is the scope of global networks, their reach and depth. Against over-generalized depictions of the changes underway, many analysts stress that the phenomenon of globalization is unevenly experienced.[6] On the one hand, globalizing processes operate unevenly across different domains of social life. In the sphere of the economy, for instance, globalization is more pronounced in some sectors than others. Whereas financial markets are highly globalized, labour markets remain to a large degree nationally based and regulated. On the other hand, globalizing processes also operate unevenly across different countries and, within countries, across different social groups. Quite patently, global networks do not engage and affect everyone to the same extent and in the same ways. Thus, for example, information, communications equipment, and opportunities for mobility are more readily available to some than to others. This illustrates a further point. The intensification of worldwide social relations is not to be equated with growing interdependence. Globalizing processes may well serve to sharpen the significance of asymmetries of access to resources, and hence to exacerbate existing relations of dependence.

---

[3] Scholte 1997, 18.   [4] Giddens 1990, 64.
[5] For a helpful overview of the 'opposed tendencies' associated with globalization, see McGrew 1992*a*, 74–6. See also Arjun Appardurai's influential account of globalization's 'disjunctures': Appardurai 1990.
[6] McGrew 1992*a*, 76.

Finally, there is the question of the novelty of the developments associated with globalization. Clearly, there have been international and transnational linkages as long as there have been nation-states. One need not subscribe to world-system theory to acknowledge that an international economy has long existed. Levels of world trade are known to have been especially high in the liberal economic order of the pre-1914 period. But while some conclude that globalization represents nothing new, theorists of globalization observe that changes have nonetheless occurred. World trade itself has become more extensive. Global financial flows have increased exponentially. Production is internationalized to an unprecedented degree. More generally, the impact of global networks on culture and society (though not, as indicated, uniform) is exceptionally widespread and penetrating. In this regard a major contributing factor is obviously technological change: improved communications, enhanced data processing, accelerated transportation. What is making the world seem to shrink more dramatically than ever is that the pathways of contact between people in different countries are not the slow and difficult means of former times, but the fast, and in many cases, instantaneous media now available.[7]

With these points in mind, we can now turn to the question of how globalizing processes affect the conditions of political life. In very broad terms, a distinction can be drawn between three approaches on this matter.[8] These may be labelled 'strong globalization', 'globalization scepticism' and 'weak globalization'.[9] The 'strong globalization' thesis is the view, noted earlier, that globalization signals a sharp decline in the power and significance of states.[10] From this perspective, the contemporary might of world market forces is such that national governments are left with few policy options. In order to maintain international competitiveness, fiscal and labour laws must be geared to the demands of multinational corporations. If overheads are too high, business will simply relocate elsewhere. Likewise, monetary policy must reflect the wishes of global financial markets. An unacceptable shift in exchange or interest rates risks provoking a crippling flight of capital. It follows that governments must accept a much more minor role than—especially in the second half of the twentieth century—many had come to expect. They can no longer hope to direct economic activity within their territories. Still less can they hope to regulate social outcomes through redistributive intervention. Their only remaining function is to provide the basic infrastructure needed to support global markets at the minimum cost. Thus, the 'end of history' is also 'the end of the nation-state' as we have come to know it.[11]

The strong globalization thesis is fairly uncontroversial insofar as it asserts that, as a result of changes in the world economy, the constraints within which national authorities operate have in some respects tightened, and the difficulties which governments face in pursuing independent policy have on some matters grown. But, as critics of this thesis point out, it is one thing to take note of tightening constraints

---

[7] See Harvey 1990.   [8] For a similar analysis, see Gray 1998, ch. 3.
[9] The strong/weak terminology is widely used (see, e.g., Weiss 1997), if not always in uniform ways.
[10] This perspective is exemplified by Ohmae 1995 and Horsman & Marshall 1994.
[11] On the 'end of the nation-state', see, e.g., Ohmae 1995.

and growing difficulties; it is quite another to conclude that the nation-state has reached the end of its life as a significant structure for the exercise of social power. From the perspective of 'globalization scepticism', the strong globalization thesis considerably overstates the extent to which economic forces are incapacitating states.[12] In doing so, it fails to take into account the possibilities for, and continuous history of, state adaptation to new circumstances. Indeed, it puts to one side the many respects in which state capacities for administration and control are undergoing expansion. It also glosses over the variable impact of international capital, the fact that some states are more vulnerable to constraints than others and that some domains of state activity are more implicated than others. And it neglects to register the degree to which economic globalization, by reinforcing social polarization, confirms the necessity and the demand for ongoing efforts at national level to secure the just allocation of collective goods. The image of uncontrollable market forces and minimal states seems, then, to be a case of wishful thinking. More than that, this image seems to be a case of ideology, working (as Paul Hirst and Grahame Thompson put it) to engender a 'pathology of over-diminished expectations' and thus to 'paralyse radical reforming national strategies, to [make them seem] unviable in the face of the judgement and sanction of international markets'.[13]

Globalization scepticism is a valuable corrective to the more fanciful—and ideological—claims of strong globalization. As some scholars argue, however, there is a danger here of bending the stick too far the other way. In dismissing the overstatements of the strong globalization thesis, it is important not to understate the scale of the challenge facing nation-states. Partly in response to the pressures noted in that thesis, important changes are occurring in the structure of world governance. The 'weak globalization' thesis seeks to clarify these changes.[14] In particular, while recognizing the enduring powers and responsibilities of national governments with respect to domestic affairs, this thesis calls attention to the many non-national contexts in which political initiative, decision-making and action now take place. A range of developments are highlighted. In the first place, the compass of these contexts has enlarged. New international organizations have been established, especially at regional level; the membership of some existing organizations has increased significantly; and other more or less institutionalized inter-governmental settings have also proliferated. Secondly, the scope of global governance has widened. A broad variety of issue areas today comes within the domain of international policy-making and regulation. A third development concerns the powers of international and regional agencies. Though trends on this matter are inconsistent, in certain spheres an expansion has occurred. Some institutions currently have considerable regulatory and other competences. Fourthly, the forms of global governance have diversified. Recent

---

[12] This perspective is exemplified by Hirst & Thompson 1996 and Weiss 1997.
[13] Hirst & Thompson 1996, 6, 1. See also 175–7.
[14] This perspective is exemplified by Scholte 1997. It should be noted that the works cited in connection with globalization scepticism are also concerned to clarify these changes. The distinction between globalization scepticism and the weak globalization thesis is one of emphasis, rather than of substance.

decades have, for instance, seen the growth of private sector regulatory agencies and of transnational networks of authorities. Finally, a striking change has occurred with regard to the actors engaged in the elaboration and implementation of international initiatives. As is frequently observed, the impact has considerably increased of global social movements (the green movement, the women's movement, etc.), international non-governmental organisations, and pressure groups of diverse kinds.

Reflected in these developments are some of the ways in which globalization can be seen to enhance both the need and the opportunity for governance to operate on a global or at least transnational basis. A diffusion, or rediffusion, of political authority and initiative appears to be occurring. This in no way spells the decline of national government, but it does compel attention to the (actual and potential) contributions of other significant actors and agencies, and to the relationship between those contributions and the exercise of state functions. In the words of one proponent of the weak globalization thesis, 'the state is still very much in the picture, although its capacities, orientations, and activities have changed . . . At the same time, however, other parties besides the state have also acquired important roles in the process of world governance'.[15]

The Limits of Pan-National Democracy

If the capacities, orientations, and activities of the state are changing and non-state governance is assuming increasing importance, then pressing questions arise about many fundamental issues of political organization, among them, democracy. Modern democracy has customarily been understood as the democracy of nation-states—in contradistinction to the ancient democracy of city-states. Historically, the development of liberal democracy is indeed inseparable from the project of building and consolidating the sovereign nation-state. The institutions associated with modern democracy were framed in connection with efforts to foster national solidarities and strengthen national polities, and modern democracy continues to be theorized as the working out of democratic principles for nationally organized political communities. Thus, in the leading accounts, the people or *demos* is conceived as the nation; legitimacy is defined in terms of consent by, and accountability to, the national citizenry; popular consent is linked with the holding of periodic national elections and other mechanisms; accountability is related to the existence of a 'public sphere' within national territory; self-government is identified with the independence of the state; and so on.

Underpinning this notion that the nation-state is modern democracy's 'container'[16] are two related ideas. One is the idea that democratic polities are territorially bounded communities. In this regard David Held highlights a series of assumptions which have tended to inform democratic thought.[17] It has been assumed

---

[15] Scholte 1997, 23.   [16] I owe this image to McGrew 1997*a*, 5.
[17] See Held 1991, 1993, 1995*a*, and 1995*b*.

that democracies can operate as self-contained units; that they are clearly demarcated from one another; that change within democracies may be explained largely by reference to internal politics; and that democratic politics is a function of the interplay of national forces. The modern democratic polity has thus been seen, in Held's phrase, as a national 'community of fate', that is to say, a community which both governs itself and is accountable solely to itself. Put differently, a symmetrical or congruent relationship has been presumed to exist between those experiencing outcomes and those taking decisions. This relationship has been held to exist above all between national electorates and their elected representatives, and between those subject to national jurisdiction and national authorities.

The second idea underpinning the notion that the nation-state is democracy's container is a corollary of the presumed boundedness of democratic polities. The world beyond the nation-state has been treated, for the most part, as a given. Democratic principles have not been seen as applicable to that world, and the lack of democracy in that world has not been seen to affect the prospects for democracy in nation-states. Thus, the modern states system has been characterized, to quote Held once again, by a 'striking tension between the entrenchment of accountability and democratic legitimacy inside state boundaries and the pursuit of power politics outside such boundaries'.[18] Democratic national arrangements have been accompanied by non-democratic international arrangements. Reflecting and reinforcing these ideas has been the emergence in the twentieth century of a disciplinary division between political theory and international relations, between the study of the politics of nation-states and the study of the relations among them. Democracy has been the 'property' of political theory. In international relations the basis for a democratic (and, on some views, any) political community has generally been supposed to be lacking, and analysis has mostly focused on issues of war and peace, survival and security.

There have, of course, always been challenges to both these ideas, and especially the first.[19] In recent years, however, the misgivings have grown, as scholars on both sides of the disciplinary divide just mentioned have begun to argue that, in the circumstances of contemporary globalization, democratic politics cannot continue to be kept apart from international relations. On the one hand, assumptions about the boundedness of democratic polities seem less tenable than ever. If globalizing processes are enhancing the extent to which action in one country has ramifications in another, and if those same processes are also augmenting the extent to which national options are shaped by action in international and other non-national settings, then the notion of the national 'community of fate' becomes extremely difficult to sustain. National democratic politics clearly cannot be understood in isolation from the global web in which national forces are enmeshed. To grasp the problems of democracy, and the possibilities for solving them, it is vital to look beyond the frontiers of the nation-state, and consider the role of other governments, inter-

[18] Held 1995a, 73.
[19] Among the most notable challenges have been those informed by world-system theory and related Marxist and neo-Marxist approaches. See Ch. 3 below.

national organizations, global markets, non-governmental organizations, etc. in set-ting the terms of collective life. On the other hand, and in consequence, the suppo-sition that (national) democracy can thrive in a sea of (international) non-democracy is called seriously into question. If national boundaries do not describe the limits of a community of fate, how can they describe the limits of democracy? However legit-imate a national political order, does national political legitimacy suffice, when in far-reaching ways citizens are affected by decisions taken in non-national settings? On what basis are *those* decisions to be held legitimate? Where is the congruence between *those* decisions and their outcomes? When globalization is taken into account, the conception of democracy as the working out of democratic principles for national polities starts to appear dramatically inadequate. Correspondingly, the idea that democracy has no application in the international domain of interstate relations, international organizations and the world economy comes to seem in urgent need of revision. The contradiction has to be confronted between 'structures of power that seem to be increasingly internationalised, globalised, in some sense universalised and processes of participation, representation, accountability and legitimation that remain rooted in the institutionalised apparatuses of states'.[20]

The central implication of this analysis is that the nation-state cannot remain democracy's container. In the first place, attention must be paid to the global context of national democracy, the various ways in which global networks may support, as well as constrain, the expansion of democracy's purchase within national communi-ties. The work on low intensity democracy discussed in Chapter 3 illustrates efforts to address this aspect.[21] Secondly, consideration must also be given to the democra-tization of global governance. To resolve the contradiction between globalized struc-tures of power and state-based democratic institutions, democracy's compass must be widened to include power relations across the world as a whole. Decision-making with global or transboundary impact—whether undertaken by governments, inter-national or regional organizations, intergovernmental associations of officials and experts, private-sector regulatory agencies, multinational corporations, or other actors—must be brought within the scope of democratic concern. If politics has become global, then so too must democracy. What could this mean? For reasons already indicated, democratic theorists have not generally broached the topic of global democracy. Where they have done so, however, one of two assumptions has generally prevailed. Either it has been imagined that global democracy is predicated upon the disappearance of the states system and its replacement by government on a world-wide scale. Or it has been envisaged that global democracy is achieved through democratization at the level of each nation-state. The first-mentioned vision of global democracy might be labelled 'world government'; the second might be termed 'pan-national democracy'. Yet, as is today argued, this rendering of the options is nei-ther necessary nor sufficient. In conjunction with the weak globalization thesis, more

[20] Walker 1993, 143.
[21] See also Cox 1997 for an instructive account of some of the ways in which globalization serves both to heighten social inequality and political disaffection, and to fuel mobilization and resistance.

theorists have begun to consider the meaning of global democracy, and many have rejected its identification both with world government and with pan-national democracy. Instead, they have begun to explore a third set of possibilities for institutionalizing democratic global governance.[22] The work of David Held is a particularly influential example of contemporary approaches.[23]

Held refutes the notion that global democracy must await the demise of the states system. As observed above, globalizing processes afford no basis for predicting the occurrence of that event. Still less is there (or has there ever been) among observers an expectation of—or wish for—world government. In any case, as Held comments, there exists ample scope for democratization within the current structures of global politics. At the same time, Held also disputes that global democracy can be presumed to follow democracy within nation-states. In this regard he notes that the widely celebrated turn to democracy in the early 1990s brought relatively limited progress in securing control of global decision-making by those affected. Indeed, inasmuch as related moves in the direction of economic liberalization served to strengthen global economic forces, the impact of the transformations was partly to weaken accountability. But even if global democracy could be presumed to follow universal national democracy, Held contends that efforts to pursue global democracy cannot be deferred until every nation-state has embraced democracy, or has reached a certain level of 'democracity'.[24] One reason is that national democracy is constrained by the undemocratic character of the international political-economic domain itself. No matter how democratic the political arrangements within a nation-state, those arrangements cannot ensure the accountability to citizens of systems of power which shape national options but yet elude national control. In this sense pan-national democracy is a self-defeating vision of global democracy. Incongruence between those experiencing outcomes and those taking decisions will always remain unless distinct endeavours are made to democratize the agencies of global governance and the structures of the global economy. Democracy within nation-states and democracy in international affairs are mutually supportive developments, which must be pursued in tandem.

Held's notion of global democracy thus goes beyond pan-national democracy, but falls well short of world government. Rather, it involves simultaneous efforts to deepen democracy within nation-states and extend it to international and transnational settings. It aims at the 'creation of a democratic community which both involves and cuts across democratic states'.[25] Held calls this twofold agenda the project of 'cosmopolitan democracy'. As he explains, '[t]he term *cosmopolitan* is used to indicate a model of political organization in which citizens, wherever they are located in the world, have voice, input and political representation in international affairs, in parallel with and independently of their own governments'. Such a model relies on a 'conception of *democracy* . . . that entails . . . not only a particular set of procedures (important though this is), but also the pursuit of democratic values involving the

[22] For an illuminating account of recent work, see McGrew 1997*b*.   [23] See esp. Held 1995*a*.
[24] Archibugi & Held 1995, 13.   [25] Ibid.

extension of popular participation in the political process'.[26] Like others who argue for an approach to global democracy which involves neither world government nor simply pan-national democracy, Held readily acknowledges that the democratization of global governance presents a formidable challenge. Cosmopolitan democracy will not spring fully formed from humanity's democratic imagination, any more than did nation-state democracy. Simply to work out how relevant decision-making processes currently operate is likely to be difficult enough. In the sphere of the world economy, for instance, Robert Cox highlights the operation of what he refers to as a *'nébuleuse'*: decisions are made within shadowy networks encompassing both national officials and international bureaucrats, intergovernmental bodies and independent experts, public institutions and private agencies, official meetings, and unofficial conclaves.[27] That said, the project cannot be dismissed as futile, for—as Cox, Held, and others also note—moves are already underway to demonstrate how transparency may be improved and accountability enhanced. In this connection a frequently cited development is the rising profile of social movements, non-governmental organizations and pressure groups. Of course, only a small, self-selecting and largely elite section of the world's population takes part in such initiatives. But, while few observers have illusions that these elements of an international civil society can alone suffice, many see in them important indications of how the circle of participation in international and transnational decision-making might begin to be enlarged.

With a view to building on current trends and drawing out potentials of existing arrangements, Held elaborates both a theoretical framework which might inform efforts to institutionalize cosmopolitan democracy and a series of recommendations for reconstructing the institutions of global governance accordingly. I outline some of the recommendations in Chapter 5. For present purposes, however, the details of Held's proposals are less important than his central claim that, if democracy is to flourish in conditions of intensifying global interconnectedness, it must become a transnational affair, linked to an expanding framework of democratic institutions and procedures. Democratizing efforts must embrace and connect all domains and levels of political interaction, just as globalizing processes do. This does *not* entail—he emphasizes—that democracy should become tied to the international arena, as it has earlier been tied to the city-state and the nation-state. Local and national arenas remain significant. Rather, what is entailed is more far-reaching than that. The notion of a democratic political community should be untied from the whole 'idea of locality and place'.[28] Is this chimerical? There can be no denying that, as William Connolly observes, precisely because it 'lacks a territorial base through which [the terms of its accountability] could be solidified, . . . the project of nonterritorial democratization necessarily exudes an air of unreality'. But then, Connolly adds, 'territorial [i.e. nation-state] democracy exudes its own aura of unreality in the late modern time'. He continues:

---

[26] Ibid. (emphasis in original).   [27] Cox 1997, 60.
[28] Held 1995a, 278. See also Mary Kaldor's assertion that, to meet the challenges of globalization, democracy needs to become '*issue based* rather than territorially based'. Kaldor 1995, 88.

Perhaps the basic issue today . . . is which unreality to attack and which to succumb to—the unreality of territorial democracy or the unreality of nonterritorial democratization. Or perhaps it is best to conclude that neither of these modalities of democratic life can thrive in this time unless it enters into an active relation with the other.[29]

INTERNATIONAL LAW AND PAN-NATIONAL DEMOCRACY

The foregoing discussion trains a spotlight on two questions which have tended to fall into the interstices of democratic theory and international relations scholarship.[30] First, in what ways does the international system support and constrain democracy within nation-states, and how might the support be strengthened and the constraint reduced? Secondly, how can democratic principles be brought to bear among and across nation-states, that is to say, in the multifarious official and unofficial settings in which rules are made and decisions taken with global, or at any rate, transnational reach? If we now turn our attention to legal scholarship, it is immediately apparent that the first question has not similarly remained in the dark. The substance of this question has long been a focus of legal analysis, whether in the context of work on human rights protection or in other contexts. More obviously still, those who currently urge recognition of an international legal norm of democratic governance can hardly be accused of failing to consider how the international system might support democracy within nation-states (even if, as suggested in Chapter 3, they may have failed adequately to consider how the international system *constrains* democracy within nation-states). But what of the second question? To what extent do moves to promote democracy through international law reflect an effort to bring democratic principles to bear among and across nation-states? On its face, the norm of democratic governance is a claim about governance within nation-states. As this confirms, the proponents of the democratic norm do not anticipate the demise of the states system and its replacement by world government. Do they nonetheless envision a multilayered process of democratization, along the lines of cosmopolitan democracy? Or do they conceive democratic global governance in more pan-national terms, as the universalization of national democracy? This section examines the relationship between the democratic norm thesis and the construction of global democracy. My argument in this regard will be that the thesis 'succumbs to the unreality of territorial democracy': *pan-national democracy* is largely what is in view.

Democratic Norm, Global Governance Reform

On one level globalization is, as Martti Koskenniemi remarks, 'old news to international lawyers, who presume an international polity, the laws of which they prac-

---

[29] Connolly 1991, 219–20.
[30] In formulating these questions, I draw on the account in Archibugi & Held 1995, 8.

tice'.[31] International lawyers are apt to find equally unremarkable the notion that the growth of this international polity does not spell the contraction of the national polity. Since international law serves as both underwriter of state sovereignty and claimant upon it, there can be little doubt from the vantage point of these observers that national authority and international governance form no zero-sum game. Rather, national and international powers develop in tandem: each fuels the other; at the same time, each marks out its own distinctive arena by setting limits to the other's operation. In presuming an international polity, international lawyers are thus also disposed to presume the continuing significance of the nation-state. To return to the language used earlier, they are disposed to prefer a 'weak' account of globalization to a 'strong' one. Yet if weak theories of globalization include the familiar points just evoked, those theories additionally go well beyond them. Even the most circumspect asserts the occurrence of changes with far-reaching implications for international and national political arrangements. On another level, then, the news is perhaps not so old. However clear international lawyers may be as to the *existence* of an international polity and its enmeshment with national polities, globalizing processes may strain assumptions about the *character* of international governance and about the political, legal, and other challenges which it occasions, and confronts.

Precisely because new conditions periodically call for revised conceptualizations (as well as for other reasons), the character of the international polity is a matter of enduring debate among international lawyers.[32] It will be valuable to begin our enquiry into the relationship between the democratic norm thesis and the construction of global democracy by considering the relationship between the thesis and this debate. What notion of the contemporary international polity underpins the claims regarding the norm of democratic governance? How is this notion held to affect these claims? How are these claims held to affect this notion? Clarifying these matters will help to elucidate the approach to global democracy that informs the democratic norm thesis and, more specifically, the bearing of the proposed norm of democratic governance with respect to the democratization of relations among and across nation-states. Quite obviously, however, no single or unified account is involved here. Moves to promote an international legal norm of democratic governance are consistent with a diversity of visions of the structures of global governance, and are related to those visions in a diversity of ways. The discussion that follows will focus on two accounts in particular. In the first Anne-Marie Slaughter discusses contemporary developments in terms of an emergent 'transgovernmentalism'; in the second Thomas Franck addresses the issue of 'fairness' in international governance.

Slaughter: transgovernmentalism as the 'real new world order'

In an essay entitled 'The Real New World Order' Slaughter refutes both the contention that national governments are declining in importance and the contention

---

[31] Koskenniemi 1991, 401.

[32] For an illuminating account of the ebb and flow of this debate, see Kennedy 1994. Recent interventions include Sur 1997, Reisman 1997, and Schachter 1997, along with the writings discussed below.

that international institutions, subnational authorities, and non-governmental actors are rising in significance.[33] Profound changes are underway in the structure of international governance, she holds. But neither of those two analyses captures them, for each is preoccupied with the wrong domain. Instead of scrutinizing national governments and international, subnational, and non-governmental bodies, the focus should be on changes at the level of transgovernmental interaction. What is occurring is best understood as a 'disaggregation of sovereignty'. In her words:

the state . . . is disaggregating into its separate, functionally distinct parts. These parts—courts, regulatory agencies, executives, and even legislatures—are networking with their counterparts abroad, creating a dense web of relations that constitutes a new, transgovernmental order. Today's international problems—terrorism, organized crime, environmental degradation, money laundering, bank failure, and securities fraud—created and sustain these relations.[34]

'Transgovernmentalism', then, is the central characteristic of Slaughter's 'real new world order'. As the passage just quoted indicates, she considers that this trend is evident in all spheres of state activity. But it is in the regulatory sphere that she seems to find government networking most advanced. As an example of networking in this arena, she cites the Basle Committee on Banking Supervision, formed in 1988 not by interstate treaty but by independent decision of twelve central bank governors. Despite the Committee's lack of official or legal competence, it exerts considerable influence: 'Wall Street looks to the Basle Committee, rather than the World Bank.'[35]

If bodies like the Basle Committee have assumed a central role in global governance, in Slaughter's analysis this is because they offer a more promising framework than international institutions for finding and implementing solutions to our most pressing global problems. In the first place, government networks have at their disposal highly flexible and efficient ways of dealing with transnational activity. More can be generally achieved by '[n]etworks of bureaucrats responding to international crises and planning to prevent future problems' than through the centralized, hierarchical, and slow-moving procedures of international institutions.[36] Secondly, government networks are likely to escape the negative attitudes which have hampered international organizations. Slaughter observes that '[e]fforts to expand supranational authority . . . have consistently produced a backlash among member states', for 'major powers [will not] cede their power and sovereignty to an international institution'.[37] Government networks, by contrast, require no formal transfer of power, and are thus able to command wider support. Finally, and for related reasons, government networks enjoy greater legitimacy than international institutions. Since transgovernmental networks have no independent competence, and serve only to enforce law made at national level, they carry the legitimacy of the national processes with which they intersect. Transgovernmentalism sidesteps the 'prospect of a supranational bureaucracy accountable to no-one' by '[leaving] the control of government institutions in the hands of national citizens, who must hold their governments as account-

---

[33] See Slaughter 1997. For an earlier intimation of this argument, see also Slaughter, 1995.
[34] Slaughter 1997, 184.   [35] Ibid. 185.   [36] Ibid.   [37] Ibid. 183.

able for their transnational activities as for their domestic duties'.[38] Slaughter recognizes that transgovernmental networking may aggravate the problem of non-transparent decision-making by unelected officials, but recalls that 'checking unelected officials is a familiar problem in domestic politics'. Established national procedures for securing accountability can thus be expected to come into play. After all, she remarks, '[c]itizens of liberal democracies will not accept any form of international regulation they cannot control'.[39]

Slaughter also recognizes, of course, that government networks do not engage officials from all parts of the world to the same extent. She observes that 'transgovernmental networks are concentrated among liberal democracies'. On the other hand, they 'are not limited to them'.[40] Some non-democratic states have institutions (regulatory agencies, judiciaries, etc.) which are capable of cooperating with counterparts from democratic states. In such cases, networking helps to strengthen the institutions and protect them from political domination, corruption, and incompetence. Viewed from this perspective, she argues, government networks not only open up the prospect of surpassing the achievements of international organizations with respect to global governance. They also offer a compelling means of achieving 'democratization, step by step', institution by institution. The inclusion in transgovernmental networks of institutions from non-democratic states serves to 'expand the circle of democracies one institution at a time'.[41] Networking in this way chimes with international and foreign policies aimed at promoting liberal democracy. At the same time, the disaggregation of the state facilitates the enforcement of an entitlement to democratic governance. It becomes possible to assess whether or not governments are democratic by reference to the quality of specific judicial, administrative, and legislative institutions. Slaughter concludes that transgovernmentalism is not only an emerging reality. It is also a 'world order ideal in its own right', a suitable 'blueprint for the international architecture of the 21st century'.[42]

In what sense is this a blueprint for a *democratic* international architecture? Slaughter's account of the norm of democratic governance is informed by a notion of global democracy that is unequivocally, indeed emphatically, pan-national. For her the democratic deficits of international organizations are a powerful reason for eschewing visions of cosmopolitan democracy and concentrating on enlarging the community of liberal democratic states. Yet, in the light of the analysis presented earlier in this chapter, the limitations of this approach are all too plain. If transgovernmental networks are as central to contemporary political life as Slaughter suggests, to what extent can global governance be deemed democratic? Slaughter argues that transgovernmental networks draw legitimacy from the national processes with which they intersect. Whereas international organizations involve the prospect of a supranational bureaucracy accountable to no-one, government networks leave control in the hands of national citizens. To be sure, she observes, government networks often promulgate their own rules; in doing so, however, the purpose is always to 'enhance

---

[38] Ibid. 186.   [39] Ibid. 197.   [40] Ibid. 194.   [41] Ibid.   [42] Ibid. 186, 197.

the enforcement of national law'.[43] With transgovernmentalism the 'makers and enforcers of rules are national leaders who are accountable to the people'.[44] All of which might well prompt one to enquire: *which* national citizens? *whose* national law? *what* people? However effectively citizens may be able to hold their own governments accountable in connection with transgovernmental activities, democratic legitimacy depends on accountability to *those affected* by such activities. In this context, those affected will necessarily include citizens of other countries, among them countries very probably not represented in the relevant network. To recall earlier discussion, the nation-state might appropriately serve as democracy's 'container' if territorial boundaries coincided with a national 'community of fate', that is to say, a community which governs itself, and only itself. But Slaughter's account of the role of transgovernmental networks precisely illustrates the point that territorial boundaries *do not* coincide with a national community of fate. A symmetrical or congruent relationship *does not* exist between those taking decisions and those experiencing outcomes. When options in one country are shaped by transgovernmental networks, which are themselves shaped by decisions in other countries, national democracy—no matter how widespread and how deep-rooted—cannot suffice. From this perspective, it is difficult to see on what basis the Basle Committee offers a more legitimate forum than the World Bank, difficult to grasp how Slaughter's real (and ideal) new world order makes up the democratic deficits of other forms of global governance.

Indeed, transgovernmentalism might plausibly be seen to push in quite the reverse direction. I have so far been stressing that, even if citizens are able to hold their own governments accountable in connection with transgovernmental activities, democratic legitimacy requires accountability to the wider constituency of all those affected. To what extent, however, are citizens likely to be able to hold their governments accountable with respect to transgovernmental networking? Slaughter acknowledges that networking may aggravate the problem of non-transparent decision-making by unelected officials. 'To many', she concedes, 'the prospect of transnational government by judges and bureaucrats looks more like technocracy than democracy'. To her, however, such a view fails to register that the challenges involved are not intrinsically different from those routinely faced in domestic democratic politics. With this in mind, she expresses confidence that citizens of liberal democracies will not accept international regulation which they cannot control. As Philip Alston contends in a response to Slaughter's account, this seems far too sanguine an assessment.[45] With transgovernmentalism as she describes it, the *nébuleuse* evoked by Cox threatens to become so nebulous as to be almost completely unassailable. He writes:

If [Slaughter] is correct, her analysis . . . implies the marginalization of governments as such and their replacement by special interest groups, which might sometimes include the relevant governmental bureaucrats. It suggests a definitive move away from arenas of relative transparency into the back rooms, . . . the bypassing of the national political arenas to which the United States and other proponents of the importance of healthy democratic institutions attach so much importance'.[46]

---

[43] Slaughter 1997, 191.   [44] Ibid. 192.   [45] Alston 1997, 442.   [46] Ibid. 441.

According to Alston, Slaughter exaggerates the decline of international institutions. While she identifies an observable trend, she overstates—or, at any rate, over-generalizes—the extent to which transgovernmental networking is replacing action within the framework of organizations. At the same time, she understates the significance of changes within the global economy. Indeed, he suggests, these two short-comings are linked. One reason why Slaughter is excessively optimistic about the prospects for national democratic control over transgovernmentalism is that she leaves out of consideration the impact of neo-liberal economic values, practices and institutions. When discussing the non-state dimensions of transnational activity, her focus is on non-governmental organizations and social movements; transnational business and associated agencies scarcely figure in her analysis. Yet, as theorists of globalization point out, the context in which governments exercise their functions has altered considerably in consequence of the whole range of developments associated with late twentieth-century globalization. Wall Street may look to the Basle Committee, but pressing questions arise as to how adequate scrutiny may be exercised over Wall Street (in addition to the questions already raised about scrutiny of the Basle Committee itself). Alongside Slaughter's government networks, then, international organizations remain important, and private economic actors also play a major part in shaping the options open to national communities. Once these phenomena are taken into account, it becomes all the harder to see on what basis national democracy can be held to suffice.

In a passage quoted earlier Slaughter provides a vivid illustration of what happens when global democracy is understood in terms of pan-national democracy, rather than in terms of an effort to create a democratic community that involves, but also cuts across and extends beyond, nation-states. As 'today's international problems' she cites 'terrorism, organised crime, environmental degradation, money laundering, bank failure and securities fraud'.[47] If these are indeed to be rated as our most pressing international problems, then—to quote Alston again—'the plight of a billion or so people living in poverty seems to become a domestic problem, or at least to have disappeared from the international agenda, perhaps to be best taken care of by the free market'; the same goes for malnourishment, lack of access to basic education, inadequate provision of health care, the persecution of minority groups, the plight of refugees and displaced persons, more effective regulation of global economic life, and other aspects of the protection of human rights.[48] Slaughter's 'largely equity-free international agenda'[49] is also a largely democracy-free international agenda. When global democracy is identified with pan-national democracy, the central democratic preoccupations—equality, inclusion, accountability, etc.—are removed from the sphere of international concern. In Slaughter's account, democracy becomes a matter of national 'institutions' (executive agencies, judiciaries, legislatures), and global governance a function of interaction among these institutions, in response to an agenda

---

[47] Slaughter 1997, 184.   [48] Alston 1997, 439.   [49] Ibid. 446.

set by 'the internationalists of the 1990s'. Who are these? 'Bankers, lawyers, businesspeople, public-interest activists, and criminals'.[50]

Slaughter's conception of the contemporary international polity might be understood as a distinctive variant of the weak globalization thesis. In keeping with that thesis, she stresses changes in the organization of global politics. At the same time, there is much in her discussion that is reminiscent of the other two approaches to globalization outlined above. She evinces a large measure of globalization scepticism, yet also makes assumptions about the minimal state which recall the strong globalization thesis. For present purposes, however, what is most significant about her analysis is that, while the transnationalization of decision-making processes is registered, the implications of this for democracy are not fully pursued. The legitimacy of a transgovernmental political order thus comes to rest on the limited ground of pan-national democracy.

Franck: fairness and the reform of global governance

Compared to Slaughter's theory of transgovernmentalism, Franck's understanding of contemporary international politics seems to stand more directly in the line of liberal internationalist traditions. This is made clear in his wide-ranging study of *Fairness in International Law and Institutions*.[51] In one of the book's early chapters Franck considers the issue of 'fairness to persons'. It is in this context that he presents his claim (reviewed in Chapter 2 above) that a 'democratic entitlement' is emerging in international law.[52] Then, after exploring his central theme from various other angles, he turns his attention in the book's final chapter to the fairness of international forums.

The discussion opens with some observations about developments affecting the structure of the international polity. Putting forward one of the propositions which Slaughter precisely seeks to refute, Franck argues that, while national governments remain pivotal, non-state actors are assuming rising salience in global political life.

What was an anarchic rabble of states has transformed itself into a society in which a variety of participants—not merely states, but also individuals, corporations, churches, regional and global organizations, bureaucrats, and courts—now have a voice and are determined to interact.[53]

This being so, his concern is to examine the extent to which international decision-making is organized in ways that can be considered fair. A wide diversity of actors may now have a voice in global affairs and be determined to interact. But—he asks—to what extent do their participation and interaction take place on fair terms? He contends that, despite changes which have occurred, two principles compromising the fairness of international decision-making processes remain dominant. First, in most international institutions each state has one vote, irrespective of the size of its population. Second, the predominant mode of organizing international decision-making is that only governments have a vote. It follows from the first principle that the citizens of small states are unfairly accorded a greater say than their counterparts in more

[50] Slaughter 1997, 185.   [51] Franck 1995.   [52] Franck 1995, ch. 4.   [53] Ibid. 477.

populous states. And it follows from the second principle that members of indigenous and other subaltern communities are unfairly deprived of adequate representation.

Franck concludes that the international system suffers from a serious 'fairness deficit'. To overcome (or at any rate reduce) this deficit, a new forum must in his view be created 'in which people rather than governments are directly represented'.[54] This would help to establish some correlation between population and representation. It would also give voice to groups that are currently disenfranchised. Franck proposes that such a forum might additionally offer a number of further benefits. It would enable excluded communities to enhance their participation in international affairs without claiming independent statehood, thus helping to curb the threat of secessionist violence. It would create a popular constituency with a stake in the activities of international institutions, and might in that way aid efforts to expand the role of the United Nations and other international organizations. It would encourage the mobilization of alliances across territorial lines, thereby serving to broaden understandings of national interest. And it would assist in monitoring compliance with an international legal norm of democratic governance. In his words, 'such a systemic reform would provide [an opportunity] for institutionalizing the democratic entitlement and certifying the authenticity of the link between people and their representatives . . .'.[55] Franck gives brief consideration to the question of how such a forum might be established. One possibility, which he endorses at least as an initial stage, is the widely mooted idea that the United Nations General Assembly might be divided into a two-chamber body, with one chamber constituted along current lines, and the other constituted through direct election and on the basis that seats are allocated in proportion to population size. Resolutions on important matters could then be required to be passed by a majority of both chambers. Since the consent of the chamber comprising governments would always be needed, he observes that 'little actual power would be transferred from governments to popular representatives at this stage of reform'. It would be 'on the ethos of the international community, not on the allocation of political power, that such reform would have its impact'.[56] Franck stresses, however, that his primary aim is less to argue for this particular reform than to highlight the need for current procedures of intergovernmental decision-making to be supplemented through the creation of a global popular forum. Insofar as global politics continues to be conceived as a 'conversation between nations', that 'limited view . . . is wrong', he holds. 'Not only is it inaccurate'; it is also unfair.[57] But is it *undemocratic?*

For all his evident concern with the shortcomings of international governance, it is striking that Franck refrains from characterizing those shortcomings as challenges for democracy, and treats them instead as instances of unfairness. He pointedly modifies a familiar phrase in calling attention to the 'fairness deficit' of the international system. More generally, he detaches the question of extending democracy's purchase from the problem of improving global decision-making processes. When presenting

---

[54] Ibid. 482.   [55] Ibid.   [56] Ibid. 484.   [57] Ibid.

his case for the democratic entitlement, he does not deal with international political structures. When addressing international political structures, he does refer to the democratic entitlement, but in a way which confirms that the latter finds expression in the arena of national politics; efforts to make the international system more fair are said to provide a means for helping to monitor compliance by national authorities with the norm of democratic governance. As in Slaughter's otherwise very different account, the assumption appears, then, to be that democracy is a form of national government, and pan-national democracy the corresponding global project. Yet, once again, such an approach sits uneasily with the recognition of changes in the international polity. While Franck in some respects sidesteps the issues raised above in connection with Slaughter's analysis, in other respects his discussion of the fairness of international forums exemplifies those issues, and also brings into relief a number of further points.

An initial concern arises from the *focus* of the effort to pass beyond a 'limited view' of global politics. In examining 'who has a voice and how decisions are reached' in global affairs, Franck takes his bearings from the procedures of international organizations.[58] What of the phenomenon to which Slaughter attaches so much importance? Transgovernmental networking, if overemphasized by Slaughter, is largely put to one side in Franck's account. On the other hand, Franck shares Slaughter's tendency to underrate the political significance of developments in the international economy. Had his analysis encompassed these 'unofficial' and 'private' settings, the scale of the problem he seeks to address might have appeared considerably larger. The fairness of international decision-making processes might have been seen as compromised not just by the failure to make allowance for disparities in the population size of states, and not just by the exclusion from consensus or vote of representatives of non-state communities. The fairness of those processes might also have been seen as compromised by the fact that decisions are taken in forums containing no representative from some of the states where outcomes are produced, as well as in private-sector forums regulated in the interests of a fraction of those affected—and in some cases scarcely regulated at all. Put differently, asymmetries of participation in institutionalized international activity might have seemed a small subset of the skewed relations that form the context for global governance today.

This then prompts reflection on the *scope* of the effort to pass beyond a limited view of global politics. As noted, Franck considers how international procedures might help to support national democracy (or at any rate to support the turn to democratic constitutions). But he does not ask how those procedures might work to constrain national democracy. The logic of his analysis is that the organization of international politics is presumptively neutral with respect to the conduct of national politics, that international political arrangements are without necessary consequence for the quality of national democratic life. Yet (to recall earlier discussion once again) globalization entails that international and national domains are less separable than

⁵⁸ Franck 1995, 478.

ever. The condition of nation-states cannot be understood in isolation from the wider web in which relationships and institutions are enmeshed. And if that is so, then correspondingly the prospects for democracy cannot be understood in isolation from that wider web. Moves to promote democracy in national polities must be accompanied by, and linked to, moves to promote democracy (not just 'fairness') in the international polity. In turn, steps to democratize 'official' international activity must be accompanied by, and linked to, steps to democratize other sites of decision-making with global or transnational impact. From this angle, Franck's unease about the international 'fairness deficit' appears an advance on Slaughter's celebration of transgovernmentalism. But it remains difficult to see how even his combination of national democracy and public-international fairness can suffice.

Finally, there is the question of the *character* of the effort to pass beyond a limited view of global politics. In order to alleviate the unfair operation of current procedures, Franck advocates the establishment of a new popular forum. He observes that such a forum might be grafted onto the existing structures of the United Nations. Whatever the merits of this idea, a different approach is required once the focus and scope of analysis are widened and the points just raised taken into account. Fairness may call for institutional and procedural reform. Democracy, however, demands change of transformative proportions. If global governance is to be democratized, proposals concerning particular institutions and procedures need to be connected to a much more far-reaching project directed to enhancing the prospects for popular participation and redressing inequalities in the extent to which, and the forms in which, opportunities to participate are made available. Such fundamental issues have to be opened to question as the character of political community, the nature of political agency, the constitution of the sovereign people, the significance of territorial boundaries. It follows that an approach centred on reform also falls short in another respect. A project of this kind cannot be pursued by remaining at the level of practical proposals and technical solutions, important as those undoubtedly are. Debate must be initiated on the theoretical, and ultimately political, question of what global democracy should mean.

The thrust of the argument presented here is that on this question Franck and Slaughter are *ad idem*, even if they are at variance on the issue of how the international polity should be characterized and evaluated. Both take global democracy to mean the universalization of national democracy. Though Franck embraces the weak globalization thesis with fewer hesitations than Slaughter seemingly does, he still shares her reluctance to pursue the implications of this thesis in the manner of David Held and others. He still pulls back from the notion that democracy should become a transnational, even non-territorial, affair. As already noted, this approach has not gone unchallenged. Alston is one of a number of international legal scholars who insist on the inadequacy of pan-national democracy to meet the challenges of contemporary circumstances.[59] For him, there is an urgent need to enhance awareness of

[59] Prominent among these scholars are Richard Falk (see esp. Falk 1995*a*, ch. 4 and Falk 1998, discussed in Ch. 5 below) and Dianne Otto (see esp. Otto 1993).

how far 'the emerging shape of the international system reflects the principles of transparency, participation and accountability' by which national arrangements are increasingly judged.[60] Remarking on the disparity between the central role of international lawyers as 'in many respects . . . the handmaidens of the changes wrought by globalization' and the marginal place within international legal debates of the ramifications of these changes,[61] Alston writes of the 'myopia' of globalization's international legal handmaidens.[62] But is this a case of inability to see, or of unwillingness to do so?

Legitimating Pan-National Democracy

The discussion so far has concentrated on clarifying the notion of global democracy that informs the democratic norm thesis. By reference to the work of two of its most prominent proponents, I have tried to show how the thesis rests on a pan-national account of global democratic governance. Global democracy is conceived as the sum of national democracies. At the same time, I have sought to illustrate the limitations of such an account, the way it neglects to register important—indeed growing—arenas of unaccountable power and sources of social disadvantage. If these are to be reduced, efforts to democratize national politics must be accompanied by specific steps to democratize systems of transnational and global decision-making. The question which must now be addressed is that of the impact of the democratic norm thesis for the prospects of this more expansive vision of democratic global governance. Some might argue that the thesis is at worst neutral with respect to cosmopolitan democracy, inasmuch as the wider issues of democratizing systems of transnational and global decision-making are simply left to be taken up on another occasion. However, just as in Chapter 3 I proposed that moves to promote democracy also serve as moves to constrain democracy, so too here my contention is that moves to promote democracy within nation-states serve as moves to constrain democracy in international and transnational affairs. Pan-national parameters work actively, even if unintentionally, to check cosmopolitan ambitions. Thus, once again, I maintain that ideology is in play, and in the paragraphs that follow I highlight some of the strategies deployed.

As in relation to low intensity democracy, perhaps the most powerful strategies operate in the mode of *naturalization*. The notion that modern democracy could be anything other than a form of nation-state government is removed from contemplation. Most straightforwardly, the democratic norm thesis accomplishes this by means of an *assumption*. It is assumed, without discussion, that democracy belongs within the national domain and that, conversely, the international domain is inherently resistant to democratization. The nation-state is taken to be democracy's container—not, of course, in the sense that national polities are impermeable, but rather in the

---

[60] Alston 1997, 447.   [61] Ibid. 435.
[62] Thus, the title of Alston 1997: 'The Myopia of the Handmaidens: International Lawyers and Globalization'.

sense that the world beyond is a distinct realm which cannot be expected to serve as the incubator for an authentic democratic community. Thus, pan-national democracy is made to appear the self-evident and incontestable meaning of global democracy. The same effect is produced through the use of *dichotomous reasoning*. Slaughter, for instance, defends her claim that a transgovernmental order is emerging, in which the democratization of global politics is achieved through the establishment and invocation of national democratic processes, on the basis that alternative analyses invite us to suppose that the nation-state is disappearing. She considers two alternative analyses. One envisions the building of world government, in the form of international institutions with centralized rule-making authority. The other imagines that state power will be replaced by private power, in the shape of informal networks of non-governmental actors and agencies of various kinds.[63] By ruling out intermediate analyses, in which the state remains pivotal but its capacities, orientations and activities are seen to have changed and other significant parties are seen to have acquired important roles in the process of governance, she makes it appear natural that the focus should be on national political institutions. The insight that the 'state is not disappearing' becomes an irrefutable argument against any suggestion that specific efforts are required to democratize transnational and international politics.[64]

A second set of ideological strategies operates in the mode of *unification*. The democratic norm thesis is linked to an account of contemporary globalization which tends to reduce the complexity and unevenness of the processes underway. As highlighted earlier, while Slaughter underrates the enduring role of international organizations, Franck pays too little regard to the significance of transgovernmental networks, and both attach insufficient importance to the 'private' domain of transnational business. Where the impact of globalization is *simplified* in this way, the scale of the democratic challenge posed is correspondingly understated. Attention is drawn away from the democratic deficits of international organizations, transgovernmental networks, and transnational business, and away from the inadequacy of national action to make up those deficits. But the problem is not just that awareness is occluded of the need to democratize particular arenas of decision-making. It is also that awareness is occluded of the ways in which globalizing processes serve to intensify existing patterns of dependency, marginalization and deprivation. By passing over the uneven dynamics and differentiated impact of globalization, these analysts foster the idea that the context for democratizing efforts, even if not unified, is at least constant. Democratization is portrayed as unfolding in a world in which subsisting gaps between haves and have-nots are unaffected by ongoing changes in the sphere of globalization, perhaps even narrowed by them. And if that is so, then the best policy seems to be 'wait and see', or, at any rate, 'carry on as usual'. The urgency of developing new approaches to global governance becomes difficult to grasp.

These ideas are further buttressed, thirdly, through strategies of *reification*, among

---

[63] See Slaughter 1997, 183–4.   [64] Ibid. 184.

them the use of particular *figurative devices*. As noted in Chapter 3, the democratic norm thesis (in common with much argumentation) structures discussion of democracy in terms of a distinctive metaphor: democracy is figured as a place. In Chapter 3 my main concern was to highlight the dehistoricizing impact of this. It makes democracy appear an event, rather than a process; a state of being, rather than an orientation for change. Societies engaged in democratic reconstruction are depicted as confronting a journey towards a predetermined end, a journey that involves the negation, rather than the transformation, of what went before. Societies of long-standing democratic commitment are depicted as having arrived, and facing only the challenge of defending existing democratic gains. Here, however, another aspect of this metaphor's impact comes into focus. In addition to these temporal implications, the idea that democracy is to be understood as a place clearly also has spatial implications. If (national) societies can travel towards, or have arrived at, democracy, then democracy appears as mapped onto, and hence coextensive with, the societies themselves. Thus, the democratic norm thesis encourages the notion that a democratic community is a nationally defined community. More generally, it encourages the notion that a democratic community is a territorially bounded community, and conversely discourages the move— articulated by David Held, William Connolly and others—to respond to the political challenges of globalization by untying democracy from the 'idea of locality and place' and reconceiving it in 'cosmopolitan' or 'nonterritorial' terms.[65]

Another figurative device which helps to make modern democracy seem necessarily national in scope is perhaps also worth highlighting. In arguments relating to the norm of democratic governance discussion is frequently structured in terms of synecdoche, such that a specific country—notably, the United States—is made to stand for the whole world. Thus, for instance, when Slaughter writes that 'nations [will not] cede their power and sovereignty to an international institution',[66] she refers to an attitude which is influential in the United States, but does not hold sway—or, at any rate, does not hold sway to the same extent—in many nations. Likewise, when she writes that 'human rights lawyers are more likely to develop transnational litigation strategies for domestic courts than to petition the UN Committee on Human Rights',[67] she again generalizes from the distinctive situation of a country that has a record of exceptional reluctance to participate in international systems for the protection of human rights. It is not possible to make complaints against the United States to the Human Rights Committee because the United States has not ratified the treaty—the (First) Optional Protocol to the Covenant on Civil and Political Rights—which would authorize the Committee to receive such complaints. Most nations of the world, however, have ratified this treaty and/or taken steps to authorize other international and regional supervisory bodies to receive complaints against them, and in these nations procedures of this kind continue to be valued and pursued when local remedies are unavailable. By making the United States appear to represent the world as a whole, Slaughter establishes the proposition that resistance to democ-

---

[65] Held 1995*a*, 278; Connolly 1991, 219–20.   [66] Slaughter 1997, 183.   [67] Ibid. 185.

ratic global governance is overriding, and that democratizing efforts must remain focused on national politics. This use of reifying synecdoche points to the deployment of a further ideological strategy, labelled in Chapter 1 *performative contradiction*. That is to say, what is claimed is at odds with the context of the utterance itself. The gap here between universal claim and parochial context is also the gap, highlighted by Rob Walker, between democracy's 'universalist aspiration and particularist realisation', and between 'structures of power that seem to be increasingly internationalised, globalised, in some sense universalised and processes of participation, representation, accountability and legitimation that remain rooted in the institutionalised apparatuses of states'.[68]

A final set of strategies works in the mode of *justification*. The identification of global democracy with pan-national democracy is *rationalized* on the basis that democracy is best pursued in national political arenas; with regard to international arenas, attention should be directed to problems of a different order, such as fairness and efficiency. Thus, discussion of global governance centres on institutional and procedural reform in the interests of improved fairness, or on the reorganization of decision-making systems in the interests of enhanced efficiency. In this way, once again the issues are made to seem largely technical; the extent to which goal-setting is implicated and distributive policies are shaped is removed from view, and democratic concerns about the relationship between those experiencing outcomes and those taking decisions are thereby marginalized. It is certainly the case, as noted earlier, that moves to democratize processes of international decision-making are difficult to specify. As Connolly observes, the 'project of nonterritorial democratization necessarily exudes an air of unreality', given the lack of any territorial base in which anchor democratic forms. As he also observes, however, the impact of globalizing processes has been to heighten the extent to which nation-state democracy 'exudes its own aura of unreality'.[69] The democratic norm thesis tends to block awareness of this latter unreality by detaching the question of changes at the level of national politics from the question of changes in the character of international polity, the prospects for national democracy from the possibilities of global democracy. Despite the claims of Fox and others that, with the emerging norm of democratic governance, popular sovereignty is replacing state sovereignty, the logic of the thesis is, then, that national sovereignty continues to define the terms of democratic citizenship.

CONCLUSIONS

In 1987 Daniel Bell offered the 'prediction' that in the succeeding decades the nation-state would be increasingly sidelined; it would become, in his much quoted phrase, 'too small for the big problems of life, and too big for the small problems'.[70] As the twenty-first century begins, states show little sign of remaining other than

---

[68] Walker 1993, 143.   [69] Connolly 1991, 219.   [70] Bell 1987, 14 (emphasis omitted).

central to the organization of political life. Yet Bell was not wholly wrong, and one reason is that his prediction was to a degree a self-fulfilling prophesy.[71] Owing in part to deregulatory moves urged by people like him, the context in which national politics occurs has altered significantly. Governments must today contend with the unprecedented might of global markets, the revolution in transnational communications, the reassertion of local solidarities and multiple identities. In some respects the nation-state is indeed challenged by the scale of the problems confronting it—too small to cope alone with the demands of economic regulation and environmental protection; too big to respond adequately to grassroots needs and cultural claims. These 'big' and 'small' issues are, moreover, the ones that now dominate political agendas; the problem of monopolizing the use of force—the nation-state's most venerable function—has declined in relative importance.

How are these developments to be characterized and evaluated? Like all keywords globalization names a much contested concept. Some celebrate it as the dawn of a free market utopia. Others dismiss what they see as so much neo-liberal myth-making. Still others neither celebrate globalization nor dismiss the concept. As they see it, to assert that the state is becoming impotent is to encourage us to believe that the market must rule. But to suggest that the state is unaffected by the changes underway is also to foster a degree of reconciliation to fate. From this third perspective, globalization serves as a critical tool, to help in highlighting the problems, as well as the possibilities, of our contemporary circumstances. One set of problems and possibilities concerns democracy. If national options are now shaped in significant ways by action in international organizations, transgovernmental networks, global markets, and transnational 'civil society', then—scholars observe—the nation-state cannot continue to be regarded as modern democracy's 'container'. National democratic politics cannot be understood without reference to international forces. Furthermore, democracy cannot flourish in nation-states unless efforts are made to democratize the processes of transnational and global decision-making as well. Since power relations do not stop at national borders, democratic principles must not be allowed to stop there either.

This chapter has re-examined the democratic norm thesis with these points in mind. I have argued that the thesis precisely does allow democracy to stop at national borders. More than that, whether intentionally or unintentionally, it encourages democracy to do so. Just as in the previous chapter I proposed that the democratic norm thesis works to stabilize existing power relations by identifying democracy with low intensity democracy, so here I have sought to show how the thesis works to stabilize existing power relations by identifying global democracy with pan-national democracy. If these arguments are compelling, then the critics of the thesis are right that the norm is problematic, and not only on the grounds reviewed in Chapter 2. The question that must now be addressed is: what then follows? For recall that critique is concerned not just to investigate how ideas sustain domination. It is also concerned to investigate how those same ideas may provide resources for transformative change.

[71] On the partly 'self-fulfilling' character of *all* social scientific analysis, see the discussion of the 'reflexivity' of modern social life in Ch. 6 below.

Chapter 5

International Law and the Project of Cosmopolitan Democracy

What happens when ideals begin to seem like illusions?[1] The preceding chapters have shown how the proposal which some international legal scholars have elaborated for an international legal 'norm of democratic governance' operates as ideology. A move to promote democracy through international law becomes a step in securing systematic inequalities among states, within states, and in global governance generally. It is a familiar story. We start out singing of autonomy, justice, and solidarity, and of the great ideas through which those aspirations might be brought to social reality (international law, democracy, even better a combination of the two), and end up legitimating domination. One obvious remedy immediately suggests itself. International lawyers should stop singing of democracy. They should drop the effort to fashion international legal norms out of democratic agendas, leave off trying to turn international law into democracy's champion, and accept that their discipline's contribution (and also their own) is best carried forward in the name of other, less illusory ideals. That may be what Martti Koskenniemi has in mind when he writes that a democratic norm is 'too easily used against revolutionary politics that aim at the roots of the existing distributionary system'. In any event, such a norm is unlikely to prove acceptable, he observes, because it is simultaneously 'both over- and under inclusive . . . too general to provide political guidance and always suspect as a neocolonialist strategy'. If international lawyers want to support emancipatory struggles, then he proposes that they would do well to put aside ideas of universal democracy and turn their attention instead to 'more concrete forms of political commitment'.[2]

Does this not concede too much, however? One of the most important reminders delivered by twentieth-century history is surely that modernity is a deeply ambiguous inheritance. Writing in Germany in the 1920s and 1930s, the theorists of the Frankfurt School were appalled to witness the way ideas which promised freedom were deployed to justify tyranny. Fascist governments came to power through competitive elections. Fundamental rights were denied in accordance with law. Genocide unfolded with the highest regard for procedural correctness and administrative efficiency. Yet these theorists resisted the conclusion that the concepts in question—among them democracy, but also rationality, equality, constitutionalism, the rule of law, and so on—should be ditched. Thomas McCarthy recalls how in 1933 Max

---

[1] I owe this formulation to Thomas McCarthy's 'Ideals and Illusions'. See McCarthy 1993.
[2] Koskenniemi 1996, 234–5. See Ch. 2 above. See also Ch. 6 below for a discussion of the relationship between scholarly enquiry and political commitment in the sphere of international law.

Horkheimer urged scholars 'not to surrender such ideas to the regressive forces who used them to justify their privileged positions and betrayed them whenever it was in their interest to do so'. Rather, he maintained that scholars should 'critically reappropriate [the ideas] for progressive purposes'.[3] In Horkheimer's words: 'The battle cries of the Enlightenment and of the French Revolution are valid now more than ever . . . Politics should not abandon those demands, but realize them . . . not, however, by clinging . . . to historically conditioned definitions of them, but in accordance with their meaning. The content of these ideas is not eternal but subject to historical change . . . because the human impulses that demand something better take [historically] different forms'.[4] A few years later, Herbert Marcuse reiterated the call to '[preserve through reconstruction] truths that past generations [had] struggled to attain'.[5] In a society that 'gives the lie to all these universals', he famously insisted, 'adherence to universality is more important than its philosophical destruction'.[6] These theorists' concern to temper scepticism for the sake of critique led them to emphasize the Janus-faced character of modernity's central concepts. Because these concepts provide an ongoing basis for opposing repression, their enduring relevance or, in McCarthy's terminology, their 'context-transcending' import, must be defended. On the other hand, because these same concepts also provide an ongoing basis for drawing us back into repression, efforts to defend their context-transcending import must take the form of steps continually to rearticulate or 'recontextualize' them for emancipatory ends.

These observations suggest a different response to the pacifying potentials of the norm of democratic governance from that described in the opening paragraph. Rather than abandoning the project of fashioning international legal norms out of democratic agendas, and thus in effect leaving such norms to be fashioned in a way which works—as Koskenniemi warns—'against revolutionary politics that aim at the roots of the existing distributionary system' and 'as a neo-colonialist strategy', international lawyers should redirect that project to emancipatory ends. They should recapture the initiative *in favour of* revolutionary politics that aim at the roots of the existing distributionary system, redeploy an alliance between international law and democracy *against* neo-colonialism. Let us not forget Koskenniemi's other warning, however, that the concept of democracy is, in any case, 'too general to provide political guidance'. Is such a move doomed on the ground that, even if the problem of under-inclusiveness can be resolved, the problem of over-inclusiveness remains? To be sure, democracy does not settle the issue of what self-rule and equality are to mean in particular contexts. It leaves open the question of how these ideas are to be inscribed in real life. From the perspective adopted here, however, that is precisely the point.[7] The fact that democracy transcends contexts means that continuous

---

[3] McCarthy 1994, 21.

[4] Quoted McCarthy 1994, 21 (Horkheimer, M., 'Materialism and Morality', trans. Hunter, G. F. and Torpey, J., 69 *Telos* (1986) 85, 108).

[5] McCarthy 1994, 23.

[6] Quoted in ibid. 20 (Marcuse, H., 'Philosophy and Critical Theory', trans. Shapiro, J. in *Negations* (Boston: Beacon, 1968), 153).

[7] On this aspect, see further Conclusion below.

recontextualization is necessary. But the fact that democracy transcends contexts also means that continuous recontextualization in the struggle against oppression is *possible*. Democratic ideas provide a framework for emancipatory claims, the content of which cannot be anticipated in advance, for, as Horkheimer remarks, 'the human impulses that demand something better take [historically] different forms'. McCarthy explains that the effect of context-transcendence is to create a tension between the real and the ideal, and, in so doing, to generate a 'normative surplus of meaning' on which we can draw in seeking to overcome the limits of our current circumstances.[8] There is considerable evidence to suggest that contemporary political analysts share this appreciation of democracy's conceptual generality. Even the severest critics of existing democratic practices and institutions appear to assume that alternatives are to be sought within the 'normative surplus of meaning' to which democratic ideas give rise. When they condemn democracy as illusion, most analysts work—as observed in Chapters 3 and 4—to renew it as ideal.

How, then, might claims concerning the emerging norm of democratic governance be redirected to more emancipatory ends? How might an alliance between international law and democracy be turned into a more potent resource for transformative change? As a contribution to the consideration of these questions, this chapter puts forward one tentative proposal. The starting-point for this proposal is the project of cosmopolitan democracy, articulated by David Held and others. In the first part of the chapter I describe efforts to bring out the implications of cosmopolitan democracy for international law. For the most part, these efforts have focused on the need for institutional change. But, as observed in earlier discussion, conceptual change is at least as important. Could the norm of democratic governance be rethought to provide a conceptual framework for connecting international law with the project of cosmopolitan democracy? The second part of the chapter outlines my proposal. The crux of it is a principle which at first sight may appear to differ from the norm of democratic governance only in that it has a slightly modified and more pretentious name. I seek to define and defend a 'principle of democratic inclusion'. But I hope that, when I explain what I have in mind, the considerable substantive differences (as well as the logic of the principle's name) will become apparent. That said, I do not intend to press the case for this particular development too hard. My main aim is simply to illustrate the possibilities that open up if we respond to the limitations of the democratic norm thesis not by renouncing the effort to promote democracy through international law, but rather—in the spirit of Horkheimer and Marcuse—by trying to reconstruct the thesis for progressive purposes.

COSMOPOLITAN DEMOCRACY AND INTERNATIONAL LAW

The project of cosmopolitan democracy is, as indicated in Chapter 4, the project of creating a global democratic community which both includes and cuts across national

---

[8] McCarthy 1994, 21.

democratic communities. In place of the idea that the nation-state is democracy's container, it seeks to entrench the idea that democracy is relevant wherever and whenever action is taken which affects the capacity of individuals and groups to determine the conditions of their collective lives. The basis for this move is a belief that democracy should be understood not just as a method of producing governments but as an ideal of popular self-rule and equal citizenship. The project of cosmopolitan democracy seeks to bring to bear on this conception of democracy an awareness of the impact of globalizing processes. The result is a call for simultaneous efforts to deepen democracy within nation-states and extend democracy to international and transnational settings. What are the implications of this for international law? Highlighted in the paragraphs that follow are comments on the relationship between cosmopolitan democracy and international law by David Held, as well as by two other analysts.

For Held far-reaching changes are needed to democratize the polity of which international law is the law.[9] In particular, he highlights three key requirements. First, systems of accountability must be extended, to enable issues which elude the regulatory capacity of individual national governments—'global financial flows, the debt burden of developing countries, environmental crises, elements of security and defence, new forms of communication and so on'—to be brought under better democratic control. Secondly, established agencies of geogovernance must be reoriented and restructured, so that they provide a more coherent and effective focus for public affairs. Thirdly, the place of an international public sphere must be acknowledged and strengthened, through the closer articulation of international civil society and its diverse associations and organizations with international political institutions.[10] Held considers that an initial step which might be taken in addressing these requirements 'lies within the grasp of the UN system'. This would consist of 'living up to' existing commitments, through (for example) enhanced efforts to implement UN Charter provisions regarding the non-use of force and collective security, and enhanced support for UN and treaty-based institutions concerned with the protection of human rights.[11] He suggests that further steps might be taken by modifications within the framework of subsisting institutions. The jurisdiction of the International Court of Justice might, for instance, be made compulsory in certain circumstances; UN General Assembly resolutions might in some contexts be made to count for more as sources of international law than is currently the case; and the composition and voting procedures of the Security Council might be altered to allow wider regional representation. But Held observes that such developments would still represent, at best, limited progress in meeting the requirements of a democratic international polity. 'This governance system would remain . . . a state-centred . . . model of international politics, and would lie at some considerable distance from what might be called a "thicker" democratic ordering of global affairs'.[12]

Held contends that a thicker democratic ordering of global affairs would depend on restructuring the existing framework of geogovernance in a number of funda-

---

[9] See Held 1995*a*, ch. 12.   [10] Held 1995*a*, 267–8.   [11] Ibid. 269.
[12] Ibid. 270.

mental respects. He suggests that the changes involved might be thought of as 'the necessary minimum components of an institutional solution to the problems of democracy in the global order'.[13] In the first place, the avenues would need to be expanded for individuals and groups to assert democratic rights before international tribunals. International judicial authorities would need to become more centrally engaged than at present in the process of building democratic systems of governance which involve, but also crosscut, nation-states. At the same time, measures would be needed to expand international legislative and executive competences. Thus, for example, existing regional parliaments might be strengthened and additional ones created. New procedures might be introduced to extend the possibilities for public control of transnational economic activity. Consideration might even be given to the use of transnational referenda on issues of transnational concern. For Held, however, a democratic framework of geogovernance also has a further minimum component which goes beyond those mentioned. There needs to be established 'an independent assembly of democratic peoples, directly elected by them and accountable to them'.[14] This could take the form of a reformed UN General Assembly, or it could be a complement to the existing General Assembly. But either way (in contrast to the assembly proposed by Thomas Franck and mentioned in Chapter 4) it would have to enjoy independent decision-making authority. Of course, were political authority to 'be "sucked" upwards in [such a] new cross-border democratic settlement', the aims of cosmopolitan democracy would hardly be served.[15] Most decisions are most appropriately taken in local, national or regional settings, rather than at global level. Thus, Held emphasizes that the establishment of new global governance institutions would need to go hand in hand with efforts to elaborate principles to direct particular issues to particular levels of decision-making.

Held is aware that his proposed 'institutional solution to the problems of democracy in the global order' is itself fraught with problems, the solution of which is in some cases extremely difficult to envisage. He suggests that a distinction should be drawn between changes that can serve as short-term objectives, such as reform of the UN Security Council, and changes that might serve as long-term objectives, such as the creation of a global popular assembly.[16] More generally, he comments on the relation between political feasibility and political ambition. While 'the question of political feasibility is of the utmost significance', he writes, it cannot be allowed to dictate the limits of political ambition, '[f]or what is ambitious today might prove feasible tomorrow'.[17] Of course, concerns about feasibility are not the only kinds of concerns to which Held's proposals might give rise. There is plenty of room for debate about the extent to which the specific reforms and innovations he advocates are indeed appropriate ambitions for those seeking the institutionalization of global democracy. Should it be, as Held recommends, a short-term objective to strengthen the legislative role of the UN General Assembly? Should it be a short-term objective to make the jurisdiction of the International Court of Justice compulsory in certain circumstances? Should it

---

[13] Ibid. 272.   [14] Ibid. 273.   [15] Ibid. 235.   [16] Ibid. 279–80.   [17] Ibid. 285.

be a long-term objective to create a global popular assembly with binding authority
in some spheres?

Whatever view is taken of the short- and long-term objectives which should govern efforts to institutionalize global democracy, one thing is certain. The success of
those efforts will depend not just on calls for institutional change. It will also depend
on (among other things) the extent to which institutional change is supported by relevant ideas and concepts. Quite patently, the prospects for restructuring global governance will be enhanced if global governance is informed by a framework of ideas
and concepts within which restructuring appears justified, and even more so if it is
informed by a framework within which restructuring appears necessary or urgent.
Conversely, those prospects will be reduced where the framework of ideas and concepts is such that restructuring appears irrational, unnecessary or unimportant. As
observed in Chapter 4, proposals for institutional reform become ideological if they
are not accompanied by moves to ground the reform at the level of consciousness.
Recognizing this, Held devotes considerable attention to the theoretical dimensions
of the project of cosmopolitan democracy, and elaborates a cluster of foundational
ideas, assembled around what he refers to as the 'principle of autonomy', and the need
to defend that principle in relation to all the various systems of power which contribute to generating conditions of 'nautonomy' (defined as the 'asymmetrical production and distribution of life-chances which limit and erode the possibilities of
political participation').[18] These ideas provide a deep grounding for the institutionalization of cosmopolitan democracy within political theory. But, since our focus here
is on this project's international legal implications, the question that must now pre-
occupy us is to what extent such a grounding also exists within international law.

The sphere of international legal activity which is most often discussed in this context is human rights. David Beetham considers that the human rights regime might
even serve as a kind of 'model for the project of cosmopolitan democracy'.[19] On the
one hand, the universalism inherent in the notion of human rights supplies a *cosmopolitan* orientation. On the other hand, that cosmopolitan orientation attaches to
a set of rights which broadly corresponds to the requirements for *democratic* citizenship. Thus, for Beetham, the human rights regime instantiates the union of cosmopolitanism and democracy itself. He observes that a certain universalism is also
inherent in the concept of democracy itself. Embodied in that concept is 'the universalist assumption that all adults are capable of making reflective choices about collective priorities, given the relevant information', and 'there is no reason why this
assumption should stop short at national boundaries'.[20] But the historical fact is that
it did come to stop short at national boundaries; in the context of the modern state
the *demos* did come to be defined in national terms. By contrast, the concept of
human rights 'has from the outset been universalist in aspiration and global in its
scope of operation'.[21] It posits that certain rights are enjoyed by virtue of humanity,
rather than citizenship. Insofar as these rights are now protected through inter-

---

[18] Held 1995*a*, 147 (principle of autonomy), 171 (nautonomy); see generally chs. 7–8.
[19] Beetham 1998, 58.   [20] Ibid. 59.   [21] Ibid.

national law and institutions, it engages a process which proceeds 'from the international to the national and local levels, rather than vice versa as is the case with democracy'.[22] At the same time, it shares the democratic concern to enable participation in the choice of collective priorities. Beetham concludes that the regime of human rights speaks precisely to the possibility which the project of cosmopolitan democracy takes as its aim—the possibility of unsettling the assumed territoriality of democracy, bridging the gap between humanity and citizenship, and pursuing a dual agenda of deepening democracy within nation-states and extending it to global governance.

That said, Beetham recognizes that the human rights regime has severe limitations. In particular, he writes, 'the weak point of this regime is that of enforcement'.[23] Efforts to enforce human rights are compromised by the fact that 'states are at one and the same time the necessary agents for the implementation of human rights, and also among their chief violators, or at least colluders in their violation'.[24] A tension exists between the supranational ambitions of the human rights system and the world of sovereign states in which that system is inserted. In the result, the recognition of human rights is consistent with the maintenance of systemic barriers to their enforcement. Yet this is by no means the only tension within the human rights regime, and enforcement is by no means that regime's only weakness. From the standpoint of cosmopolitan democracy, at least two further strains are surely significant. In the first place, there is the widely remarked tension between the proclaimed indivisibility of civil, political, economic, social, and cultural rights and the priority accorded to some of those rights. This affects the prospects for deepening democracy within nation-states for, if equality is to be secured in the opportunities for political participation, all categories of human rights need protection. Secondly, there is the tension between the universalism inherent in the concept of human rights and the state-centric scope of these rights' implementation. This affects the prospects for extending democracy to global governance for, if accountability is to be secured in transnational and international affairs, human rights must be seen to create relationships of entitlement and obligation that cross national boundaries. The first of these two strains is reflected in the fact that, as demonstrated in Chapter 3, the recognition of human rights is consistent with the promotion of low intensity democracy. The second is reflected in the fact that, as demonstrated in Chapter 4, the recognition of human rights is consistent with the pursuit of pan-national democracy. Beetham, then, may be right that the human rights regime instantiates the union of cosmopolitanism and democracy. But if so, that union is clearly not without unresolved issues. Just as he proposes that those concerned with the project of cosmopolitan democracy should look to the regime of human rights, perhaps those concerned with the regime of human rights would also do well to look to the project of cosmopolitan democracy.

Richard Falk is the international legal scholar who, arguably more than any other, has looked to the project of cosmopolitan democracy. He writes of the way 'traditional [i.e. territorial] democracy becomes increasingly marginalized and formalized

[22] Ibid. 59–60.   [23] Ibid. 64.   [24] Ibid. 58.

insofar as authority over an integrated world economy and information order is shaped by extraterritorial forces'. At the same time, 'such democracy may be accompanied by varying degrees of social regression as a result of the impact of capital-driven geogovernance'.[25] Given '[t]he realities of globalization', he argues, 'democratization efforts [must] be extended to geopolitical and market arenas, as well as "internalized" at all levels of political organization'.[26] Falk shares Held's assessment that this in turn requires that new systems of transnational accountability be developed, existing structures of geogovernance be democratized, and the role of international civil society be strengthened. As to how these aims might be advanced, he comments that 'it is difficult to be more than heuristic at this stage, pointing to the need and to possible directions of democratizing efforts, but being hazy about means and effects . . .'. Extending democracy to geopolitical and market arenas 'is more problematic to depict in situational terms than is the familiar political terrain of state/society relations'.[27] The obvious reason is that democratic practices and institutions have only been developed for particular national settings, and one of the few certainties of international and transnational democracy is presumably that they cannot entail the simple transposition of national forms. The main focus of his discussion is on the possibilities for enhanced enforcement of international legal commitments and for the restructuring of international agencies, especially the United Nations.[28]

Falk also shares Held's concern to support these changes at the level of ideas and concepts. He seeks to ground his call to extend and internalize democracy by means of the concept of 'humane governance'.[29] By this he intends a model of global governance which departs from earlier forms of geopolitics, both in that it is more concerned with justice (including social justice) and in that it is more concerned with public control of political–economic systems. Thus, humane governance refers to 'the effective realization of human rights, including economic and social rights, and the extension of participatory mechanisms and accountability procedures to the arenas of decision in which geopolitical and global market forces are operative'.[30] The concept of humane governance, were it to take root, could certainly help in justifying efforts to deepen democracy within states and extend democracy to international and transnational settings. To what extent, however, could it help in harnessing the resources of international law to that endeavour? To what extent could it lay a basis for reshaping international legal doctrines and processes, so as not only to justify moves to democratize global politics, but even to compel such moves and demand that they be given priority? As a means of grounding the project of cosmopolitan democracy within international law, Falk's notion of human governance seems, to use his word, relatively hazy. Is this the price which must be paid for overcoming the limitations of the democratic norm thesis? Or is there a way of connecting international law with democratic struggles which avoids both the critical haziness of the

---

[25] Falk 1995a, 107.   [26] Ibid. 131.   [27] Ibid.
[28] Ibid., esp. chs. 4 and 7. See also Falk 1995b and 1998.   [29] See generally Falk 1995a.
[30] Ibid. 125.

concept of humane governance and the ideological restrictiveness of the norm of democratic governance?

In this section I outline a proposal for what I shall term the 'principle of democratic inclusion'.[31] Let me begin by explaining why I call it this. I use the expression 'democratic inclusion' to signal the distinctive conception of democracy which is to inform the principle. This is a very different conception from that which informs the norm of democratic governance. As noted in earlier discussion, the norm of democratic governance rests on the supposition that democracy is to be understood, in this context, as a method of producing legitimate governments. What characterizes that method is the holding of periodic multiparty elections, within the framework of institutions which guarantee respect for the rule of law and safeguard civil rights. In Franck's words, '[t]he term "democracy", as used in international rights parlance, is intended to connote the kind of governance that is legitimated by the consent of the governed'.[32] Though conscious of the shortcomings of this conception, Franck considers that it 'probably represents the limit of what the still frail system of states can be expected to accept and promote as a right of people assertable against their own, and other, governments'.[33] In Chapters 3 and 4 I highlighted the ideological, and partly self-fulfilling, character of assertions such as this. In any event, as will be explained below, I do not seek to argue that democratic inclusion is the basis of a distinct right of people assertable against their own, and other, governments. Thus, even if low intensity democracy and pan-national democracy did reflect the necessary limit of what the international system might be expected to accept and promote as such a right, my proposal would not be affected.

With these points in mind, I tie the principle of democratic inclusion to a conception of democracy along the lines of that which underpins the project of cosmopolitan democracy. In this conception—to recall Held's account—democracy is seen to entail not only a particular set of institutions and procedures, but also, and more generally, an ongoing call to enlarge the opportunities for popular participation in political processes and end social practices that systematically marginalize some citizens while empowering others. In turn, these goals are seen, under conditions of intensifying globalization, to require 'a model of political organization in which citizens, wherever located in the world, have voice, input and political representation in international affairs, in parallel with and independently of their own governments'.[34] The concept of democratic inclusion refers, then, to the belief that democracy is to be understood as an ideal of popular self-rule and political equality, and that this ideal has relevance not

---

[31] I am indebted to the LL M International Human Rights Law class of 1998–9 at the University of Cambridge for help in framing the arguments of this section. I wish to record my thanks to the members of that class.

[32] Franck 1994, 75. See Ch. 2 above.   [33] Ibid. 75.   [34] Archibugi & Held 1995, 13.

just in national politics, but in international and indeed all other political settings as well. It refers to the notion that democratic politics is less a matter of forms and events than an affair of relationships and processes, an open-ended and continually recontextualized agenda of enhancing control by citizens of decision-making which affects them and overcoming disparities in the distribution of citizenship rights and opportunities. Why specify this approach in terms of 'inclusion'? Because inclusion is a theme of many contemporary attempts to capture the problem which this particular conception of democracy seeks to address. For Andrew Linklater, for example, global politics can be viewed as a constellation of systems of exclusion and inclusion, operating both within societies and among them, and the issue is always how to make those systems more inclusory. As he puts it, the challenge is to '[widen] the moral boundaries of political communities' and '[enlarge] the sphere in which human beings treat one another as equals'.[35] This is not to say, of course, that all exclusionary practices must be regarded as unjust. It is just to say that 'decisions about the justice of exclusionary practices [should not be] monopolised by dominant groups'.[36]

I use the word 'principle' to signal the distinctive status within international law which this concept of democratic inclusion is to enjoy. This is a very different status from that which is involved in the norm of democratic governance. As once again noted in earlier discussion, the democratic norm thesis postulates that democratic governance should be, and is arguably becoming, a criterion of international legal legitimacy. Only democratic governments will be recognized for international legal purposes as the legitimate representatives of states. More than that, however, the thesis postulates that democratic governance should be, and arguably is becoming, an international legal entitlement. Thus, Franck writes of the emerging 'right to democratic governance', and tries to mobilize international lawyers to the task of developing mechanisms for monitoring and enforcing this right. For him and other proponents of the democratic norm thesis, a new consensus has arisen with respect to the right to vote and stand as a candidate in periodic multiparty elections, the impact of which has been to extend the scope of universally recognized human rights. In Chapters 3 and 4 I called attention to the danger that a right to democratic governance might instead serve to *reduce* the scope of universally recognized rights, by reinforcing pressures to detach, on the one hand, civil and political rights from economic, social, cultural, and group-based rights and, on the other, legal relationships within nation-states from legal relationships which stretch across national boundaries. Would this danger be obviated if the democratic entitlement were conceived not as an extension of the existing corpus of universally recognized rights, but as a synthesis of the various rights that comprise that corpus? As the history of the 'right to development' confirms, synthetic rights carry a serious risk of diminishing, rather than enhancing, their constituent elements.[37] Rights to rights seem best avoided. Thus, even leaving aside the question of whether democratic inclusion could plausibly form

---

[35] Linklater 1998, 2, 4.   [36] Ibid. 101.
[37] See, e.g., Ghai 1989. For a vigorous defence of the right to development, see, however, Mansell & Scott 1994.

the basis of an international legal entitlement, I do not propose that it should do so.

Rather, my proposal is that the concept of democratic inclusion should function as a *principle*, to guide the elaboration, application, and invocation of international law. Sovereign equality of states and non-interference in domestic affairs are two examples of concepts which have long functioned in this way. Each has operated as a reference point in international legal argument, moulding the agenda of international law-making, shaping the interpretation of international legal norms, and influencing the procedures for asserting international legal rights and enforcing international legal duties. In the process, each has itself been reshaped, as contradictions have spawned new laws, new interpretations, new procedures, and new principles. I propose the principle of democratic inclusion as a new principle, which might serve to reshape such established international legal norms as the principle of sovereign equality of states and the principle of non-interference in domestic affairs, and also to orient future international legal developments in a particular direction. I envision the principle as weaving into the fabric of international law a kind of bias in favour of popular self-rule and equal citizenship, that is to say, a bias in favour of inclusory political communities.

Though I refer to this as a new principle, it is in no way a new departure. For one thing, as repeatedly emphasized, the concern here is with emancipatory possibilities already present in accepted logics and processes. Moreover, these possibilities are widely perceived, and form the basis of a range of contemporary claims. Furthermore, as a result of these claims, the concept of democratic inclusion is reflected in many important trends in international law today. My aim in elaborating the principle of democratic inclusion is to reinforce these trends, encourage reflection on how they might be broadened and intensified, and, in doing so, help to vindicate the claims to which they respond. How might the principle do these things? Were it to become a reference point in international legal argument, how might this affect the agenda of international law-making, the interpretation of international legal norms and the procedures for asserting international legal rights and enforcing international legal duties? Let me now try to clarify and illustrate the significance which the principle of democratic inclusion might have. I begin with one extended example, and then offer some comments of a more general nature.

My extended example relates to the *right of peoples to self-determination*. One of the most familiar clichés of commentary on this subject is Judge Dillard's dictum in the *Western Sahara* Advisory Opinion of the International Court of Justice: 'It is for the people to determine the destiny of the territory and not the territory the destiny of the people.'[38] It is the kind of neat reversal that makes for a quotable quote. And, in the circumstances of the *Western Sahara* Opinion, it was an important affirmation of the implications of the right to self-determination in the context of decolonization: the Saharan people must have the ultimate say as to their political status

---

[38] ICJ Reports 1975, 12, 122.

upon decolonization, irrespective of any pre-colonial ties that may have linked other nations to Saharan territory. When taken out of this context, however, and used as a statement of the central idea involved in the right of self-determination, Judge Dillard's dictum can be seriously unhelpful. The problem is not just that, as many have observed, it begs all the questions (which people? what territory? destiny in what sense?), but that it begs the wrong questions. Approached in this way, the right of self-determination revolves around the relationship between people and territory, and the establishment of that relationship as one of sovereignty. Yet this scarcely captures what is at stake in a significant proportion of cases. For, as commentators have likewise observed, appeals to the principle of self-determination frequently stem from concerns which can be met without the creation of new states. To depict the central issue in terms of territorial sovereignty is to fuel the kind of conversation at cross purposes which so often occurs when claims to self-determination are made. Subaltern groups assert claims that do not entail independent statehood; governments respond to those claims on the basis that territorial integrity is threatened. To depict the central issue in these terms is thus to distract attention from the changes needed to end subalternity, and turn self-determination into an all-or-nothing matter of whether secession is permissible or not.

How could the principle of democratic inclusion help here? In the first place, it could serve to shift the focus from territorial sovereignty to political community, from relationships between people and territory to relationships among individuals and groups.[39] If the right to self-determination were oriented towards extending the opportunities for participation in political processes and overcoming barriers to the exercise of such opportunities, this would clearly indicate that the choice is not between the creation of new states and the preservation of existing arrangements. Transformative change has to be considered, but it can be realized in a wide variety of ways. In turn, this call to consider various options would encourage moves to develop imaginative solutions to self-determination demands, and to experiment with diverse forms of self-government and diverse structures of association.[40] Secondly, and in consequence, the principle of democratic inclusion could help to avoid the all too common conversation at cross purposes described above. Some commentators contend that the only means of avoiding such miscommunication is to drop the language of self-determination altogether. Thus, it is argued, indigenous groups should desist from asserting a right to self-determination, and concentrate instead of gaining recognition for the specific rights they seek with respect to land, natural resources, traditional law, and so on.[41] Indigenous groups are understandably reluctant to take this step, however, for the language of self-determination carries powerful justificatory force; to concede that it does not apply to their circumstances would be to diminish the strength of their claims. The principle of democratic inclusion might point to the possibility of using the language of self-determination in a

[39] On the development of self-determination from 'an instrument of decolonization towards a more nuanced and participatory ideal', see Simpson 1996, 258.

[40] See, e.g., Hannum 1996.   [41] See, e.g., Corntassel & Primeau 1995.

manner that is forceful, but not so forceful as to constitute a presumptive threat to territorial integrity.

These things said, the right to self-determination is, of course, sometimes claimed with a view to secession. A third function which the principle of democratic inclusion might perform is to help in explaining cases in which secession has been accepted, and might in the future be acceptable. A number of commentators have highlighted that the concept of self-determination cannot of itself do this. For that concept lends support simultaneously for secessionist arguments and anti-secessionist ones. It can rationalize both the liberatory struggles of oppressed groups and the totalizing projects of their oppressors, both the communitarian visions that underpin nationalist movements and the liberal visions that are invoked to build and defend pluralist polities.[42] If, however, the issues were set against the background of the goal of combatting unjust exclusion, it might become possible to differentiate between liberatory struggles and communitarian visions, and to suggest reasons why, in the case of the former, secession may in extreme circumstances be acceptable, while, in the case of the latter, there may be less prospect of justifying secession. Finally, the principle of democratic inclusion might serve to reshape approaches to the right to self-determination so as to reflect the realities of contemporary globalization. Informing those approaches has been a distinction between 'external' and 'internal' self-determination. External self-determination refers to the right of peoples to choose their international political status, and applies in the context of colonial and trust territories, and perhaps also in the context of territories subject to belligerent occupation. Internal self-determination applies in all contexts to uphold the right of peoples to choose their national constitution, and set their national goals, without either outside interference or domestic coercion.[43] As discussed in Chapter 4, the impact of globalizing processes is to make it harder than ever to sustain the sharp distinction implied here between the external order of international relations and the internal order of national politics. The principle of democratic inclusion might call attention to the inadequacy of both universal decolonization and pan-national democracy to protect the right of peoples to self-determination.

Let me now leave behind the principle of self-determination, and try to elucidate in a more general way the impact which the principle of democratic inclusion might have in relation to the three spheres of elaboration, application and invocation. I do this with the aid of a range of brief examples. First, with respect to the *elaboration* of international law, the principle of democratic inclusion would support and promote moves to make the processes of international law-making more inclusory. On the one hand, it would provide reasons for widening the circle of participation. Thus, it would endorse calls for representation in norm-making of communities and identities of diverse kinds. More specifically, it would help to justify the efforts of nongovernmental organizations to take up a central role in the framing of international legal norms, while at the same time giving impetus for such organizations themselves

---

[42] See, e.g., Berman 1988 and Koskenniemi 1994.   [43] Cassese 1981.

to develop and network in ways that broaden their horizons. On the other hand, it would provide a basis for delegitimizing traditions of international legal paternalism. That is to say, it would help to entrench in international law what David Beetham has termed democracy's 'anti-paternalist argument, to the effect that there are no "superiors" competent to decide for us what is for our own good, . . . except in so far as we specifically, and within clearly defined limits, authorise them to do so'.[44] In this way, the principle would explain, for instance, why the participation of indigenous peoples in the elaboration of the draft UN Declaration on the Rights of Indigenous Peoples means that the eventual Declaration is likely to have greater legitimacy than earlier instruments concerned with the indigenous peoples, which were drafted with no, or less, active involvement on the part of the latter.[45]

To influence the processes of international law-making is, of course, indirectly to influence the agenda of international law-making. But the principle of democratic inclusion would also have direct implications for this agenda. This can be illustrated by reference to debates about the limits of national jurisdiction. A major focus of these debates is the question of whether national jurisdiction includes the right to make foreign businesses operating in foreign territory liable in respect of activities which have the effect of impeding free competition in domestic or international trade. If approaches to this issue were oriented to the goal of enhancing congruence between decisions and their outcomes, this might help to elucidate the dilemma that is faced here. For congruence is lacking when those in one country are made subject to the jurisdiction of another. But, from the perspective of the latter, congruence is also lacking when those in one country undertake activities which constrain the options available to another country, yet escape its control. Viewed in this light, neither the assertion of jurisdiction over foreign businesses, nor the restriction of regulatory concerns to domestic activities, will do. *International* regulation is required. Inasmuch as a practice has indeed emerged of concluding bilateral treaties that provide for consultation and cooperation among regulatory authorities, the principle of democratic inclusion might encourage this trend.[46] At the same time, however, the principle might create pressure to go further. If the starting-point is that decisions about the justice of exclusionary practices should not be monopolized by dominant groups, this might argue for the development of more broadly based forms of international governance and accountability than the intergovernmental pairings and transgovernmental networks established hitherto.

With respect to the *application* of international law, the principle of democratic inclusion would support and promote interpretations that are conducive to extending the opportunities for self-rule and overcoming barriers to the exercise of such

[44] Beetham 1995, 7.

[45] For the Draft Declaration on the Rights of Indigenous Peoples, see UN Doc. E/CN.4/1995/2. Representatives of indigenous peoples also participated, to a more limited degree, in the elaboration of ILO Convention 169 (27 June 1989). See 28 ILM (1989) 1382.

[46] See, e.g., Agreement between the European Communities and the Government of the United States of America on the Application of Positive Comity Principles in the Enforcement of Competition Laws, OJ 1998 L.173, 18 June 1998, 28.

opportunities. This would have implications for the way particular terms are understood. An example might be the term 'non-discrimination', as used in human rights norms. At least three understandings of this word compete for ascendancy. On one understanding, non-discrimination means that everyone should be treated as if they were the same; distinctions among people should be ruled out of account. On a second understanding, non-discrimination means that active steps should be taken to ensure that distinctions among people arising from membership of different social groups do not entail systematic disadvantage. On a third understanding, non-discrimination means that structural changes should be implemented so that no-one is systematically excluded from participation in processes of decision-making that affect them. The principle of democratic inclusion would lend support for calls by commentators—now reflected in the work of some supervisory organs, such as the Committee on the Elimination of All Forms of Discrimination against Women—to go beyond the first understanding of non-discrimination just mentioned, and entrench the second or, better still, the third.

But, of course, the significance of international legal norms is not just a function of the abstract definition of particular terms. It is also a function of the way norms can be made meaningful in particular contexts. The principle of democratic inclusion would have implications for this aspect of the interpretive process as well. Another example taken from the sphere of human rights law will serve to illustrate this. A persistent argument advanced to refute the application of human rights norms in specific contexts is that those norms cannot apply in those contexts because they are inappropriate to the society concerned. Typically, the features said to account for this are that the community is more important than the individual; duties are more important than rights; faith is more important than reason; economic prosperity is more important than civic engagement. This argument often meets with considerable scepticism, especially insofar as it tends to be advanced by representatives of repressive governments. On the other hand, our world is indeed characterized by a tremendous diversity of traditions, forms of life, and belief systems, and few observers would wish to suggest that culture is irrelevant to the way human rights apply. For Arati Rao the central issue is 'the *politics* of any argument based on culture in human rights discourse'. Culture, she emphasizes, is 'a series of constantly contested and negotiated social practices whose meanings are influenced by the power and status of their interpreters and participants'. Thus, of any claim to restrict the application of human rights on cultural grounds, it is necessary to ask: 'what is the status of the speaker? . . . in whose name is the argument from culture advanced? . . . what is the degree of participation in culture formation of the social groups primarily affected by the cultural practices in question?'.[47] If the relationship between universality and diversity were viewed in the light of the principle of democratic inclusion, this move to introduce democratic considerations into the calculation of cultural legitimacy would merit very close attention.

---

[47] Rao 1995, 168 (emphasis in original), 173.

Finally, with respect to the *invocation* of international law, the principle of democratic inclusion would support and promote moves to expand the avenues for vindicating human rights. If the overall goal is to make political communities more inclusory, this helps to explain why securing respect for all categories of human rights must assume priority as an international concern. At the same time, it might also help to explain why in some circumstances non-prosecution of human rights offenders may be acceptable. There is a serious argument to the effect that, where evidence exists that gross and systematic human rights abuses have been committed, amnesties granted to members of a former regime in connection with a process of 'national reconciliation' are unlawful under international law. However, insofar as such amnesties might remain acceptable, the principle of democratic inclusion could lend support for proposals to connect their legitimacy with the extent to which they are embedded in a democratic process.[48] Thus, for instance, the principle might aid efforts to distinguish between exemption from prosecution granted in the context of proceedings such as those of the post-apartheid South African Truth and Reconciliation Commission and exemption from prosecution in the context of a 'self-amnesty' of the kind enacted in Chile in 1978. More generally, the principle of democratic inclusion would support and promote moves to expand the range of interests taken into account when international legal rights are invoked. If the procedures of international legal courts and tribunals were informed by the goal of reducing the extent to which people are excluded from decision-making that affects them, this might bring into focus the limitations of bilateral processes. Thus, for instance, the principle might encourage the use of *amicus curiae* briefs and third party intervention procedures. It might also foster the development of new procedures for dealing with international legal claims in ways that provide scope for the expression of diverse perspectives. And it might add impetus to moves to enhance the opportunities for individuals and groups to assert international legal rights against their own, and other, governments.

What, then, might be the impact of the principle of democratic inclusion? In the first place, it could lend coherence to a variety of developments that may otherwise appear unrelated. It might explain that what unites them is a wish to deploy international law to advance the prospects of self-rule on a footing of equality among citizens, both within and across nation-states. In this sense the principle of democratic inclusion might serve as a connecting thread, linking a range of familiar arguments, trends, ideas, approaches, and initiatives with one another, and with the project of cosmopolitan democracy. Secondly, it might provide a principled basis for extending these developments. That is to say, it might not only explain them, but also give reasons why their logic should be further pursued. Just as Held puts forward the 'principle of autonomy' as a means of grounding the project of cosmopolitan democracy within political theory, so too the principle of democratic inclusion might serve as a means of grounding efforts to direct international law to the democratization of global politics. Following the lead of Falk's notion of 'humane governance', the pro-

---

[48] See, e.g., Dugard 1998, esp. 288–90.

posed principle might offer a focused way of making such efforts appear justified, and even necessary and urgent. A third aspect of the principle's potential impact recalls Beetham's claim that the human rights regime might serve as a model for the project of cosmopolitan democracy. If the mirror of cosmopolitan democracy were likewise held up to the human rights regime, this might help to bring into view the contradictions affecting enforcement, as well as those surrounding the proclaimed indivisibility and universality of human rights (among others). In turn, this might provide impetus for renewed attention to the possibilities of supranational enforcement. It might also provide impetus for renewed attention to the need for all categories of human rights to be protected, and to be protected not only against violations within national political communities, but also against violations attributable to those acting in international and transnational arenas.

Fourthly, the principle of democratic inclusion might serve as a counterweight to a process which Anne-Marie Slaughter has characterized as the 'nationalization of international law'.[49] By this she means that international law is increasingly the servant, rather than the master, of national law. Thanks to the emergent mode of global governance which she terms 'transgovernmentalism', the scope for international law to serve as a framework for setting goals and launching initiatives is on the wane. As she explains, 'transnational regulatory organizations do not aspire to exercise power in the international system independent of their members. Indeed, their main purpose is to help regulators apprehend those who would harm the interests of American voters. Transgovernmental networks often promulgate their own rules, but the purpose of those rules is to enhance the enforcement of national law'.[50] The principle of democratic inclusion might prompt reflection on the elision here of 'American voters' with 'national law' and, more generally, on the hegemonic dimensions and democratic deficits of transgovernmentalist trends. If a bias in favour of inclusory politics were woven into international law, this might help to signal the urgent need for these new structures of power to be linked to new approaches to participation and new forms of accountability. Finally, and connectedly, the principle might assist with respect to a larger issue. Responding to Slaughter's account of the 'nationalization of international law', Philip Alston observes that this account risks, so to speak, writing international law out of global affairs. If policy is made in national arenas (or some of them), and the function of international processes is to help in meeting the technical challenges associated with implementation and enforcement, then, he remarks, this 'seems to leave increasingly little significant or relevant space for international law'.[51] The principle of democratic inclusion might work to reverse this contraction of international law's 'significant space'. It might work to show how global and national are linked—but also distinct. By enhancing the sensitivity of international law to the problem of unjust exclusion—within states, among states, and in transnational affairs—the proposed principle would define a set of concerns that is irreducibly global and irrepressibly ongoing. Zygmunt Bauman has urged a form of moral life

---

[49] Slaughter 1997, 192.   [50] Ibid. 191.   [51] Alston 1997, 446.

that is 'always haunted by the suspicion that it is not moral enough'.[52] Through the principle of democratic inclusion an international legal dynamic might be fuelled, such that international law is always haunted by the suspicion that it has not done enough to ensure that all can participate, on a footing of equality with others, in all of the many and various processes of decision-making which affect them.

I have sketched the barest outline of a proposal for what I have called the principle of democratic inclusion. No doubt many questions and objections arise, and would still arise even if the proposal were further elaborated. Of these at least one is easy to anticipate and answer. 'You have developed the principle of democratic inclusion in the context of an effort to bring out and pass beyond the ideological dimensions of the norm of democratic governance. But could not the principle of democratic inclusion come to serve as ideology too?' The answer to this is certainly 'yes'! The principle of democratic inclusion is no less susceptible of being deployed in the service of relations of domination than is the norm of democratic governance. Indeed, it may well be more so, for the most effective ideology is that which has the most convincing cover. To recall the discussion of ideology in Chapter 1, ideology is never an inherent quality, but it is always a possible eventuality. If, as John Thompson explains, nothing can be regarded as ideological *per se*, then equally, as Theodor Adorno emphasizes, nothing can be regarded as non-ideological *per se*. Once the mystifications of ideology have been exposed, there is no invisible hand which comes down to guide domination inexorably towards emancipation, and actuality towards its ideals. The question is always how systems of meaning operate in specific contexts.[53]

Ideology critique, then, does not purport to remove us to some kind of ideology-free zone, or promise the transcendence of ideology in general. (Indeed, it seeks to highlight the ideological significance of assertions that such a state has now been reached.) Rather, its aim is to criticize and transcend particular instances of ideology, on the understanding that there can be no guarantee that the result will be emancipatory, for ideology can always reappear in different guises—including the guise of critique. Thus, the central point of ideology critique is that, since ideology is a permanent possibility, critique must be permanent too. Because we cannot anticipate a world in which meaning no longer serves power, we must ensure that the ways in which meaning serves power are exposed to unremitting critical scrutiny. We must remain constantly alert to the danger, highlighted by Slavoj Žižek, of sliding back into ideology just as we seem to step out of it.[54] From this perspective, the principle of democratic inclusion must be seen as part of an ongoing process of critique. It *draws out* emancipatory potentials. But, since it can also become a vehicle for *closing off* emancipatory potentials, it requires to be approached with the same critical attitude out of which it was born.

---

[52] Bauman 1993, 80 (emphasis omitted), quoted Linklater 1998, 67.
[53] See Ch. 1 above.   [54] Žižek 1994a, 6, 17.

CONCLUSIONS

When ideals begin to seem like illusions, we can jettison and replace them. Or we can reassert and reclaim them. In this chapter I have tried to respond to the limitations of the democratic norm thesis in the manner of the second approach, by reasserting and reclaiming the ideals around which it turns. To this end, I have put forward a proposal for reframing the suggested alliance between international law and democracy in terms of a 'principle of democratic inclusion'. As indicated, the phrase 'democratic inclusion' is used to refer to the idea that all should have the right to a say in decision-making which affects them, and that systematic barriers to the exercise of that right should be acknowledged and removed. For this purpose, the relevant processes of decision-making and barriers to participation include not only those operating within nation-states, but also those operating among nation-states and in transnational arenas. The principle of democratic inclusion seeks to build this idea into the framework of ideas and concepts that informs international legal agendas, interpretations, and procedures. In this way it seeks to support claims, reinforce trends, and provide a principled basis for further developments, that orient international law to the realization of democratic inclusion. With the argument of earlier chapters in mind, the aim here is to reach beyond low intensity democracy and pan-national democracy, and connect international law with the project of cosmopolitan democracy articulated by Held and others.

Though the principle of democratic inclusion is a response to the limitations of the democratic norm thesis, the fact that it is a response suggests that the thesis already anticipates it. This is further confirmed by acknowledgements such as Franck's that the conception of democracy which underpins the democratic norm thesis is 'not ambitious, it is not necessarily unambiguous, and it is almost certainly not the one an American would prefer'.[55] That the thesis, in this sense, points beyond itself is also confirmed by the many references in accounts of the norm of democratic governance to 'political participation', 'participatory political processes', 'meaningful political choice', and so on. The ambiguity of these phrases, and of the central concept of democracy itself, is what enables the principle of democratic inclusion to turn the progressive dimensions of the democratic norm thesis against its unnecessary constraints. As discussed in Chapter 1, the distinctiveness of critique lies in the effort to eschew blueprints and encourage instead investigation of the unrealized potential within existing conceptual resources. The premise of this approach is that ideology is never a seamless monolith, but contains both ideas 'internal' to itself and other ideas which run counter to its ruling logic. Thus, in Marx's analysis, capitalist labour relations both mask economic exploitation and provide the context for overcoming that exploitation. For it is through the contradictions of those relations that 'men become conscious of this conflict and fight it out'.[56] As Eagleton expresses this point, ideology, like dreams, 'reveals and conceals at once'.[57]

---

[55] Franck 1994, 75.   [56] Marx (Tucker) 5.   [57] Eagleton 1991, 134.

It is important to note that what is revealed here is the *possibility* of other ways of linking international law and democracy which overcome the constraints of current formulations. The effect of ideology critique, as again highlighted in Chapter 1, is to unsettle particular meanings and shift them onto a larger field of alternative possibilities. Of these possibilities the proposal for a principle of democratic inclusion is, quite patently, only one. Much more work would be needed to develop that proposal, and to test its value as a means of placing international law at the service of those struggling against domination. Likewise, more work is needed to explore other ways of rearticulating the alliance between international law and democracy. Thus, this discussion of the claim that a right to democratic governance should be recognized as a norm of international law ends with a question. How can the move to promote democracy through international law be carried forward in a way that reduces the ideological dimensions of the democratic norm thesis? But there is also another discussion here, opened with the account of ideology critique in Chapter 1, to which I wish, finally, to revert. This has to do with the general perspective within which such a question arises. Why analyse international legal proposals in terms of their 'ideological dimensions'? What form of enquiry is involved? What sort of theory is engaged? What kind of knowledge is produced?

Chapter 6

Afterword: Critical Knowledge

Introducing a survey of theories of world politics, Steve Smith and John Baylis make the following observations.

> [W]e do not think that theory is an *option*. It is not as if you can say that you do not want to bother with a theory, all you want to do is look at the 'facts'. We believe that this is simply impossible, since the only way in which you can decide which of the millions of possible facts to look at is by adhering to some simplifying device which tells you which ones matter the most. We think of theory as such a simplifying device.[1]

From this perspective, 'a theory is not simply some grand formal model with hypotheses and assumptions'. Rather, a 'theory is a simplifying device that allows you to decide which facts matter and which do not' (or, to put the point slightly differently, which facts count as facts).[2] That device may be made explicit, or it may be left implicit, but either way it is an inescapable dimension of knowledge. What you hold to be true about the world depends on what you take into account, and what you take into account depends on what you think matters. Thus, according to the criteria used by Baylis and Smith (along with many others), the criteria used for deciding what matters themselves matter; the device deployed to sort significant facts from insignificant ones—that is to say, the *theory* which informs enquiry—is itself a significant fact.

Theory in this sense is the subject of this chapter. In what follows I seek to render explicit the evaluative standards which have animated my arguments in this book. I seek to clarify—and, more than that, to justify—the approach I have adopted to the question of 'which facts matter and which do not'. This approach has already been adumbrated in the context of remarks concerning the critique of ideology. If ideology critique seeks to elucidate the ways in which meaning serves to establish and sustain relations of domination, it does this not just for the sake of discovering those ways. Rather, as noted in Chapter 1, the intention is to criticize those ways, and contribute to reshaping the relations of domination they support. Enquiry is motivated not by curiosity alone, but also by a sense of injustice, a wish to break down barriers to the enjoyment of social goods. Ideology critique thus proceeds on the basis that the 'facts which matter' are the practices through which asymmetrical power relations are constituted, reproduced—and, potentially, transformed. Its premise is that, by calling attention to the signifying practices which help to constitute and reproduce those relations, the critic undertakes an activity that can itself have transformative effect. By showing how that which appears necessary perpetuates historical injustice, that which

---

[1] Smith & Baylis 1997, 3 (emphasis added).　　[2] Ibid. 3 (emphasis omitted).

seems universal serves particular interests, and that which claims to be rational functions as an argument against change, ideology critique can help to make us see things in a new way, and act accordingly.

The succeeding discussion extends these initial theoretical observations by reference to a series of seminal expositions of critical approaches to the pursuit of social scientific knowledge. Though these expositions are directed to fields of social enquiry other than international law, they clarify the distinctiveness and contribution of knowledge in the mode of critique in a manner that remains highly instructive for international legal scholars. To grasp fully in what respects they are instructive, it would be necessary to consider their implications in relation to the whole range of established traditions of international legal scholarship. In turn, this would entail an investigation of the many and complex ways in which those various traditions cut across, and overlap with, a critical approach of the kind described in this chapter. However, that investigation must be left for another occasion. Instead, I take up at the end the more specific question of how critique affects analysis of the international legal issues around which earlier chapters of this book have revolved. My limited goal in the succeeding pages is, as indicated, to explain and defend my own approach to these issues. Of course, even were I to provide the kind of wide-ranging account just alluded to, I would have to recognize that not all those engaged in the study of international law can be persuaded of the merits of critique. To repeat, how the world is studied is bound up with what is held to matter, and what matters a great deal to me may matter less, or not at all, to others. Perhaps it is not too much to hope, however, that all can be persuaded at least of the connection between epistemological concerns and ethical ones, between ideas about the good analysis and ideas about the good life, and between academic debates and political struggles. And if international legal scholars can be persuaded of this, who knows what changes might follow?

CRITICAL KNOWLEDGE

In exploring critical approaches to knowledge, this section first revisits Marx to note the contrast highlighted in his work between the speculative theorizing of the German 'idealist' philosophers and the more practical form of enquiry which Marx himself sought to define and undertake. The remainder of the section is concerned with twentieth-century perspectives. To keep the discussion within manageable proportions, I concentrate on four specific accounts, presented respectively by Max Horkheimer, Jürgen Habermas, Robert Cox, and Michel Foucault. Each develops a theme articulated, like Marx's, in terms of a contrast: between 'critical' theory and 'traditional' theory; between 'emancipatory cognitive interests' and other 'cognitive interests'; between 'critique' and 'problem-solving'; and between 'genealogy' and 'history'. I have chosen these accounts because they offer exceptionally clear signposts within the difficult—and, to a non-specialist, at times disorienting—terrain that I shall refer to as 'critical knowledge'.

'The Point is to Change the World'

Marx's claim that the 'idealist' philosophers of his own time treated consciousness as if it determined material life and, to this extent, saw the world 'upside down, as in a *camera obscura*', was recalled in Chapter 1. This seems to suggest that, when the world is viewed the correct way up, material life is determinative of consciousness. If Marx was indeed intending to suggest that ideas are simply the outcome of material conditions, then—as also noted in that chapter—this seriously underestimates the extent to which ideas themselves shape material reality. In doing so, it denies the potential of ideas to help in challenging and transforming existing conditions. Clearly, however, Marx cannot have doubted that potential. Otherwise, he would not have expended his own energies in the way he did. That he was in fact acutely conscious of the social significance of ideas is confirmed by the content of his analyses, some of which were, again, touched upon in Chapter 1. Thus, Marx's scepticism seems to have been directed not so much at theorizing *per se*, as at the particular form of theorizing favoured in his day and epitomized in the work of the Young Hegelians. For Terry Eagleton, Marx might be thought of as belonging to a 'distinguished lineage of "anti-philosophers" ', who question the value, and seek to 'deflate the . . . pretensions', of dominant philosophical approaches, with a view to either '[transcending] the whole project for reasons which remain *philosophically* interesting or [as in Marx's case] . . . [re-casting] it in a new key entirely'.[3]

What, then, are the pretensions of the Young Hegelians which Marx seeks to deflate? And what is the new key in which he seeks to re-cast enquiry? The form of theorizing exemplified in idealist philosphy is characterized, according to Marx, by a focus on questions of human nature, the relationship between human beings and God, and so on.[4] The Young Hegelians seek to disabuse us of 'false notions' about ourselves. In doing so, they claim, or at any rate assume, that it is those notions which are at the root of society's problems. Thus, they suppose that, if only we can be delivered 'from the phantoms, the ideas, dogmas, imaginary beings under whose yoke [we] languish', injustice will end. If only 'illusions' can be exchanged 'for thoughts that conform to the nature of man', the old order 'will crumble' and universal human flourishing will be assured. Yet, Marx insists, the Young Hegelians are 'sheep who take themselves, and are taken, to be wolves'. Far from presenting a threat to privileged sections of society, their 'philosophic bleatings are simply echoes of the opinions of the German bourgeois'.[5] For deprivation is not simply a function of misconceptions about human nature or erroneous interpretations of the world. Insofar as the idealist philosophers suggest otherwise, they simply peddle a conservative myth. To achieve social justice, material conditions need to be changed. And contemplation of such issues as the nature of being cannot help us do that. Indeed,

---

[3] Eagleton 1997, 5 (emphasis in original). As Eagleton explains, an anti-philosopher is still a philosopher: 'an anti-philospher of this kind differs from a mere opponent of philosophy in much the same way that an "anti-novel" like Ulysses differs from a non-novel like the telephone directory'.

[4] See Marx (O'Malley) 1994, esp. 119–22.   [5] Ibid. 119.

where—as in the case of the Young Hegelians—contemplation of such issues is made to seem 'earth shaking' in its implications, philosophy may even hinder efforts to bring about material change.[6] Marx encapsulates these objections in a famous sentence: 'The philosophers have only *interpreted* the world in different ways; the point is to *change* it.'[7]

With this is mind, Marx sought to develop a new form of enquiry that would have a better prospect of contributing to redistributive change than the speculative investigations of the Young Hegelian philosophers. In this new form of enquiry theorizing is recast as a '"practical-critical" activity',[8] geared to engagement with 'practical' questions, as distinct from purely abstract or 'scholastic' ones. In Marx's words:

The question of whether human thinking obtains objective truth is not a question of theory but a *practical* question. It is in practice that man must prove the truth, the actuality and power, the subjective aspect and validity of his thinking. Argument about the actuality or non-actuality of thinking, where thinking is taken in isolation from practice, is a purely *scholastic* question.[9]

The distinctive character of the 'practical-critical activity' to which Marx refers, and which his own work instantiates, is explained in succinct terms by Terry Eagleton.[10] Marx's aim, writes Eagleton, is to 'fashion a kind of practical philosophy which will help to transform what it is seeking to comprehend'—a kind of philosophy in which '[s]ocial and intellectual change go together'. What results is a 'special kind of action-oriented theory . . . sometimes known as "emancipatory knowledge" '. Eagleton highlights four features of this. First, it is concerned with self-understanding. To change their situation, individuals and groups must first understand that situation. In doing this, however, they inevitably change the latter, for 'to know yourself in a new way is to alter yourself in that very act'. Secondly, then, emancipatory knowledge is 'a peculiar form of cognition in which the act of knowing alters what it contemplates'. In the process of pursuing self-knowledge, both the self who is seeking to know and the self known are different from what they were before. Thirdly, 'since such knowledge also moves people to change their situation in a practical way, it becomes itself a kind of social or political force'. While the reflections of idealist philosophers help to stabilize actuality, this kind of knowledge intervenes in, and disrupts, historical conditions to press emancipatory claims. In this way, finally, practical-critical theorizing blurs traditional distinctions between 'knowing *that*' and 'knowing *how*', between comprehension of facts and assertion of values. 'It is not just that this kind of knowledge can be put to valuable use', Eagleton explains, 'but that the motivation for understanding in the first place is bound up with a sense of value'.

As this brief summary makes clear, Marx's quarrel with his philosophical contemporaries is not that they interpret the world, but that they *only* interpret the world. Since the point is to change it, an approach is required in which interpretation is

---

[6] Marx (O'Malley) 1994, 122.   [7] Ibid. 118 (emphasis in original).   [8] Ibid. 116.

[9] Ibid. (emphasis in original) (quoted, in a different translation, at Eagleton 1997, 3).

[10] See Eagleton 1997. All the quotations in this paragraph are from pp. 3–4 of this text.

harnessed to change, understanding to transformative action, theory to emancipatory practice. Thus the issue, for Marx, is: how can change be pursued *through* interpretation (among other means)?

Traditional Theory v. Critical Theory, and Other Distinctions

Since Marx's time efforts to connect scholarly activity with emancipatory practice have been pursued in many directions. In what follows I highlight four twentieth-century accounts in particular, each of them enormously—and enduringly—influential. Though expressed in different terms, and put forward as interventions in different debates, the four discussions complement one another in elucidating the distinctive character of critical knowledge.

Traditional theory and critical theory

I begin with Max Horkheimer's famous essay, 'Traditional and Critical Theory'.[11] Published in 1937, the essay is a call by a founding member of the Frankfurt School to recognize the limits of, and alternatives to, dominant approaches to social-scientific research. Horkheimer uses the term 'traditional theory'—or 'positivism'—to refer to approaches underpinned by an assumption that the study of social phenomena should proceed in the same way as the empirical study of natural phenomena. That is to say, he understands traditional theory as resting on the notion that social enquiry should be conducted by testing hypotheses, with the aim of describing, explaining, and predicting regularities. Horkheimer observes that during the formative stages of capitalism this notion served a transformative purpose in helping to delegitimize ideas and institutions associated with feudal society; in his words, it 'tended chiefly to the break-up of the status quo'.[12] But, he argues, what was once radical has become conservative. In contemporary circumstances traditional theory 'concentrates on the problems which it meets in the wake of technical development'. To this extent, it retains a certain value, but '[does] not . . . further the interests of any important sector of society in the present age'. Rather, it '[belongs] to the existing order and [helps] make it possible'.[13]

   Horkheimer identifies a number of ideological moves through which, in his analysis, traditional theory works to supports the existing order. To begin with, traditional theory universalizes empirical enquiry. A single form of analysis appears to answer to all investigative purposes, and that form appears necessarily to correspond to empirical science. As Horkheimer explains it, positivism 'absolutizes' its own conception of knowledge 'as though [this] were grounded in the inner nature of knowledge as such or justified in some other ahistorical way'.[14] In turn, this provides a basis for naturalizing particular social arrangements. Traditional theory depicts regularities in the domain of society and politics as given facts, rather than historical artefacts. The injustices and contradictions of bourgeois society thus come to appear a state of affairs

[11] Horkheimer 1972.   [12] Ibid. 205.   [13] Ibid. 205–6.   [14] Ibid. 194.

that we must accept and adapt to, but cannot hope to transform: 'The whole process, with all its waste of work-power and human life, and with its wars and all its sense-less wretchedness, seems to be an unchangeable force of nature, a fate beyond man's control.'[15] Linked with this naturalization of actuality is a reification of human endeavours. Traditional theory treats individuals as if they were spectators of their circumstances, recipients rather than active producers of their world. In consequence, knowledge comes to seem a matter of observation or perception, without the capacity to affect material reality. Through this 'dualism of thought and being', traditional theory fosters 'quietism or conformism', as 'men see themselves only as onlookers, passive participants in a mighty process which may be foreseen but not modified'.[16] Finally, and connectedly, traditional theory helps to sustain the existing order by masking its own role as a stabilizing force. With traditional theory social research appears an autonomous activity, detached from the social processes that are its object, and independent too of the contexts in which it is undertaken and received. In Horkheimer's words, 'the genesis of particular objective facts, the practical application of the conceptual systems by which [traditional theory] grasps the facts, and the role of such systems in action, are all taken to be external to the theoretical thinking itself'.[17]

In highlighting these ideological moves associated with traditional theory, Horkheimer seeks to exemplify, and to promote, another approach to the study of social phenomena. This approach, which he refers to as 'critical theory', draws inspiration from Marx's conception of theorizing as a 'practical–critical activity'. What is distinctive about critical theory? In the first place, Horkheimer explains, it takes into account the systemic character of social problems. The aim of critical theory is 'not simply to eliminate one or other abuse, for it regards such abuses as necessarily connected with the way in which the social structure is organized'. Put differently, critical theory sets out not so much to secure 'the better functioning of any element in the structure', as to help bring about structural change.[18] To this end, a second aspect of critical theory is that its focus is on relationships among individuals and communities. Traditional theory treats the 'activity of society [as] blind and concrete, that of individuals [as] abstract and conscious'.[19] Critical theory, by contrast, recognizes that 'individuality [cannot be] separated off from events' and that in bourgeois society events occur in a setting which is itself 'internally rent'. Critical theory thus takes as its subject 'a definite individual in his real relation to other individuals and groups, . . . and . . . in the resultant web of relationships with the social totality and with nature'.[20] This provides the basis for a third feature. Eschewing both the 'detached' standpoint of liberal thought and the 'deeply rooted' perspective of totalitarian thought,[21] critical theory proceeds from an awareness of the contradictory character of life in bourgeois societies and fixes its attention on the gap between legitimating ideas and social realities. Horkheimer cites the example, extensively analysed in Marx's work, of the bourgeois economy: 'The bourgeois economy was concerned that

[15] Horkheimer 1972, 204.   [16] Ibid. 231, 229, 231.   [17] Ibid. 208.   [18] Ibid. 207.
[19] Ibid. 200.   [20] Ibid. 210–11.   [21] Ibid. 223–4.

the individual should maintain the life of society by taking care of his own personal happiness. Such an economy has within it, however, a dynamism which results in a fantastic degree of power for some . . . and in material and intellectual weakness for many others. . .'.[22] Following Marx's lead, critical theory seeks to 'take seriously the ideas by which the bourgeoisie explains its own order—free exchange, free competition, harmony of interests, and so on—and [to] follow them to their logical conclusion'. Those ideas can then be shown to 'manifest their inner contradiction and therewith their real opposition to the bourgeois order'.[23]

A fourth facet of critical theory is its concern to highlight the ideological manœuvres through which that opposition is masked, or at any rate stabilized. Horkheimer's analysis of traditional theory reflects this concern. More generally, he proposes that a central aim of critical theory is to bring to consciousness the 'two-sided character' of contemporary existence. '[T]he limited freedom of the bourgeois individual puts on the illusory form of perfect freedom and autonomy.'[24] The world appears our own; yet at the same time we experience society as 'comparable to nonhuman natural processes'.[25] Critical theory seeks to foster awareness of the tension between freedom and constraint, between the possibilities for transforming social conditions and the pressures to keep things as they are. To note this is to point to a fifth characteristic. Critical theory hitches social research to emancipatory practice. That is to say, scholarship is produced which serves not just as 'an expression of the concrete historical situation but also as a force within it to stimulate change', not just as 'a cog in an already existent mechanism', but as 'an element in action leading to new social forms'.[26] That said, as Horkheimer emphasizes, critical theory cannot itself specify those new social forms. Only those asserting emancipatory claims can do that, for 'one and the same subject who wants a new state of affairs, a better reality, to come to pass, also brings it forth'. Besides, the idea of society 'as a community of free men . . . is constantly being renewed amid prevailing conditions'.[27] A final feature of critical theory is implicit in the other points mentioned. Horkheimer observes that traditional theorists separate their activities as scholars and as citizens. While as citizens they may take an active interest in 'social reality and its products', as scholars they regard political issues as 'extrinsic' to their concerns.[28] As he puts it, traditional theory 'speaks not of what theory means in human life, but only of what it means in the isolated sphere in which for historical reasons it comes into existence'.[29] Critical theory, by contrast, unites the theorist's experience as scholar and as citizen. Rejecting the separation of 'value and research, knowledge and action', it explicitly, and indeed emphatically, relates theorizing to life.[30]

Just as Marx set out to expose the conservatism behind the 'earth shaking phrases' of idealist philosophy and to recast theorizing as a practical–critical activity, so, then, Horkheimer sought to reveal the ideological dimensions of positivist social science and to promote—under the banner of critical theory—a new departure in social-scientific research. During and after the War Horkheimer himself came to take a

---

[22] Ibid. 212–13.   [23] Ibid. 215.   [24] Ibid. 211.   [25] Ibid. 207.
[26] Ibid. 215–16.   [27] Ibid. 217.   [28] Ibid. 209.   [29] Ibid. 197.   [30] Ibid. 208.

more pessimistic view of the prospects of academic enquiry contributing to emancipatory change. His notion of transformative theory was, however, taken up and reformulated by later scholars.

Technical, practical and emancipatory cognitive interests

In an inaugural lecture delivered in 1965 Jürgen Habermas addresses the theme of 'Knowledge and Human Interests'.[31] Through this theme, the leading member of the second generation of Frankfurt School theorists revisits the question of positivism and its limits. His discussion revolves around a distinction between three forms of enquiry. Habermas wants to show how each of these forms of enquiry is oriented to a different 'interest'. In doing so, he seeks to illustrate the more general point that knowledge and interests are linked; the interest that motivates enquiry and justifies the particular methods used—in Habermas's terminology, the 'cognitive' interest—cannot be separated from the knowledge produced. Whereas positivist approaches leave that point out of the frame of analysis, critical theory regards it as significant and, indeed, central. What then, are the three forms of enquiry that Habermas has in mind, and what are the cognitive interests that correspond to them?

In the first place, there are the 'empirical-analytical sciences', as Habermas calls them. The natural sciences are his model for these. Empirical–analytical enquiry aims to describe, explain and, above all, predict. By formulating and testing hypotheses, it seeks to identify regularities. On the basis of those regularities, it seeks to develop predictions about future conditions. The result, he highlights, is a distinctive kind of knowledge. What makes predictions valuable is that they offer the possibility of expanded control over material reality. They provide information which enlarges our capacity to direct events, or at least to manage them. In his words, the 'meaning' of predictive propositions is a function of their 'technical exploitability'.[32] Restating the point in terms of 'interests', Habermas argues that this form of enquiry is geared to an 'interest in technical control over objectified processes'.[33] Corresponding to empirical-analytical knowledge is, thus, a 'technical' cognitive interest.

Secondly, Habermas discusses the 'historical-hermeneutic sciences'. His model for these comes from disciplines such as history and literary studies. Here the central concern is not so much verification as interpretation. While empirical-analytical enquiry aims to predict, historical-hermeneutic enquiry aims to comprehend. Again, a distinctive kind of knowledge is involved. Habermas considers that, as in the case of predictive propositions, interpretive propositions acquire significance from their bearing on material reality. But unlike the case of predictive propositions, their meaning is not so much a function of their technical exploitability as it is a function of their cultural or 'practical' value. By explicating the traditions that frame our interaction, historical-hermeneutic knowledge helps us to interact more competently. It reduces the scope for miscommunication, and in this way speaks to the possibility of mutual understanding, and hence consensus, among actors within an established framework.

---

[31] Reprinted at Habermas 1987, 301.   [32] Ibid. 308.   [33] Ibid. 309.

Habermas infers that what guides such enquiry is a 'practical' interest 'in the preservation and expansion of . . . intersubjectivity'.[34] The correlate of historical-hermeneutic knowledge is, accordingly, a 'practical' cognitive interest.

Finally, Habermas turns to the social sciences. In the spirit of Horkheimer's discussion of traditional and critical theory, he distinguishes between two approaches, which he refers to as 'positivist' and 'critical' social science. By positivist social science he understands dominant approaches in the fields of economics, sociology and political science. For Habermas this form of enquiry belongs with the empirical-analytical sciences. That is to say, it adapts methods and logics commonly used in those sciences. More than that, it shares those sciences' orientation to a technical cognitive interest. In Habermas's assessment, the overall aim of positivist social science is to enhance the prospects for controlling social outcomes. Analysis is geared to elaborating predictions about social structures, with a view to improving the way those structures function. By identifying chains of causation, for instance, scholars put forward a basis on which we may anticipate the impact of particular courses of action, and hence pursue our goals with greater efficiency. Against this form of social-scientific research, Habermas counterposes an approach which seeks to go beyond predictive knowledge. Critical social science is concerned not simply to predict, nor indeed to comprehend. Rather, it intends to transform. In his words, the objective is 'to determine when theoretical statements grasp invariant regularities of social action as such and when they express ideologically frozen relations of dependence that can in principle be transformed'.[35] As this implies, Habermas takes the critique of ideology to exemplify the methods of critical social science. What is characteristic of these methods is, for him, that they are directed to 'self-reflection'. That is to say, critical social science engages social actors in a process of reflecting on their own situation. In the case of ideology critique, this entails inviting us to consider the possibility that our ideas both make us accomplices to oppression (including that of which we are ourselves the victims) and also place at our disposal weapons for resisting oppression. Where empirical-analytical enquiry is concerned with verification, and historical-hermeneutic enquiry with interpretation, Habermas thus considers that critical enquiry is centrally concerned with self-reflection. Correspondingly, the knowledge attained through critical enquiry has a distinctive kind of value. The 'meaning' of self-reflection lies not in its capacity to generate technical information, nor in its practical role as a basis for mutual understanding and expanded consensus. What makes it significant is, instead, its potential to mobilize emancipatory action. In inviting us to reflect on our situation with respect to oppression, the critique of ideology challenges complicity and fosters resistance. Through this form of enquiry, scholars help to open up possibilities for human self-realization occluded in current conditions. Critical knowledge, then, is addressed to an 'emancipatory' cognitive interest.

Habermas explains that his aim in introducing the concept of 'cognitive interests' is to counter the prevailing tendency to mask the interests lying behind knowledge.

[34] Ibid. 310.   [35] Ibid.

Inasmuch as objectivity is held to require that those interests be masked, he contends that this points up the double mystification associated with positivist approaches. On the one hand, positivist scholarship fails to admit the impetus it draws from particular interests. On the other hand, it also fails to register that such interests provide the very 'conditions of possible objectivity themselves'. The three cognitive interests he describes represent three 'specific viewpoints from which we can apprehend reality as such in any way whatsover'.[36] Depending on where we stand, our effort to capture objective reality will take a different form. It follows that decisions about how objectivity should be achieved are 'neither arbitrary nor compelling', but rather 'appropriate or inappropriate' to the cognitive interest involved.[37] For Habermas, the distinctiveness of critical knowledge arises from the fact that the emancipatory cognitive interest is best served by making all this a matter of conscious reflection. Critical knowledge takes interests explicitly into account. By contrast, empirical-analytical and historical-hermeneutic knowledge, for all their differences, join together in identifying objectivity with disinterestedness. Pursued in these sciences is a 'pure' kind of knowledge that seeks to 'derive everything from itself'.[38] However, purity here is not innocence. By placing interests beyond the pale of enquiry, these sciences also support efforts to remove transformative change from the agenda of politics. Empirical-analytical enquiry '[squeezes] the conduct of life into the behavioral system of instrumental action', while historical-hermeneutic enquiry 'locks up history in a museum'.[39] As only critical enquiry can show, each 'succumbs to unacknowledged external conditions and becomes ideological'.[40]

With this inaugural lecture, then, Habermas renewed Horkheimer's critique of 'traditional' approaches to social science and sought to promote awareness that 'critical' approaches are also possible. Enquiry can respond, he recalled, not just to technical and practical interests, but to an interest in emancipation as well. Habermas later wrote that his aim in contrasting these three cognitive interests was to 'help to recover the forgotten experience of reflection' and, in this way, to counteract the prevailing 'disavowal' of critique.[41] As he sees it, positivist social science has 'taken . . . knowledge into the service of the internalization of norms and thus estranged it from its legitimate task'.[42] Habermas's subsequent work is less preoccupied than this early contribution with exposing the limitations of positivism. He has come to view critical theory as more appropriately explained in terms of communication than in terms of knowledge. In consequence, he invests less in the concept of cognitive interests, and also dwells more on the evident interrelation of prediction, interpretation, and self-reflection.[43] One thing he has not modified, however, is his conception of the 'legitimate task' of social enquiry. The notion that knowledge should respond to an emancipatory interest in transforming relations of domination remains as germane today as it ever was—and not only for Habermas and others whose central concern might be described as social theory.

---

[36] Habermas 1987, 311 (emphasis omitted).   [37] Ibid. 312.   [38] Ibid. 314.
[39] Ibid. 316.   [40] Ibid. 314.   [41] Ibid. vii.   [42] Ibid. 304.
[43] For some later reflections, see Postscript, Habermas 1987, 351. On the relationship between his work on 'knowledge and human interests' and his later writing, see Outhwaite 1994 and Held 1980, chs. 11–13.

Problem-solving and critique

In an article published in 1981 Robert Cox presents an unconventional analysis of approaches to the study of world politics.[44] Later to be widely cited, the analysis illuminates the bearing of an emancipatory conception of knowledge for international relations theory. Cox's starting-point is the observation that '[t]heory is always *for* someone and *for* some purpose'.[45] One aspect of this is the point that knowledge is always pursued from a perspective. Theorists may (and, as he later argues, should) attain a certain distance from their perspective, by reflecting on it and by taking other perspectives into consideration. But the pertinence of perspectives can never be wholly eliminated. It follows that there is 'no such thing as theory in itself, divorced from a standpoint in time and space'. When any theory holds itself out as such, it is, he suggests, 'the more important to examine it as ideology, and to lay bare its concealed perspective'.[46]

Cox next observes that, from each perspective, social reality appears to throw up a distinct set of issues, a distinct array of problems to be grappled with. To use his word, each perspective suggests a distinct 'problematic'.[47] The question then becomes: what approach does that problematic suggest? What sort of challenge is posed for theorists by the particular issues and problems confronted? Cox draws a distinction between two purposes which theory might serve. One is to 'be a guide to help solve the problems posed within the terms of the particular perspective which was the point of departure'. The other is 'to become clearly aware of the perspective which gives rise to theorising, and its relation to other perspectives (to achieve a perspective on perspectives); and to open up the possibility of choosing a different valid perspective from which the problematic becomes one of creating an alternative world'.[48] To each of these purposes he contends that there corresponds a different kind of theory, which he terms respectively 'problem-solving' theory and 'critical' theory.

The concern of problem-solving theory is to remove the strains, tensions and confusions that disrupt, or threaten to disrupt, the operation of social processes. That is to say, the effort is to ameliorate social and political structures by correcting specific failings or weaknesses. The structures themselves, however, are not part of the problematic. In Cox's words, problem-solving theory

takes the world as it finds it, with the prevailing social and power relationships and the institutions into which they are organised, as the given framework for action. The general aim of problem-solving is to make these relationships and institutions work smoothly by dealing effectively with particular sources of trouble.[49]

This kind of theory thus considers the world in relation to discrete arenas of social life, compartmentalizing enquiry into specialized fields of study. As Cox comments, that is, indeed, its strength. By isolating issues and putting wider questions to one

---

[44] Cox 1981. The account that follows focuses on the opening sections of this article, where the analysis appears.
[45] Ibid. 128 (emphasis in original).   [46] Ibid.   [47] Ibid.   [48] Ibid.
[49] Ibid. 128–9.

side, problem-solving theory limits the range of variables which must be taken into account and, correspondingly, augments the prospects for establishing causal linkages and developing general propositions. With the aid of those propositions, social actors are able to make informed decisions about problems and their solutions.

Critical theory, by contrast, does not take the prevailing social and power relationships, and the institutions into which they are organized, as the given framework of action. Rather, it regards those relationships and institutions as aspects of the problematic. With this kind of theory, writes Cox, scholarly effort 'is directed towards an appraisal of the very framework for action ... which problem-solving theory accepts as its parameters'.[50] Of course, critical enquiry necessarily begins, like problem-solving, by focusing on some specific arena of social life. But while problem-solving works inwards, reducing the frame of reference so as to concentrate attention on a restricted issue, critical theory works outwards, enlarging the frame of reference so as to bring into view the broader field of which the specific arena forms a part. One consequence of this is that critical theory may seem to lack the rigour of problem-solving; it cannot deliver the kind of precision which is possible when the area under investigation is more circumscribed. Cox recalls, however, that problem-solving achieves precision only by relying on the (counterfactual) assumption that social structures are fixed. From the perspective of critical theory, this assumption is not just false; it also reflects an 'ideological bias' in favour of those 'comfortable within the given order'.[51] To resolve particular problems that affect the functioning of relationships and institutions is to stabilize those relationships and institutions. In treating social structures as if they were fixed, problem-solving theory thus helps to make them so. Critical theory differs in that it has the character of a 'theory of history'.[52] That is to say, it is centrally concerned with change. But it is not just concerned with describing or explaining change. If problem-solving is a 'guide to tactical actions which, intended or unintended, sustain the existing order', the ambition of critique is to be a 'guide to strategic action for bringing about an alternative order'. To this end, critical theory seeks to identify both possibilities and constraints. It seeks to '[allow] for a normative choice in favour of a social and political order different from the prevailing order, but it limits the range of choice to alternative orders which are feasible transformations of the existing world'.[53]

In presenting this analysis, Cox's aim is to promote a critical approach to the study of world politics. This is not so much a matter of replacing problem-solving with critique as of shifting the balance in favour of the latter. As he observes, '[c]urrents of theory which include works of sophistication usually share some of the features of both problem-solving and critical theory, but tend to emphasize one approach over the other'.[54] He summarizes the orientation of an approach that emphasizes critique in terms of five propositions, five premises on which enquiry is based. The first is that social life occurs within a framework, which must itself be called into question. The second is that theorizing likewise occurs within a framework. While critical theory

---

[50] Cox 1981, 129.   [51] Ibid.   [52] Ibid.   [53] Ibid. 130.   [54] Ibid.

may achieve a broader perspective than problem-solving theory, it still remains necessarily limited and, thus, necessarily incomplete. The third premise is that the framework for action must be studied in the light of its changing character. The fourth premise is that this framework can be understood as a kind of structure. While not determining reality, existing relationships and institutions shape action by providing a context of constraints, norms, expectations, and so on. Finally, theorizing is premised on the notion that the proper way of viewing this structure is, in Cox's words, 'not from the top in terms of the requisites for its equilibrium or reproduction . . . but rather from the bottom or from outside in terms of the conflicts which arise within it and open the possibility of its transformation'.[55] What are the prospects of an approach to global politics that rests on these premises? Cox proposes that different historical epochs may foster different kinds of theory. He suggests that the appeal of critical theory may be greater during periods experienced as times of flux than during periods when relationships and institutions seem more durable or rigid. Writing in 1981 he considers that conditions are already propitious for challenging the Cold War dominance of problem-solving in international relations theory.

Cox's account stands, like Habermas's, fairly directly in the line of Horkheimer's 1937 study of social-scientific ideology. The latter's distinction between traditional theory and critical theory seems an obvious precursor to the effort to show in what ways problem-solving and critique are each 'for someone and for some purpose'.[56] By contrast, one of the most important twentieth-century contributions on the subject of knowledge and its relation to emancipatory action is that of a theorist whose work proceeds along a somewhat different path.

History and genealogy

Michel Foucault, as noted in Chapter 1, was dismissive of the study of ideology. However, as also noted, what he sought to dismiss was not the study of ideology in the sense used here. His objection was, rather, to a concern with ideology conceived as false—or 'alienated'—consciousness. For him, such a conception misses the point, inasmuch as the barriers to freedom lie not in falsehood, but in truth.

Foucault explains this claim, and clarifies its implications for a critical approach to scholarship, in a celebrated discussion of the relationship between truth and power.[57] His explanation begins in memorable terms.

Truth isn't outside power or lacking in power: . . . truth isn't the reward of free spirits, the child of protracted solitude, nor the privilege of those who have succeeded in liberating themselves. Truth is a thing of this world: it is produced only by virtue of multiple forms of constraint. And it induces regular effects of power.[58]

For Foucault, then, truth and power are mutually dependent, or at any rate mutually reinforcing. What counts as truth is produced through 'forms of constraint'. That is

---

[55] Ibid. 135.

[56] This is by no means to suggest that Horkheimer is the only precursor. In this article Cox himself cites Giambattista Vico and Antonio Gramsci as his more significant points of reference.

[57] Foucault 1980, 109, esp. 131 *et seq.*   [58] Ibid. 131.

to say, it is the outcome of structured social processes. At the same time, truth itself induces 'effects of power'. It helps to establish and sustain the social structures within which its validity is secured. Thus, truth is constituted through power, and power is partly constituted and reproduced through truth. Foucault refers to the various rules, procedures, expectations and other 'forms of constraint' that govern the production, distribution, and circulation of truth in a society as its 'regime of truth'. Analysed in this way, regimes of truth can be seen to be 'linked in a circular relation with systems of power', depending on those systems, while also supporting them.[59] And if regimes of truth and systems of power can be seen to stand together, then will they not also fall together? To challenge the one is, surely, to challenge the other.

With this in mind, Foucault argues that scholars seeking to transform relationships of power are misguided to focus on 'error, illusion, [or] alienated consciousness'; they should turn their attention instead to regimes of truth. In place of the study of 'ideology' (in this Engelsian sense), he proposes the analysis of the 'politics of truth' or, as his alternative term is generally rendered in English, 'power/knowledge'. In his words, '[t]he essential political problem for the intellectual . . . is [to change] the political, economic, institutional regime of the production of truth'. This is not simply a matter of 'changing people's consciousness—or what's in their heads'. Nor is it a matter of 'emancipating truth from every system of power (which would be a chimera, for truth is already power)'. Rather, the critical task is to detach 'the power of truth from the forms of hegemony, social, economic and cultural, within which it operates at the present time', and elucidate 'the possibility of constituting a new politics of truth'.[60] What does this task entail? Foucault's own path-breaking studies, on subjects such as madness and criminality, serve to illustrate his answer. At the same time, however, his published work contains many discussions of the strategies involved. One concept that is central to these discussions is 'genealogy'. In an essay entitled 'Nietzsche, Genealogy, History' Foucault explicates this Nietzschean-inspired notion by contrasting it with what he refers to as 'history in the traditional sense'.[61] As he conceives it, conventional historical enquiry is directed to discovering origins, and explaining how they set a course that can be traced in a coherent, linear fashion. History, for him, describes a steady, patient unfolding of events. Genealogy, on the other hand, eschews the search for origins, and relates instead a story of accidents, surprises, miscalculations, and deviations. Its ambition is to grasp the piecemeal and disorderly construction of things.

To clarify further the distinctiveness of genealogy, Foucault underlines a number of specific differences between these two approaches to historical investigation. While history tends to present reality as the rational effect—and hence in some sense the necessary outcome—of specified causes, genealogy depicts current conditions as dramatically contingent. Genealogical writing does not announce the culmination of historical processes; in Foucault's words, it 'does not resemble the evolution of a species and does not map the destiny of a people'.[62] This points to another difference.

---

[59] Foucault 1980, 133.   [60] Ibid.   [61] Foucault (Rabinow) 1984, 76, 86.   [62] Ibid. 81.

While history lends support to present arrangements by showing them to rest on firm foundations, genealogy works to demonstrate the fragility of inherited institutions and practices. Genealogical enquiry 'disturbs what was previously considered immobile; it fragments what was thought unified; it shows the heterogeneity of what was imagined consistent with itself'.[63] In turn, this brings out a further point of distinction. While history concerns itself with the forging of identities, the resolution of problems and the reconciliation of differences, a genealogical approach homes in on exclusions, tensions, and disparities. Genealogy goes beyond the 'consoling play of recognitions', to point up the 'hazardous play of dominations'.[64] There is also one final aspect to be noted. While history tries to remove all trace of the standpoint from which it proceeds, genealogy claims no transcendental status. Genealogical enquiry is 'explicit in its perspective'. It accepts without apology that its 'perception is slanted', for it is 'not given to a discreet effacement before the objects it observes and does not submit itself to their processes'.[65] Rather, its hallmark is indiscretion in the face of prevailing regimes of truth and systems of power.

Alongside genealogy, Foucault develops a number of other concepts for use as tools in the analysis of power/knowledge. In his later writing, the strategy of 'problematization' assumes particular prominence.[66] This refers to the procedure of turning givens into problems; calling assumptions into question; in Foucault's words, shifting background conditions into 'the play of the true and false'.[67] As with Cox's conception of critical theory, the aim here is to make regimes of truth part of the problematic. The significance of such a move, for Foucault, is that it brings those regimes into the domain of 'thought'. By 'thought' he intends something quite specific: not just 'that which inhabits a certain conduct and gives it meaning', but rather that which 'allows one to step back from this way of acting or reacting, to present it to oneself as an object of thought and question it as to its meaning, its conditions and its goals'. Viewed in this light, thought is 'freedom in relation to what one does, the motion by which one detaches oneself from it, establishes it as an object, and reflects on it as a problem'.[68] Like the other scholars whose work has been discussed, then, Foucault seeks to tap into the emancipatory potential of knowledge. What marks out problematization from 'hegemonic' investigation, and genealogy from conventional history, is also what marks out critical theory from traditional theory, emancipatory knowledge from technical and practical knowledge, and critique from problem-solving: enquiry is linked to transformative action. Foucault sums up this approach in a way that carries a striking echo of Marx's riposte to the philosophers (and, to that extent, bears witness to Foucault's own conflicted intellectual ancestry): '[K]nowledge is not made for understanding; it is made for cutting'.[69]

---

[63] Ibid. 82.
[65] Ibid. 90.
[67] Foucault 1989, 456–7.
[69] Ibid. 88 (cf. Marx (O'Malley) 1994, 118).

[64] Ibid. 88, 83.
[66] See, e.g., ibid. 381 *et seq.*
[68] Foucault (Rabinow) 1984, 388.

In summary

Whether considered individually or in terms of their interrelation, the accounts discussed in this section patently prompt many questions. This is amply confirmed by a body of relevant literature from which whole libraries could be (and no doubt are) filled. But I have said enough perhaps to bring a few points into focus.

To begin with, it is clear that the various accounts differ in important respects. One reason is that they proceed from different concerns. Whereas Marx's target is idealist philosophy, Horkheimer and Habermas set their critical sights on positivist social science; Cox takes aim at the leading traditions of international relations theory; and Foucault attacks Marxist preoccupations with false consciousness. With these concerns in mind, the theorists frame their central issue in diverse terms. If for Marx the issue is the link between philosophy and practical questions, for Horkheimer it is the extent to which empirical natural science should serve as a model for other forms of enquiry; for Habermas it is the role of cognitive interests in relation to knowledge; for Cox it is the scope of what counts as the global political problematic; and for Foucault it is the politics of truth, the relationship between truth and power. In turn, these issues point to challenges which the theorists clarify through diverse conceptual pairings. Where Marx opposes idealist philosophy to practical-critical theorizing, Horkheimer's contrast is between traditional theory and critical theory; Habermas's is between practical or technical knowledge and critical theory; Cox's is between problem-solving and critique; and Foucault's is between history and genealogy.

Rather than go more deeply into these and other differences, however, let me now try to highlight some commonalities. For it is equally clear that there exists a considerable area of overlap among the various accounts. Each seeks to define and promote a particular approach to the study of contemporary social arrangements, a particular conception of knowledge about collective life—'critical knowledge', it might be labelled. What does this entail? At least seven points emerge from the writings considered in this section. The starting-point is an awareness of the extent to which social enquiry is implicated in the world it studies. Claims about social reality do more than simply grasp or perceive that reality. They help to shape it. Thus, Foucault writes of the way regimes of truth are bound up with systems of power. This is a function of what social theorists refer to as the 'reflexivity' of modern life. In one seminal account, reflexivity is defined as the process by which 'social practices are constantly examined and reformed in the light of incoming information about those very practices, thus constitutively altering their character'. The result is that material conditions are 'partly constituted by actors' knowledge of them'.[70] Secondly, critical knowledge seeks to pursue the implications of this reflexivity with respect to social enquiry itself.[71] Just as social practices generally are examined and reformed in the light of

[70] Giddens 1990, 38.
[71] I draw here on a discussion of Horkheimer's 1937 essay in McCarthy 1994, 14 *et seq.*, in which McCarthy explains how 'critical social theory breaks with ["traditional" approaches] by, among other things, taking the reflexivity of social inquiry explicitly into account' (16).

incoming information about them, so—from a critical standpoint—scholarly practices should be examined, with a view to determining how, for their part, they should
be reformed in light of information about their reflexive relation with material reality. What information is relevant?

A third feature of critical knowledge is that it approaches the reformation of social
enquiry on the basis that the aim of such enquiry should be to transform unequal power
relations. In consequence, one piece of information about social enquiry and its reflexive relation with the world assumes particular importance. This is Marx's insight that,
if ideas shape reality, they by no means determine it. The problem with idealist philosophy is that it indulges in the 'fantasy [of] striving to attain in the mind what cannot yet be achieved in historical reality'.[72] Thus, a flock of sheep imagine themselves to
be, and parade to the world as, a ferocious pack of wolves. What critical knowledge
takes from this is a recognition that it is as ideological to overstate the role of ideas with
respect to collective life as it is to understate that role. If social enquiry is to play a part
in transforming unequal power relations, it cannot neglect to consider the conditions—the framework of institutions, practices, norms, and so on—in which those
relations are enabled and reproduced. Focusing on specific difficulties that arise in the
operation of social processes, without investigating relevant constraints, will not serve.

Fourthly, critical knowledge pursues its aim by operating upon the self-perception
of social actors, engaging them in a process of reflection on their circumstances.
Through ideology critique, for instance, contradictions between social practices and
legitimating principles may be brought into view. Practices accepted as justified, necessary or natural may be shown to be simply options in favour of the *status quo*. In
this way social actors may come to see themselves as complicit in perpetuating injustice—and, in turn, to revise their conduct. Critical knowledge thus trades on the
reflexivity of modern life, the awareness that knowledge feeds back into action. Of
course, there are no guarantees as to precisely how it feeds back, and whether the
result will be beneficent. But then, as Foucault points out, to call into question social
conditions that were previously taken for granted is already to achieve a kind of freedom; the first emancipatory step comes with the knowledge that things need not be
as they are. This points to a fifth feature. Critical knowledge does not itself seek to
specify what counts as emancipation. It takes changing social realities to preclude any
fixed definition. In any event, it recognizes that the meaning of emancipation is not
a matter of scholarly *fiat* but a process of social struggle. To recall Marx's distinction
mentioned in Chapter 1, the effort here is not to undertake criticism, but immanent
critique. Rather than proposing blueprints or advancing formulae of its own, critical
knowledge urges us to consider anew the significance and implications of our existing standards. By encouraging self-reflection, the aim is to mobilize potentials for
change that subsist, but remain unrealized, in current conditions.

How does critical knowledge relate to more 'traditional' approaches to the study
of social phenomena? A sixth aspect is that, in Horkheimer's phrase, critical knowledge speaks openly of 'what theory means in human life'. Insofar as traditional

[72] Eagleton 1997, 16.

approaches tend to assert their disinterestedness, critical theory is profoundly sceptical of this claim. This is not because critical theory considers that enquiry must necessarily be informed by narrow, sectional interests. As Cox observes, the aim of critical approaches is precisely to enlarge the field of vision, so as to achieve, as he puts it, a certain 'perspective on perspectives'. Rather, critical theory is sceptical of traditional claims to disinterestedness because it holds that there is no 'news from nowhere'. Narrow self-interest is not the sole alternative to disinterestedness. But a 'perspective on perspectives' is, after all, itself still a perspective. Thus, Cox insists that theory is always 'for someone and for some purpose', and Habermas calls attention to the way cognitive interests shape efforts to comprehend objective reality. With this in mind, critical knowledge invites us to connect our studies with our values, our activities as scholars with our experience as citizens. It proposes that, if we are going to intervene in the world as scholars, we should do so purposefully, and in ways that carry forward our projects as citizens. Writing in 1930s Germany, Horkheimer had reason to be emphatic about this. 'The future of humanity', he proclaims, 'depends on the existence today of the critical attitude. . . . Mankind has already been abandoned by a science which in its imaginary self-sufficiency thinks of the shaping of practice, which it serves and to which it belongs, simply as something lying outside its borders and is content with this separation of thought and action.'[73]

In writing this, Horkheimer also touches on another aspect of the relationship between critical and 'traditional' knowledge, which will serve as my final point. After asserting that the future of humanity depends on the existence of the critical attitude, he adds that that attitude 'of course contains within it elements from traditional theories'.[74] What makes traditional theory ideological for Horkheimer is (*inter alia*) that it 'absolutizes' its own conception of knowledge 'as though [this] were grounded in the inner nature of knowledge as such'.[75] In doing so, it blocks awareness that other forms of enquiry are possible. As with Marx's objections to idealist interpretation, Horkheimer's concern is not that positivist social scientists deploy empirical methodologies, but that they *only* deploy empirical methodologies. Critical theory, by contrast, does not absolutize its own conception of knowledge. It does not deny the possibility, and the value, of other forms of analysis. Indeed, all the theorists whose work is discussed in this section assert the indispensability of traditional methods and logics, and quite plainly draw heavily upon them. Critical knowledge does not—and could not—claim to serve as a substitute for received approaches. Its claim is, instead, to offer a way of relativizing those approaches, and of highlighting and eventually transcending the limitations they involve.

In this regard the guiding idea is Marx's premise: the point is to change the world. Of course, not everyone shares this premise. Some are content with the world as it is and, while recognizing that things will inevitably change, would prefer to minimize the extent to which they do. But most people have more mixed feelings, and are unable to rest content with arrangements in which some members of society are very

[73] Horkheimer 1972, 242.   [74] Ibid.   [75] Ibid. 194.

much more equal than others. At any rate, to scholars desiring change, the writings just reviewed deliver a clear message. Traditional approaches (whether exemplified in terms of idealist philosophy, positivist social science, problem-solving international relations theory, or conventional history) cannot suffice. A distinctive, explicitly emancipatory approach to knowledge—critical knowledge—is required.

CRITICAL KNOWLEDGE AND INTERNATIONAL LAW

It is this explicitly emancipatory approach to knowledge that has informed my arguments about the proclaimed 'norm of democratic governance'. To explore further the significance of that approach for those arguments, let us now turn from the study of social practices in general to the study of one social practice in particular: international law. How are we to understand the specificity of a critical conception of international legal knowledge? Before continuing, it should be stressed that the term 'critical' has a distinctive resonance here, which does not necessarily coincide with the term's resonance in other contexts. Thus, for instance, the various 'new approaches to international law' exemplify the critical conception of knowledge I describe to diverse extents and in diverse ways.[76] The account that follows intersects with discussions of those approaches at an oblique angle, so to speak, highlighting strengths and weaknesses that may appear less significant from other perspectives. What, then, sets critical enquiry, as I understand it, apart from other forms of international legal investigation? In this section I draw a distinction between three contemporary approaches to the study of international law: 'problem-solving', 'scepticism', and 'critique'. With these three categories I do not claim—and certainly do not manage—to capture the entire spectrum of international legal scholarship, or even the entire spectrum of scholarship considered in this book. Nor do I identify bodies of writing which are altogether discrete; most work clearly cannot be so easily pigeonholed. As in the case of the various contrasts considered earlier in this chapter, the distinctions I draw are not based on differences of kind, but rather on differences of emphasis. And as in the case of those contrasts too, the point is not to cover the field of available approaches, but simply to elucidate the distinctive character of critical knowledge by setting it against the foil of competing traditions.

Problem-Solving and Scepticism

Borrowing Cox's term, then, I refer to an initial mode of enquiry as *problem-solving*. As in his account, enquiry in this mode is so named because its concern is to isolate problems—gaps, disjunctures, inconsistencies, etc.—and propose remedial action. The scholar expounds an international legal rule or glosses an international instrument with the aim of showing how strains which have arisen can be removed.

[76] For an illuminating discussion of these approaches, see Cass 1996.

This form of enquiry emerged within the framework of nineteenth-century liberal-ism, and is today the most familiar style of international legal scholarship. It might even be called international law's 'traditional theory'.

An example of problem-solving scholarship is the thesis discussed in this book, the call to recognize a right to democratic governance. What is the problem isolated in this thesis, and what is the remedial action proposed? For Thomas Franck, among others, the problem lies with the traditional doctrine according to which inter-national law accepts as legitimate any government with effective control over sover-eign territory. The persistence of this doctrine entails that international law has fallen out of alignment with its supposed basis in international practice. When relevant developments (especially recent developments with regard to international electoral assistance) are taken into account, it becomes apparent that international law is beginning to accept as legitimate only democratic governments. A norm of democra-tic governance is emerging. Anne-Marie Slaughter also considers that the problem lies with the doctrine to which Franck refers. For her, however, the main source of strain is that international law has fallen out of alignment with advances in the field of inter-national relations. When insights concerning the link between democratic govern-ment and peace are taken into account, it becomes clear that international law should accept as legitimate only democratic governments. A world of democratic states is likely to become a peaceful world.

Writing of her concern to connect international law with work in the field of inter-national relations, Slaughter declares a commitment to improving the 'conceptual fit between international law and politics'.[77] This might serve as a summary of the aims of problem-solving scholarship more generally. Such scholarship seeks to strengthen international law by identifying and correcting misalignments between international norms on the one hand and international practice and theory on the other. For some international legal scholars, however, this preoccupation with misalignments goes hand in hand with a relative neglect of other important matters. As soon as these mat-ters are allowed to enter the equation, the conclusions reached in problem-solving scholarship become difficult to accept. Enquiry in the mode of *scepticism* is oriented to puncturing the confidence with which problem-solving proceeds, debunking the claims that make coherence appear possible, and exposing the intractability of inter-national legal problems, the irremediable weakness that afflicts all international legal norms. This form of enquiry gained prominence in the 1980s and 1990s in the con-text of efforts to bring to the study of international law the methods of deconstruc-tion, discourse analysis, and related approaches.

Within the compass of this book, sceptical scholarship is exemplified in some of the misgivings to which the democratic norm thesis has given rise. One issue is the indeterminacy of the central concept, democracy. Noting the many meanings that vie for ascendancy, Roth observes: 'No term can mean so many things and continue to mean anything.' For him, 'the consequence of this indeterminacy is that "democracy"

---

[77] Slaughter 1995, 506.

becomes identified with whichever choice engages our sympathies . . . The idea of an emerging right to democratic governance transfers this problem from the realm of rhetoric to the realm of legality'.[78] Another concern is the adoption of an imperious posture with respect to democracy's significance. Thus, Koskenniemi expresses discomfort at the 'initial positioning of the author him/herself, as possessing a transparent view of the essential meaning of democracy and constructing an argument to impose it on "them" '. Rather than trying to develop general international legal principles about democracy, he suggests that international legal scholars would be better advised to search for 'more concrete forms of political commitment' which might '[engage them] in actual struggles, both as observers and participants' and '[bring] in a wealth of historical experience, [while also] taking the participants' self-understanding seriously'.[79] Finally, there is the worry about the norm's potential to serve as an agent of neo-colonialism. This is reflected in Koskenniemi's contention, recalled in the previous chapter, that a democratic norm is undesirable on the additional ground that it is too easily turned against redistributive claims and towards hegemonic agendas.

Scepticism, then, directs attention to the indeterminacy of the language in which international law trades, and especially some of it. At the same time, it highlights the need for scholars to take seriously the self-understanding of those whose words and actions are implicated in their analyses. And it stresses the importance of remaining attentive to the tendency, or at any rate the potential, for ambiguities to be resolved in real-life contexts on the side of oppression. To those working in the tradition of primary interest in this chapter, these are valuable points. As in the case of problem-solving, however, insufficient regard is paid to a number of other matters, the result of which is, once again, to call into question the conclusions that are reached. Before turning to these matters, let us first revisit problem-solving from the perspective of enquiry in the mode of *critique*.

Critique

In the first place, recalling Cox's discussion, it might be observed that problem-solving scholarship largely takes 'the world as it finds it'. The aim is to make prevailing arrangements 'work smoothly by dealing effectively with particular sources of trouble'.[80] Thus, (to use Slaughter's word) the focus is on problems of 'fit', and systemic issues are addressed only as functional components of a larger structure which is not itself in question. In consequence, the relationships and institutions that shape what can be achieved through international law form the horizon of enquiry. On the one hand, constraints affecting the development of international legal norms are treated as given facts. On the other hand, constraints affecting the impact of international legal norms are regarded as extraneous concerns; norms are considered on the basis of a working assumption that, provided they can be made actually to apply (through

---

[78] Roth 1996, 236.   [79] Koskenniemi 1996, 234–5.   [80] Cox 1981, 128–9.

adequate mechanisms of enforcement and so on), no relevant constraints affect the character and scope of the difference they may make. In this sense, as Horkheimer writes of 'traditional theory', problem-solving international legal scholarship tends to treat the activity of international society as 'blind and concrete', the activity of those who hold international legal rights and duties as 'abstract and conscious'.[81]

Another feature of international legal problem-solving is that a key part is played by explanations in the style of what Foucault refers to as conventional 'history'.[82] Legal problem-solving is less focused than some important traditions of empirical social science on generating predictive knowledge via causal explanations. Instead, it achieves a measure of control over outcomes by means of interpretive knowledge based on narrative explanations which—to recall Foucault's phrase—'resemble the evolution of a species [or] . . . map the destiny of a people'.[83] Thus, Franck explains the emergence of the norm of democratic governance as an edifice built from three key building blocks, successively put in place. His analysis of the problem and its solution evokes a story that begins with the principle of self-determination, develops with efforts to codify human rights, and eventually—with electoral assistance—leads to the norm proposed. Inasmuch as Slaughter explains the desirability of a democratic criterion of governmental legitimacy in terms of the liberal peace, 'history' is once again at work. Her analysis of the problem and its solution evokes a story that begins with a small zone of peace, develops as that zone steadily (and, more recently, exponentially) enlarges, and portends the zone's continued growth, until one day all might be brought within it. In portraying a 'world of liberal states' as the sole alternative to sacrificing universalism and 'recognizing that States in the international system inhabit very different worlds',[84] she is especially explicit in tying her proposal to the forging of identities, the reconciliation of differences, and the culmination of historical processes.

A further characteristic of problem-solving is that it approaches knowledge as a matter of observation or apprehension of facts which are, in some sense, immediate and evident to anyone who cares to look. When, for example, the claim is put forward that democratic government is becoming normative, it is treated as obvious what is to count as evidence of this. Though all are aware that democracy is a contested concept, associated with a wide diversity of political arrangements, only a passing assertion is made about the meaning of democracy for international legal purposes. Beyond this, it is not considered necessary to go more deeply into discussion of the basis on which the 'facts' of democratic government may be supposed to count as such. As Horkheimer explains with regard to traditional theory, the 'genesis of particular objective facts' and the 'practical application of the conceptual systems' by which those facts are grasped are taken to be external to the enquiry itself.[85]

This points to another aspect. While problem-solving scholarship frequently aims to influence legal developments, it does so on the basis of a clear distinction between description and prescription, commentary and advocacy, facts and values. From this

---

[81] See Horkheimer 1972, 200.   [82] See Foucault (Rabinow) 1984, 76.   [83] Ibid. 81.
[84] Slaughter 1995, 538. See Ch. 3 above.   [85] Horkheimer 1972, 208.

perspective, it is one thing to assert knowledge of things as they are; quite another to intervene in, and seek to affect, the social processes through which they are constituted. In familiar language, scholarship is a 'source' of international law, but only a 'secondary' or 'law-evidencing' source, not a primary or 'law-making' one.[86] Thus, for instance, Franck puts his case largely in descriptive terms, as a claim about how international law now stands, if properly understood; he then reinforces this claim by adding that current trends should be encouraged, in view of the findings to which Slaughter attaches importance. Slaughter, for her part, advances her argument primarily in prescriptive terms, referring in support to Franck's contention that the state of affairs which she advocates is already materializing.

Finally, as this highlights, problem-solving scholarship customarily proceeds from a detached standpoint, such that objectivity is equated with disinterestedness and knowledge is uncoupled from interests. Yet, as Habermas emphasizes, knowledge and interests are inextricably linked. Not only does knowledge draw impetus from distinct interests; those interests also provide the very conditions of possibility of objectivity, the very basis for apprehending 'reality in any way whatsoever'.[87] In Habermas's account, different interests suggest different ways of apprehending reality, and what 'technical' and 'practical' cognitive interests suggest is the pursuit of a 'pure' kind of knowledge that claims to 'derive everything from itself'.[88] Here, of course, it is not possible to cite examples from writing associated with the democratic norm thesis, for the thesis illustrates this aspect of problem-solving scholarship only by omission. Attention is *not* called to the interests motivating enquiry. The relationship between these interests and the investigative methods used is *not* made a matter of conscious reflection. More specifically, the thesis masks the extent to which it is connected to a technical and practical cognitive interest in the integrity of prevailing relationships and institutions. In this way, as earlier chapters of this book have sought to demonstrate, the democratic norm thesis 'succumbs to unacknowledged external conditions and becomes ideological'.[89] The project of fixing or repairing becomes an obstacle to efforts at redesigning or remodelling. What sets out to be a 'guide to help solve the problems posed within the terms of the particular perspective which was the point of departure' thus comes to serve as a 'guide to tactical actions which, intended or unintended, sustain the existing order'.[90]

So much a sceptical scholar might likewise wish to argue. Whereas problem-solving seeks to make the international legal system work better, scepticism asserts the need to put the system into question. Whereas problem-solving relates narratives of progress, resolution, and coherence, scepticism tells stories of contingency, provisionality, and contradiction. Whereas problem-solving models itself after technical knowledge and uses methods geared to the observation of facts, scepticism maintains that international legal enquiry is an inescapably interpretive activity. Whereas problem-solving uncouples description from argument, scepticism stresses the way description functions as argument, law shapes politics. And whereas, in uncoupling

---

[86] Statute of the International Court of Justice, article 38(1).   [87] Habermas 1987, 311.
[88] Ibid. 314.   [89] Ibid.   [90] Cox 1981, 130.

description from argument, problem-solving claims to achieve objectivity, scepticism casts doubt on that claim. What, then, are the respects in which, according to critique, scepticism falls short? The key to grasping these lies in the fourth and fifth features of critical knowledge highlighted in the previous section. For all that sets it apart from problem-solving, scepticism joins the latter in presenting its analyses as 'news from nowhere'. Critical knowledge, by contrast, takes up enquiry with a view to engaging social actors in a process of reflection on their circumstances. By inviting consideration of contradictions between social practices and legitimating principles, it intends to challenge complicity and promote resistance.

Enquiry in the mode of critique is thus characterized by a desire to involve international law in the process of social transformation. As in Horkheimer's account of critical theory, the aim is to serve not just as 'an expression of the concrete historical situation', but as a 'force within it to stimulate change', not just as a 'cog in an already existent mechanism', but as an 'element in action leading to new social forms'.[91] If critique shares the sceptical determination to put systemic issues into question, it does so with a clear focus. Rather than flitting with scepticism's gadfly, it holds fast to a preoccupation with the transformation of relations of domination. Cox calls this the 'view from below': the analyst 'tries to look at the world from the perspective of those who cannot be content with things as they are'.[92] To this end, whereas scepticism directs attention to the limitations of existing institutions and ideas, critique concerns itself with their transformative possibilities as well. Of crucial importance in this regard is the insight that nothing is ever 'identical to itself'. Reconstruction need not be the baffling, high-handed and wholly arbitrary process it is often made to seem in sceptical analyses, for institutions and ideas themselves provide resources for their own remaking; there is always a plurality of logics in play, including some which point beyond those currently dominant. Thus, critique seeks to show how international law can serve to stabilize oppression but also to unsettle it, to obstruct emancipation but also to enable it. Viewed in this light, indeterminacy is at one level international law's weakness, at another its greatest strength. It is precisely because principles are contradictory that we are able to find in them counter-systemic logics. It is precisely because norms are unstable that we can lead them to 'surpass themselves'.[93] And it is precisely because words are ambiguous that we have the chance to make them mean more than they currently want to mean. From a critical perspective, then, the issue is not just whether we perceive indeterminacy, but what we do with it.

In seeking to harness the power of indeterminacy in the struggle against domination, critique endorses the sceptical insistence that the self-understanding of those whose language and actions are implicated in international legal analyses must be taken seriously. (Sceptics typically insist on this in order to dissociate themselves from some of the more extreme, decontextualized forms of discourse analysis.) But if critical approaches take the participants' self-understanding seriously, they do not take that self-understanding so seriously as to lose the basis for critically engaging with it. As Thomas McCarthy explains, critique regards 'participants' views of their practices'

[91] Horkheimer 1972, 215–16.   [92] Cox 1997, 70.   [93] See Eagleton 1991, 171.

neither as irrelevant nor as the 'last word'. Rather, it 'treats [those views] dialectically: the dialectical critique of reason does not abstractly negate ideas of reason but seeks critically to appropriate them and to enlist them in the struggle for a better world'.[94] Adopting the posture of Eagleton's *faux naïf* evoked in the Introduction to this book, the critic thus reminds us of our lofty principles and asks why it is that those principles do not enter more on our material circumstances. The false naivety of this enquiry is reflected in the fact that there is no need to spell out what follows. The critic has already said enough to disturb our tranquillity, and stir us to confront the further question of how this state of affairs can be changed so as to make our ideals less like illusions.[95]

Likewise, critique does not abstractly negate other investigative approaches. Just as the theorists discussed earlier in this chapter rely in their analyses on 'traditional' methods and logics, so too the international legal critic draws on the methods and logics of problem-solving and scepticism. A critical approach to international legal scholarship is not a replacement for those approaches. Its function is, instead, to highlight their shortcomings, as well as their contingency, as methods of pursuing international legal knowledge.

One of the most prominent forms of critical legal scholarship is feminist analysis, and it is not surprising, therefore, that an exceptionally clear summary of this mode of enquiry can be found in the work of a feminist scholar. Noting that rights are open to misappropriation and abuse, that rights provoke counter-claims and invite exceptions, and that rights are linked to unjust conceptual structures, Carol Smart observes—as many critics of rights have done—that this is not a cause for quitting the terrain of law or renouncing the effort to win recognition of rights. It is, however, a reason for remaining alert to law's enmeshment with politics and articulation with morality. For, she writes, law might be seen 'both as a means of "liberation" and, at the same time, as a means of the reproduction of an oppressive social order', both as a '[facilitator of] change and [as] an obstacle to change'. An emancipatory approach to international legal knowledge starts with the knowledge that law is not a unity, but '[operates] on a number of dimensions at the same time'.[96]

CONCLUSION

For Max Horkheimer, as indicated above, one of the features that distinguishes a 'critical' approach to social enquiry from a 'traditional' one is that the latter speaks only of what knowledge means 'in the isolated sphere in which for historical reasons it comes into existence'. The former, by contrast, speaks of what knowledge means 'in human life'.[97] Drawing on work by Horkheimer and others, I have sought in this chapter to describe a critical approach to the study of international law, in which scholarship is addressed openly, and indeed insistently, to life. I have done so as a way

---

[94] McCarthy 1994, 20.   [95] Eagleton 1991, 172.   [96] Smart 1986, 117.
[97] Horkheimer 1972, 197.

of articulating the theoretical underpinnings of my own investigations in this book, but also as a way of defending the value of investigations of this kind.

Concern about the artificiality of 'traditional' forms of international legal scholarship is as old as those forms themselves. To some international legal analysts, however, this concern has particular urgency today. David Kennedy develops this theme in an essay published in 1994.[98] His starting-point is the observation that international law is nowadays valued less for its potential role in relation to 'particular places, people or causes' than out of enthusiasm for some generalized notion of 'the international'.[99] By this he means that reform proposals are not so much geared to achieving specific outcomes; rather, their point is to enhance the authority of international law and institutions as an end in and of itself. Attention to the level of governance has overtaken attention to the consequences of governance. Kennedy observes that the aspiration for an autonomous 'international'—'detached from politics, above redistributive debates'[100]—is linked to a long-standing ambivalence about sovereignty. 'Although international institutionalists have been announcing the death of the State for generations, they have sold their institutional innovations as the products of State consent, deferential to State will'.[101] But the drive to autonomy is also linked to the displacement of politics by a fresh and distinctive wave of disciplinary self-promotion. 'Specific political choices' have come to seem insignificant, in the face of a 'primary reform commitment . . . to the international itself'.[102]

Against this background, Kennedy evokes the idea of inaugurating a 'new wave' of enthusiasm for international law 'after ambivalence about sovereignty and agnosticism about politics'. We might return, he suggests, to earlier traditions, 'more insistent about redistributional consequences, about points of view and cultural perspectives, about centers and peripheries, winners and losers'.[103] We might begin to invest less in disciplinary autonomy and more in context-sensitive interventions in life: '[s]ometimes we would promote the State, insist on form, sometimes champion an international institution, a local court, or a corporate player'.[104] Or perhaps, he continues, what is needed is not a 'whole new wave', but simply 'a little vigilance, vigilance among current international enthusiasts about treating the international as a substitute for politics'. For 'it is all too easy for internationalists to forget that the question is not what will further the international, but which international to further'.[105] I share Kennedy's disquiet about the abstractions, or evasions, of international legal scholarship, and in this book have joined him in considering how these tendencies might be reversed. The corrective I have proposed adds a third possibility to the two he suggests. Something less grand than a new wave, yet more substantial than an exhortation to vigilance. 'Which international to further' is precisely the sort of enquiry with which *ideology critique* is concerned. In moving the issue of asymmetrical power relations to the centre of our deliberations, critique prompts us to pose this question—and also guides us in answering it.

---

[98] Kennedy 1994. [99] Ibid. 338. [100] Ibid. 369. [101] Ibid. 349.
[102] Ibid. 339. [103] Ibid. 374. [104] Ibid. [105] Ibid. 375.

Conclusion

My starting-point in this book was the claim, elaborated in the 1990s, that a norm of democratic governance is emerging in international law. The time has arrived, it is said, to discard traditional assumptions of international legal neutrality with respect to constitutions. Government which is the result of free and fair elections should now be regarded as a universal legal entitlement and legal standard of legitimate authority.

This claim well captures the mood of celebration which followed the fall of the Berlin Wall and the project of political and economic reconstruction that was thereby set in train, or given impetus, in many countries. It well captures the experience of first-time electors, no longer denied the most basic rights of citizenship, and of political dissidents, no longer constrained to live with their backs turned to the state.[1] But it fails to reflect the sense of melancholy, which has been the celebration's widely remarked accompaniment.[2] The sources of this melancholy are very familiar. In part it is a function of the enduring disappointments associated with Western political life, and of the perception—expressed in low voter turnouts and often voiced distrust of politicians—that democratic institutions have become distant and irrelevant. In part it is a function of the limited character of change in post-authoritarian societies, the persistence of political and economic structures largely closed to popular participation. In part it is a function of the course of events in areas of Eastern Europe: as post-communist enthusiasms spiralled into nationalist violence, liberal democracy was forced to confront its discomforting susceptibility, in Slavoj Žižek's words, to '[open] up the space for . . . organicist populism'.[3] And in part democratic melancholy is a function of the way globalizing processes are putting strain on the very capacity of existing democratic arrangements to secure public control and political equality with respect to the terms of collective life.

As also recalled at the outset of this book, the claim that a norm of democratic governance is emerging in international law has not gone unchallenged. But if the sceptical responses it has elicited succeed in capturing the spirit of dissatisfaction, for their part they miss the extent to which there are indeed grounds for celebration. They fail to register the very real advances that are fostered and facilitated through the global circulation of democratic ideas. How is an analyst to keep in view *both* these facets of our contemporary circumstances? How is she to retain a sense of democracy's achievements and potentials, while also remaining alert to its very considerable omissions and limitations? I have proposed that the critique of ideology might help in this regard. Ideology critique suggests a dialectical approach that enables us, as Terry

---

[1] I owe this latter image to Michael Walzer's evocative account of the 'anti-political politics' described and practised in the 1970s and 1980s by Georg Konrad, Vaclav Havel, and others: 'a way of living alongside the totalitarian state but, so to speak, with one's back turned toward it'. See Walzer 1995, 21.

[2] I take the expression 'democratic melancholy' from Bruckner 1990. For a sampling of observations along these lines, see also Walker 1993, 145 and Held 1995a, 21.

[3] Žižek 1994a, 3. See also Žižek 1993, ch. 6.

Eagleton puts it, to 'grasp . . . emancipatory and oppressive aspects together, as elements of a single logic'.[4] It invites us to view ideas in more than one dimension, and to consider both their part in supporting power and their role in promoting resistance. It initiates, or at any rate fuels, a process of reflection on the contradictions between the ideals we espouse and the realities we live, and on the possibilities that arise for resolving those contradictions.

In this book, after reviewing (in Chapter 1) the method of ideology critique, I have used that method to analyse the claim (outlined in Chapter 2) that a norm of democratic governance is emerging in international law. The result (presented in Chapters 3 and 4) was to bring into focus both limitations and further potentials. With these in mind, I have put forward (in Chapter 5) a tentative proposal for rearticulating the relationship between international law and democracy, in the shape of a 'principle of democratic inclusion'. I have also elaborated a little (in Chapter 6) on the character and significance of critique. The axes around which the discussion has turned, then, are, firstly, the critique of ideology and, secondly, the limitations and further potentials of the democratic norm thesis. It remains now to say something about how these two axes—the one methodological and theoretical, the other normative—interrelate. Are they connected only contingently, or is there some deeper logic that ties them together? Does the critique of ideology operate on a purely instrumental level, as a particular method of analysis informed by a particular theory? Or is it linked in some intrinsic fashion with the object of analysis, the normative question of democracy and its meaning and status within international law?

THE UNSOLVED RIDDLE OF ALL CONSTITUTIONS

Democracy and ideology make an intriguing pair. On the one hand, they stand in apparently antithetical relation. Just as in former decades democracy belonged here and ideology there, democracy was what we had and ideology what they had, so today democracy seems to be everywhere and ideology nowhere, democracy seems to represent now and ideology then. On the other hand, these two concepts also have much in common. Each came to prominence as a revolutionary idea. Each has been the object of ongoing efforts to trim or neutralize its transformative dimensions. Each has also been the object of ongoing efforts to sideline it, with or without some replacement (polyarchy, power/knowledge, etc.). Each nonetheless retains enduring appeal in the struggle against oppression. For each offers an exceptionally effective strategy: the same unflattering mirror that makes us recognize ourselves as oppressors and accomplices to oppression, and, not liking what we see, commit ourselves to change.

To explore further the interrelation of democracy and ideology and the implications that follow for the present study of international law, let us return one last time to Karl Marx, whose work on the critique of ideology I have discussed, but whose

[4] Eagleton 1997, 43–4.

writings on democracy I have not so far touched upon. As hardly needs stating, this is not the place, and I am certainly not the author, to attempt an account of Marxian views on the subject of democracy. I wish simply to recall a famous passage that appears in one of Marx's early works.

Democracy is the solved *riddle* of all constitutions. Here not merely *implicitly* and in essence but *existing* in reality, the constitution is constantly brought back to its actual basis, the *actual human being*, the *actual people*, and established as the people's *own* work.[5]

Eagleton contends that Marx consistently emphasized the 'dynamic, open-ended, interactive nature of things, detested those overweening systems of thought which . . . believed that they could somehow stitch up the whole world within their concepts'. He adds that it is 'darkly ironic that [Marx's] own work would, among other things, give birth in time to just such sterile system-building'.[6] For many contemporary theorists, however, Marx contributed to his own traducement by failing adequately to pursue the implications of his attachment to the critique of ideology. From this perspective, Marx was right to identify democracy as a riddle that challenges *all constitutions*. In doing so, he helped to theorize the universality of experiences of oppression and struggles for emancipation. But he was wrong to identify democracy as the *solution* to that riddle. In doing so, he lent unintended aid to such later exercises in sterile system-building as 'people's democracy'.

Whatever the more compelling interpretation of Marx's position, the point here is that ideology critique suggests a distinctive approach with respect to democracy. Thomas McCarthy summarizes the general thrust of this approach in the following terms. Acknowledging concerns about the susceptibility of big ideas or 'grand narratives' like democracy to support all-encompassing systems, he writes that the way to meet these concerns is not to eschew grand narratives. Rather, it is to adopt a provisional approach to their significance, to conceive them 'as *ongoing accomplishments. They are never finished, but have to be constructed, deconstructed and reconstructed in ever-changing circumstances'. Through critique, he contends, we can 'develop and deploy practically interested, theoretically informed, general accounts in a fallibilistic and open manner, that is, without claiming closure'.[7] What does this imply where democracy is concerned?

Insofar as democracy offers a powerful argument against domination, the critique of ideology affirms the importance of holding onto that argument. This translates into a claim that the democratic ideals of self-rule and political equality must not be wasted. 'Realism' must not be allowed to corrode them; statism must not be allowed to confine them; scepticism must not be allowed to overwhelm them. On the other hand, insofar as this argument will be called upon to do service in ever-changing circumstances, the critique of ideology also affirms the importance of keeping open the question of what counts as domination. This translates into a claim that the democratic ideals of self-rule and equality must not be reduced to any particular set

---

[5] Marx (Tucker), 20 (emphasis in original).   [6] Eagleton 1997, 8.
[7] McCarthy 1994, 19 (emphasis in original).

of institutions and practices. Instead, they must be permitted to retain their character as tools for criticizing actuality and orienting change. Thus, in an often cited passage, Jacques Derrida proposes that democracy should be seen as having the 'structure of a promise'. It is 'never simply given', but is rather something that always 'remains to be thought and *to come* [*à venir*]: not something that is certain to happen tomorrow, not the democracy . . . of the *future*, but . . . *the memory of that which carries the future, the to-come, here and now*'.[8] Viewed in this light, democracy's failures and omissions appear not as broken promises to be written off, but as promises that remain permanently executory, never to be fully performed.[9] With democracy we 'summon the very thing that will never present itself in full presence, . . . [await] what [we] do not expect . . .'.[10]

I noted a moment ago that for some scholars the fact that work by Marx got caught up in sterile system-building may not be as ironic as Eagleton suggests. What is surely ironic, however, is that at the end of the twentieth century Marx's idea that democracy is the consummate formula for collective life, the great discovery which at last resolves the mystery of constitutions, should have resurfaced in the writings of Francis Fukuyama. Of course, the conception of democratic politics that is involved is very different. But the notion is again advanced that democracy is the final form of human government, that which fits political authority to the measure of humankind. For Fukuyama, as noted in Chapter 2, recent events confirm the existence of a 'common evolutionary pattern for *all* human societies— . . . something like a Universal History of mankind in the direction of liberal democracy'.[11] He explains this on the basis that liberal democracy satisfies certain fundamental human needs—captured by Hegel in the notion of a desire for 'recognition'—which other modes of government leave unfulfilled.[12]

If Marx neglected adequately to pursue the implications of his attachment to the critique of ideology, Fukuyama is quite explicit in declaring that democracy's rise spells ideology's fall. With liberal democracy now unrivalled, he holds, the end of ideology—or, as he puts it, the end of 'history'—has arrived. 'What we may be witnessing is not just the end of the Cold War, or the passing of a particular period of postwar history, but the end of history as such: that is, the end point of mankind's ideological evolution . . .'[13] In earlier chapters I highlighted some of the ways in which scholars are likewise seeking to theorize the replacement of ideology by democracy within international law, likewise seeking to detach democracy from history and fix it in international law as an event and 'place'. I tried to show how such moves to declare the end of ideology themselves operate ideologically. Through them we are invited to put aside democratic melancholy, and celebrate the occurrence of a worldwide liberal revolution.

In response to these moves I have put forward a proposal geared to lodging within international law a permanent reminder of the need to grasp emancipatory and

---

[8] Derrida 1992, 78 (emphasis in original).   [9] Cf. Bobbio 1987, 18, 37.

[10] Derrida 1994, 65.   [11] Fukuyama 1992, 48 (emphasis in original).

[12] See Fukuyama 1992, Part III.   [13] Fukuyama 1989, 4.

oppressive aspects together, a permanent trace of critique. The principle of democratic inclusion aims to affirm democracy's pertinence in all contexts, while also keeping its meaning open to ongoing recontextualization. It aims to acknowledge democracy's metapolitical appeal,[14] while also recognizing that it is rooted in political struggles. And it aims to take note of democracy's historical legacies, while also defending its character as an ideal, transformative tool and executory promise, always 'to come'. Whatever the merits or demerits of this particular proposal, the argument comes down to this. International law should not seek to establish democracy as the *solution* to the question of constitutions. But neither should it baulk at the prospect of asserting democracy's universal significance. Its ambition should be, rather, to help in entrenching democracy as the endlessly tantalizing, perpetually unsettling, continuously confounding *riddle* of all constitutions.

[14] See Held 1995*a*, 282.

References

ABERCROMBIE, N., HILL, S., & TURNER, B., *The Dominant Ideology Thesis* (London: Allen & Unwin, 1980).

AKE, C., 'Devaluing Democracy', in Diamond, L. & Plattner, M. F. (eds.), *Capitalism, Socialism and Democracy Revisited* (Baltimore, MD: Johns Hopkins University Press, 1983) 26.

ALSTON, P., 'The Myopia of the Handmaidens: International Lawyers and Globalization' 8 *European Journal of International Law* (1997) 435.

ALTHUSSER, L., *For Marx* (London: Allen Lane, 1969).

——, 'Ideological State Apparatuses (Notes Towards an Investigation)', in Žižek, S. (ed.), *Mapping Ideology* (London: Verso, 1994) 100.

AMSDEN, A., KOCHANOWICZ, J., & TAYLOR, L., *The Market Meets its Match: Restructuring the Economies of Eastern Europe* (Cambridge, MA: Harvard University Press, 1994).

APPARDURAI, A., 'Disjuncture and Difference in the Global Cultural Economy' 2 *Public Culture* (1990) 1.

ARCHIBUGI, D. & HELD, D., 'Editors' Introduction', in Archibugi, D. & Held, D. (eds.), *Cosmopolitan Democracy: An Agenda for a New World Order* (Cambridge: Polity Press, 1995) 1.

BALL, T., & DAGGER, R., *Political Ideologies and the Democratic Ideal* (New York: HarperCollins, 1995).

BARBER, B., *Strong Democracy—Participatory Politics for a New Age* (Berkeley, CA: University of California Press, 1984).

BARRETT, M., *The Politics of Truth, from Marx to Foucault* (Cambridge: Polity Press, 1991).

BAUDRILLARD, J., *Simulacra and Simulation,* trans. Glaser, S. E. (Ann Arbor, MI: University of Michigan Press, 1994).

BAUMAN, Z., *Postmodern Ethics* (Oxford: Blackwell, 1993).

BEETHAM, D., *Human Rights and Democracy: A Multifaceted Relationship* (Leeds: Centre for Democratization Studies/Leeds University Press, 1995).

——, 'Human Rights as a Model for Cosmopolitan Democracy', in Archibugi, D., Held, D., & Köhler, M. (eds.), *Re-imagining Political Community: Studies in Cosmopolitan Democracy* (Cambridge: Polity Press, 1998) 58.

BELL, D., *The End of Ideology,* rev. ed. (Glencoe, IL: Free Press, 1962).

——, 'The World and the United States in 2013', in *Daedalus* (Summer 1987), vol. 116, No. 3, 1.

BENHABIB, S., *Critique, Norm, and Utopia: A Study of the Foundations of Critical Theory* (New York: Columbia University Press, 1986).

BERMAN, N., 'Sovereignty in Abeyance: Self-Determination and International Law' 7 *Wisconsin International Law Journal* (1988) 51.

BOBBIO, N., *The Future of Democracy: A Defence of the Rules of the Game,* Bellamy, R. (ed.), trans. Griffin, R. (Cambridge: Polity Press, 1987).

BOUTROS-GHALI, B., 'Democracy: A Newly Recognized Imperative' 1 *Global Governance* (1995) 3.

BROWN, C., '"Really Existing Liberalism", Peaceful Democracies and International Order', in Fawn, R. and Larkins, J. (eds.), *International Society After the Cold War: Anarchy and Order Reconsidered* (Basingstoke/London: Macmillan Press, 1996) 29.

BROWN, M., LYNN-JONES, S., & MILLER, S. (eds.), *Debating the Democratic Peace* (Cambridge, MA: MIT Press, 1996).

BRUCKNER, P., *La Mélancolie démocratique* (Paris: Editions du Seuil, 1990).

BURNS, T. (ed.), *After History? Francis Fukuyama and His Critics* (London: Rowman & Littlefield, 1994).

BURTON, J., *World Society* (Cambridge: Cambridge University Press, 1972).

CAROTHERS, T., 'Empirical Perspectives on the Emerging Norm of Democracy in International Law', *Proceedings of the American Society of International Law* (1992) 261.

CASS, D., 'Navigating the Newstream: Recent Critical Scholarship in International Law' 65 *Nordic Journal of International Law* (1996) 341.

CASSESE, A., 'The Self-Determination of Peoples', in Henkin, L. (ed.), *The International Bill of Rights: the Covenant on Civil and Political Rights* (New York: Columbia University Press, 1981) 92.

CERNA, C., 'Universal Democracy: An International Legal Right or the Pipe Dream of the West?' 27 *New York University Journal of International Law and Politics* (1995) 289.

CONNOLLY, W., *Identity/Difference: Democratic Negotiations of Political Paradox* (Ithaca, NY: Cornell University Press, 1991).

CORNTASSEL, J. & PRIMEAU, T., 'Indigenous "Sovereignty" and International Law: Revised Strategies for Pursuing "Self-Determination" ' 17 *Human Rights Quarterly* (1995) 343.

COX, R., 'Social Forces, States, and World Orders: Beyond International Relations Theory' 10 *Millennium* (1981) 126.

——, 'Democracy in Hard Times: Economic Globalization and the Limits to Liberal Democracy', in McGrew, A. (ed.), *The Transformation of Democracy? Globalization and Territorial Democracy* (Cambridge: Polity Press/Open University Press, 1997) 49.

CRAWFORD, J., *Democracy in International Law: Inaugural Lecture* (Cambridge: Cambridge University Press, 1994).

DERRIDA, J., *The Other Heading*, trans. Brault, P.-A. & Naas, M. B. (Bloomington, IN: Indiana University Press, 1992).

——, *Specters of Marx*, trans. Kamuf, P. (New York/London: Routledge, 1994).

DOYLE, M., 'Kant, Liberal Legacies and Foreign Affairs' 12 *Philosophy and Public Affairs* (1983) 205 & 323.

DRYZEK, J., *Discursive Democracy: Politics, Policy, and Political Science* (Cambridge: Cambridge University Press, 1990).

DUGARD, J., 'Reconciliation and Justice: the South African Experience' 8 *Transnational Law and Contemporary Problems* (1998) 277.

DUNN, J. (ed.), *Democracy: The Unfinished Journey, 508 BC to AD 1993* (Oxford: Oxford University Press, 1992).

EAGLETON, T., *Ideology: An Introduction* (London: Verso, 1991).

——, *Marx and Freedom* (London: Phoenix Press, 1997).

FALK, R. (1995a), *On Humane Governance: Toward a New Global Politics* (Cambridge: Polity Press, 1995).

—— (1995b), 'The World Order Between Inter-State Law and the Law of Humanity: the Role of Civil Society Institutions', in Archibugi, D. & Held, D. (eds.), *Cosmopolitan Democracy: An Agenda for a New World Order* (Cambridge: Polity Press, 1995) 163

——, 'The United Nations and Cosmopolitan Democracy: Bad Dream, Utopian Fantasy, Political Project', in Archibugi, D., Held, D., & Köhler, M. (eds.), *Re-imagining Political Community: Studies in Cosmopolitan Democracy* (Cambridge: Polity Press, 1998) 309.

FOUCAULT, M., *Power/Knowledge: Selected Interviews and Other Writings, 1972–1977,* Gordon, C. (ed.), trans. Gordon, C. *et al.* (Brighton, NY: Harvester Press, 1980).

——, *The Foucault Reader,* Rabinow, P. (ed.) (London: Penguin, 1984).

——, *Foucault Live: Collected Interviews* Lotringer, S. (ed.), trans. Hochroth, L. and Johnston, J. (New York: Semiotext(e), 1989).

FOX, G. (1992*a*), 'The Right to Political Participation in International Law' 17 *Yale Journal of International Law* (1992) 539.

—— (1992*b*), 'The Right to Political Participation in International Law', in 'National Sovereignty Revisited: Perspectives on the Emerging Norm of Democracy in International Law', *Proceedings of the American Society of International Law* (1992) 249.

—— & NOLTE, G., 'Intolerant Democracies' 36 *Harvard International Law Journal* (1995) 1.

FRANCK, T., 'United Nations Based Prospects for a New Global Order' 22 *New York University Journal of International Law & Politics* (1990) 601.

——, 'The Emerging Right to Democratic Governance' 86 *American Journal of International Law* (1992) 46.

——, 'Democracy as a Human Right' in Henkin, L., & Hargrove, J. L., *Human Rights: An Agenda for the Next Century* (Washington D.C.: American Society of International Law, 1994) 73.

——, *Fairness in International Law and Institutions* (Oxford: Clarendon Press, 1995).

FUKUYAMA, F., 'The End of History?' *National Interest,* (Summer 1989) 3.

——, 'A Reply to My Critics', *National Interest,* (Winter 1989/90) 21.

——, *The End of History and the Last Man* (New York: Free Press, 1992).

GEERTZ, C., *The Interpretation of Cultures: Selected Essays* (London: Fontana Press, 1993).

GEUSS, R., *The Idea of a Critical Theory: Habermas and the Frankfurt School* (Cambridge: Cambridge University Press, 1981).

GHAI, Y., *Whose Human Right to Development?* (Commonwealth Secretariat: Series of Occasional Papers on the Right to Development, 1989).

GIDDENS, A., *The Consequences of Modernity* (Cambridge: Polity Press, 1990).

GILLS, B., ROCAMORA, J., & WILSON, R., 'Low Intensity Democracy', in Gills, B., Rocamora, J., & Wilson, R. (eds.), *Low Intensity Democracy: Political Power in the New World Order* (London: Pluto Press, 1993) 3.

GRAY, J., *False Dawn: The Delusions of Global Capitalism* (London: Granta, 1998).

GROTIUS, H., *De jure belli ac pacis libri tres (1646),* Vol. II, Brown Scott, J. (ed.), trans. Kelsey, F. W. *et al.* (New York, Oceana Publications, 1964).

HABERMAS, J., *Knowledge and Human Interests,* trans. Shapiro, J. (Cambridge: Polity Press, 1987).

——, *Between Facts and Norms: Contributions to a Discourse Theory of Law and Democracy,* trans. Rehg, W. (Cambridge, MA: MIT Press, 1996).

HANNUM, H., *Autonomy, Sovereignty and Self-Determination: the Accommodation of Conflicting Rights,* 2nd edn. (Philadelphia, PA: University of Pennsylvania Press, 1996).

HANSON, R., 'Democracy', in Ball, T., Farr, J., & Hanson, R. L. (eds.), *Political Innovation and Conceptual Change* (Cambridge: Cambridge University Press, 1989) 68.

HARVEY, D., *The Condition of Postmodernity: An Enquiry into the Origins of Cultural Change* (Oxford: Basil Blackwell, 1990).

HELD, D., *Introduction to Critical Theory: Horkheimer to Habermas* (Cambridge: Polity Press, 1980).

——, 'Democracy, the Nation-State and the Global System', in Held, D. (ed.), *Political Theory Today* (Cambridge: Polity Press, 1991) 197.

HELD, D., 'Democracy: From City-States to a Cosmopolitan Order?', in Held, D. (ed.),
    Prospects for Democracy: North, South, East, West (Cambridge: Polity Press, 1993) 13.
—— (1995a), *Democracy and the Global Order: From the Modern State to Cosmopolitan
    Governance* (Cambridge: Polity Press, 1995).
—— (1995b), 'Democracy and the New International Order', in Archibugi, D. &
    Held, D. (eds.), *Cosmopolitan Democracy: An Agenda for a New World Order* (Cambridge:
    Polity Press, 1995) 96.
——, *Models of Democracy,* 2nd edn. (Cambridge: Polity Press, 1996).
HIRST, P. & THOMPSON, G., *Globalization in Question: The International Economy and the
    Possibilities of Governance* (Cambridge: Polity Press, 1996).
HOBDEN, R. & WYN JONES, R., 'World-System Theory', in Baylis, J. & Smith, S. (eds.), *The
    Globalization of World Politics* (Oxford: Oxford University Press, 1997) 125.
HORKHEIMER, M., *Eclipse of Reason* (New York: Oxford University Press, 1947).
——, *Critical Theory: Selected Essays,* trans. O'Connell, M. *et al.* (New York: Herder & Herder,
    1972).
HORSMAN, M. & MARSHALL, A., *After the Nation-State: Citizens, Tribalism and the New World
    Disorder* (London: HarperCollins, 1994).
JAMESON, F., *Postmodernism, or, The Cultural Logic of Late Capitalism* (London: Verso, 1991).
JAY, M., *The Dialectical Imagination* (Berkeley, CA: University of California Press, 1973).
KALDOR, M., 'European Institutions, Nation-States and Nationalism', in Archibugi, D. &
    Held, D. (eds.), *Cosmopolitan Democracy: An Agenda for a New World Order* (Cambridge:
    Polity Press, 1995) 68.
——, 'Introduction', in Kaldor, M., & Vashee, B. (eds.), *Restructuring the Global Military
    Sector, Vol. 1: New Wars* (London/Washington: Pinter, 1997) 3.
KANT, I., 'Perpetual Peace' (1795), in Reiss, H., (ed.) *Kant: Political Writings,* 2nd edn., trans.
    Nisbet, H. B. (Cambridge: Cambridge University Press, 1991) 93.
KENNEDY, E., *A 'Philosophe' in the Age of Revolution: Destutt de Tracy and the Origins of
    'Ideology'* (Philadelphia: American Philosophical Society, 1978).
KENNEDY, D., 'Turning to Market Democracy: A Tale of Two Architectures', 32 *Harvard
    International Law Journal* (1991) 373.
——, 'A New World Order: Yesterday, Today, and Tomorrow', 4 *Transnational Law and
    Contemporary Problems* (1994) 329.
KLARE, M. T., & KORNBLUH, P. (eds.), *Low Intensity Warfare* (London: Methuen, 1989).
KOSKENNIEMI, M., 'The Future of Statehood' 32 *Harvard International Law Journal* (1991)
    397.
——, 'National Self-Determination Today: Problems of Legal Theory and Practice' 43
    International and Comparative Law Quarterly (1994) 241.
——, ' "Intolerant Democracies": a Reaction' 37 *Harvard International Law Journal* (1996) 231.
LENIN, V. I., 'Imperialism: The Highest Stage of Capitalism : a Popular Outline', in *Collected
    Works,* vol. 22, Hanna G. (ed.), trans. Sdobnivok, Y. (London: Lawrence & Wishart, 1964)
    185.
——, *What Is To Be Done?* (1902), trans. Fineberg, J., and Hanna, G. (London: Penguin,
    1988).
LEVY, J., 'Domestic Politics and War' 18 *Journal of Interdisciplinary History* (1988) 653.
LINKLATER, A., *The Transformation of Political Community: Ethical Foundations of the Post-
    Westphalian Era* (Cambridge: Polity Press, 1998).
LIPSET, S. M., *Political Man* (London: Heinemann, 1964).

LUKÁCS, G., *History and Class Consciousness* (London: Merlin Press, 1971).

MANNHEIM, K., *Ideology and Utopia: An Introduction to the Sociology of Knowledge, Collected Works of Karl Mannheim*, vol. 1., trans. Wirth, L., and Shils, E. (London: Routledge, 1997 (1936)).

MANSELL, C., & SCOTT, J., 'Why Bother About the Right to Development?' 21 *Journal of Law & Society* (1994) 171.

MARKS, S. (1997*a*), 'The End of History? Reflections on Some International Legal Theses' 8 *European Journal of International Law* (1997) 449.

—— (1997*b*), 'The "Emerging Norm": Conceptualising "Democratic Governance" ' *Proceedings of the American Society of International Law* (1997) 372.

—— 'Guarding the Gates with Two Faces: International Law and Political Reconstruction' 6 *Indiana Journal of Global Legal Studies* (1999) 457.

MARX, K., *Later Political Writings*, Carver, T. (ed. & trans.) (Cambridge: Cambridge University Press, 1996).

—— *Early Political Writings*, O'Malley, J. (ed. & trans.) (Cambridge: Cambridge University Press, 1994).

—— *The Marx-Engels Reader*, 2nd edn., Tucker, R. (ed.) (New York: Norton, 1978).

MCCARTHY, T., *Ideals and Illusions: On Reconstruction and Deconstruction in Contemporary Critical Theory* (Cambridge MA & London: MIT Press, 1993).

——, 'Philosophy and Critical Theory: A Reprise', in Hoy, D. C., and McCarthy, T. (eds.), *Critical Theory* (Oxford & Cambridge, MA: Blackwell, 1994) 5.

MCGREW, A. (1992*a*), 'A Global Society?', in Hall, S., Held, D., & McGrew, A. (eds.), *Modernity and its Futures* (Cambridge: Polity Press/Open University Press, 1992) 61.

—— (1992*b*), 'Conceptualizing Global Politics', in McGrew, A., & Lewis P. (eds.), *Global Politics: Globalization and the Nation-State* (Cambridge: Polity Press, 1992) 1.

—— (1997*a*), 'Globalization and Territorial Democracy: An Introduction', in McGrew, A. (ed.), *The Transformation of Democracy? Globalization and Territorial Democracy* (Cambridge: Polity Press/Open University Press, 1997) 1.

—— (1997*b*), 'Democracy Beyond Borders?: Globalization and the Reconstruction of Democratic Theory and Politics', in McGrew, A. (ed.), *The Transformation of Democracy? Globalization and Territorial Democracy* (Cambridge: Polity Press/Open University Press, 1997) 231.

MCLELLAN, D., *Ideology*, 2nd edn. (Buckingham: Open University Press, 1995).

OHMAE, K., *The End of the Nation-State: The Rise of Regional Economies* (London: HarperCollins, 1995).

OPPENHEIM, L., *International Law*, Vol. 1 (1st edn.) (London: Longman, Green & Company, 1905).

ORWELL, G., 'Politics and the English Language', in *A Collection of Essays* (New York: Doubleday, 1954).

OTTO, D., 'Challenging the "New World Order": International Law, Global Democracy and the Possibilities for Women' 3 *Transnational Law and Contemporary Problems* (1993) 371.

OUTHWAITE, W., *Habermas: A Critical Introduction* (Stanford, CA: Stanford University Press, 1994).

PARRY, G., *Political Elites* (London: Allen & Unwin, 1969).

PATEMAN, C., *Participation and Democratic Theory* (Cambridge: Cambridge University Press, 1970).

PLAMENATZ, J., *Ideology* (London: Macmillan, 1979).

RAO, A., 'The Politics of Gender and Culture in Human Rights Discourse', in Peters, J., & Wolper, A. (eds.), *Women's Rights, Human Rights: International Feminist Perspectives* (London: Routledge, 1995) 168.

REAGAN, R., *Public Papers of the Presidents of the United States: January 1–July 2, 1982* (Washington, DC: US Government Printing Office, 1983).

REISMAN, W. M., 'International Law After the Cold War' 84 *American Journal of International Law* (1990) 859.

—— 'Designing and Managing the Future of the State' 8 *European Journal of International Law* (1997) 409.

ROBINSON, W. I., *Promoting Polyarchy: Globalization, US Intervention and Hegemony* (Cambridge: Cambridge University Press, 1996).

RORTY, R., 'Feminism, Ideology and Deconstruction: A Pragmatist View' in Žižek, S. (ed.), *Mapping Ideology* (London: Verso, 1994) 227.

ROTH, B., 'Democratic Intolerance: Observations on Fox and Nolte' 37 *Harvard International Law Journal* (1996) 235.

——, 'Popular Sovereignty: The Elusive Norm' *Proceedings of the American Society of International Law* (1997) 363.

RUSSETT, B., *Grasping the Democratic Peace* (Princeton, NJ: Princeton University Press, 1993).

SCHACHTER, O., 'The Decline of the Nation-State and its Implication for International Law' 36 *Columbia Journal of Transnational Law* (1997) 7.

SCHOLTE, J., 'The Globalization of World Politics', in Baylis, J. & Smith, S. (eds.), *The Globalization of World Politics* (Oxford: Oxford University Press, 1997) 13.

SCHUMPETER, J., *Capitalism, Socialism and Democracy*, 6th edn. (London: Unwin Paperbacks, 1987).

SHILS, E., 'The End of Ideology?' 5 *Encounter* (Nov. 1955) 52.

SIMPSON, G., 'The Diffusion of Sovereignty: Self-Determination in the Post-Colonial Age' 32 *Stanford Journal of International Law* (1996) 255.

SLAUGHTER, A.-M., 'Revolution of the Spirit' 3 *Harvard Human Rights Journal* (1990) 1.

—— (1992*a*), 'Towards an Age of Liberal Nations' 33 *Harvard International Law Journal* (1992) 393.

—— (1992*b*), 'Law Among Liberal States: Liberal Internationalism and the Act of State Doctrine' 92 *Columbia Law Review* (1992) 1907.

—— (1992*c*), 'Law and the Liberal Paradigm in International Relations Theory' *Proceedings of the American Society of International Law* (1992) 180.

——, 'International Law and International Relations Theory: A Dual Agenda' 87 *American Journal of International Law* (1993) 205.

——, 'International Law in a World of Liberal States' 6 *European Journal of International Law* (1995) 503.

——, 'The Real New World Order' 76 *Foreign Affairs* (Sept./Oct. 1997) 183.

——, TULUMELLO, A. and WOOD, S., 'International Law and International Relations Theory: A New Generation of Interdisciplinary Scholarship' 92 *American Journal of International Law* (1999) 367.

SLOTERDIJK, P., *Critique of Cynical Reason*, trans. Eldred, M. (London: Verso, 1988).

SMART, C., 'Feminism and Law: Some Problems of Analysis and Strategy' 14 *International Journal of the Sociology of Law* (1986) 109.

SMITH, S., & BAYLIS, J., 'Introduction', in Baylis, J. & Smith, S. (eds.), *The Globalization of World Politics* (Oxford: Oxford University Press, 1997) 1.

STEINER, H. J., 'Political Participation as a Human Right' 1 *Harvard Human Rights Yearbook* (1988) 77.

SUR, S., 'The State Between Fragmentation and Globalization' 8 *European Journal of International Law* (1997) 421.

TESÓN, F., 'The Kantian Theory of International Law' 92 *Columbia Law Review* (1992) 53.

TEXTOR, J., *Synopsis of the Law of Nations (1680)*, vol. 2, trans. Bate, J. (Washington, DC: Carnegie Institution, 1916).

THOMPSON, J. B., *Ideology and Modern Culture: Critical Social Theory in the Era of Mass Communication* (Cambridge: Polity Press, 1990).

VATTEL, E. DE, *The Law of Nations, Or, Principles of the Law of Nature, Applied to the Conduct and Affairs of Nations and Sovereigns (1758)*, vol. 3, trans. Fenwick, J. (Washington, DC: Carnegie Institution, 1916).

WALKER, R. B. J., *Inside/Outside: International Relations as Political Theory* (Cambridge: Cambridge University Press, 1993).

WALLERSTEIN, I., *The Modern World System, Vol. 1.: Capitalist Agriculture and the Origins of the European World-Economy in the Sixteenth Century* (New York, London: Academic Press, 1974).

——, *The Modern World System, Vol. 2.: Mercantilism and the Consolidation of the European World-Economy, 1600–1750* (New York, London: Academic Press, 1980).

——, 'The Inter-State Structure of the Modern World-System', in Smith, S., Booth, K. & Zalewski, M. (eds.), *International Theory: Positivism and Beyond* (Cambridge: Cambridge University Press, 1996).

WALZER, M., 'The Concept of Civil Society' in Walzer, M. (ed.), *Toward a Global Civil Society* (Providence, RI: Berghahn Books, 1995) 7.

WEBER, M., 'Politics as a Vocation', in Gerth, H. H. & Wright Mills, C. (eds. & trans.), *From Max Weber: Essays in Sociology* (New York: Oxford University Press/Galaxy, 1958) 77.

WEISS, L., 'Globalization and the Myth of the Powerless State' 225 *New Left Review* (1997) 3.

WILLIAMS, R., *Keywords: a Vocabulary of Culture and Society*, 2nd edn. (New York: Oxford University Press, 1983).

WOOLSEY, T., *Introduction to the Study of International Law* (Boston, MA: James Munro & Company, 1860).

YOUNG, I., 'Communication and the Other: Beyond Deliberative Democracy', in Benhabib, S. (ed.), *Democracy and Difference* (Princeton, NJ: Princeton University Press, 1996) 120.

ŽIŽEK, S., *Tarrying with the Negative* (Durham, NC: Duke University Press, 1993).

—— (1994*a*), 'Introduction: The Spectre of Ideology', in Žižek, S. (ed.), *Mapping Ideology* (London & New York: Verso, 1994) 1.

—— (1994*b*), 'How Did Marx Invent the Symptom?', in Žižek, S. (ed.), *Mapping Ideology* (London & New York: Verso, 1994) 296.

Index

Lightning Source UK Ltd.
Milton Keynes UK
07 January 2011

165296UK00001B/48/A